Beasts and Babies

By the same author

THE BEASTS OF MY FIELDS

Beasts and Babies

by

DAVID CREATON

ST. MARTIN'S PRESS   NEW YORK

B
Creaton

Library of Congress Cataloging in Publication Data

Creaton, David.
  Beasts and babies.

  Continues The beasts of my fields.
  1. Creaton, David. 2. Farmers—England—Kent—
Biography. 3. Farm life—England—Kent. I. Title.
SF33.C73A32 636'.0092'4 [B] 78-3961
ISBN 0-312-07047-0

To My Wife

She always insisted her diaries
would come in useful one day.

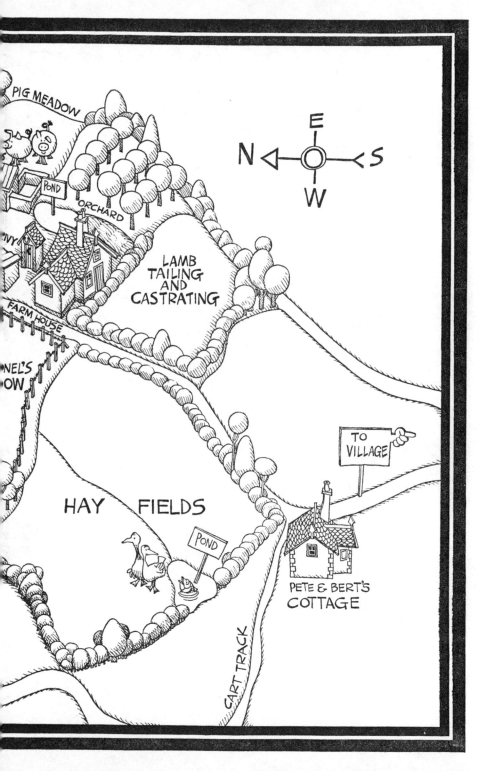

Beasts and Babies

1

DAISY WAS MY best cow. She was old, she was not pedigree, in fact she was not any particular breed. She was just a brown cow with an immense white udder from which milk flowed unstintingly. So much so that it was a job to dry her off at the end of a lactation, to give her time to prepare for the flood that came with each new calf.

Today she was due to calve again. She was out with the other cows, across the meadow on the other side of the lane. I could just see her if I stood on tiptoe outside the cowshed door to look over the hedge. All the other nine cows had their heads down, curling out their rough tongues, tearing off the grass and packing it away as though there wasn't a moment to lose. But Daisy was a little apart, moving away on her own, now grazing, now looking about her and slowly making her way to the far corner of the meadow.

She calved regularly every autumn and knew perfectly well what she was about. All the same, I thought I would pay her a quick visit to try and get the estimated time of arrival. As I walked over the lane, climbed the gate and moved through the other cows, I worked out that this would be Daisy's seventh calf. I had bought her with her second calf, soon after I had come to Maywood, my sixty-five acre farm in the Weald of Kent, which I had bought shortly after the war. I was establishing my dairy herd with the best second-hand cows my limited resources allowed. Daisy had been cheap, a real bargain, except that when I had got her home from the market and sat down to milk her, she had sent the first full bucket of milk flying with a kick of stunning accuracy.

That had been the first of many pails of wasted milk, many torrents of abuse at which Daisy had merely flicked back her long ears, rolled her liquid eyes at such language and continued chewing her cud. But with patience she and I had come to an understanding, and by the time she'd had her fourth calf a pail of spilt milk was a thing of the past. Anyway, I was milking with a machine by then and that seemed to take all the fun out of it so far as Daisy was concerned. There was nobody sitting at her side for her to pit her wits against. The milk she poured forth was now trapped and sealed in a strangely-shaped bucket sprouting rubber tubes. It was just out of reach. She couldn't send it clattering in a glorious white splash and see me leap to my feet in anger. At best she could only raise her leg to flick off the cluster gripping her teats and stamp on it as it lay spread-eagled and hissing at her feet. Nowadays, with her advancing years, she seldom even bothered to do that.

She looked up as she saw me walking across the meadow. She lowed quietly and strutted on a bit further away, her belly huge and low and her back legs forced apart by her swelling udder. By the way she was walking, seeming always to be on the point of pausing for a pee, I knew she would not be long. And she kept swishing her tail, almost as though she was waving me away, telling me to clear off because she would be all right.

'Get on with it then,' I muttered. 'If that's how you feel I've got plenty to do without bothering about you, old girl.'

And I had. Everything seemed to be happening today. Indoors, Olive was swaying around as well, threatening to give birth to our second child. It had been a race with Daisy all the way along, ever since my dear wife had been to the doctor and he had done his arithmetic and given her the date.

I had laughed when she'd told me. 'Oh, old Daisy's due with her annual event about then. She's always the first of the autumn calvers. Perhaps you'll have the honour this year. Cows and humans both take nine months!'

Now it looked as though we were in for a dead heat.

I hurried back to the lane, walked down it past the cowshed and through a gate that led across a yard to the back door of the farmhouse. It led straight into the kitchen and the room was

8

empty with that 'back in a moment' feeling. The new Rayburn cooker stood in the ingle-nook, looking smug in cream vitreous enamel, its towel rail airing some snow-white nappies. I was still not used to seeing it there in place of the old black kitchener, with its cheery red face and the cavernous oven door that swamped the room with heat when you opened it on a cold day. But the Rayburn was more efficient, cleaner, heated the water as well and was now urging a whistling kettle to give vent to its feelings. The dial on the oven was well into the red section and the room smelt of baking bread. The central table showed every sign of a sizeable baking session in progress, with strewn flour, greased bun tins, packets of this and that and a yellow mixing bowl complete with wooden spoon left in mid stir. Washing-up soaked in the long, glazed sink under the window and the big brass cold water tap dripped on it thoughtfully. A toy tractor had run into one of the empty dog baskets on the brick floor and, apart from the dripping tap and the threatening scream from the kettle, there was no sound.

I took in the whole scene in a second and immediately concluded the baby must have started coming. Why else would my methodical wife disappear in the middle of a baking session? Fancy even starting such a task today! But then it was Friday and she always baked on a Friday. She had been trained as a nurse and had just qualified when we were married, nearly four years ago now. And she had left the strict discipline of the hospital in exchange for the haphazard life at Maywood. It had been an uphill battle for her to establish a routine and a pregnancy had to take its place along with everything else.

I called as I started through into the living room in search of her.

She answered 'just coming' from the top of the stairs and I felt relieved.

The stairs led up from a little hall just inside the front door. 'I thought you'd started,' I explained, as I watched her come down, moving with surprising agility. Her dark, shoulder-length hair was swept up, piled up and pinned.

As she reached me she opened her large brown eyes wide and smiled. 'Not yet. You're too impatient — as usual. I've only just been upstairs putting the finishing touches to the room while I was waiting for the bread to come out and the buns to go in.'

9

'Fancy doing all that baking today!'

She put her arm round me, quickly tickled my ribs and walked on ahead into the kitchen. 'Where's Donald? I thought you were meant to be keeping an eye on him.'

'He's okay. He's busy playing with the chickens. The dogs are with him.'

She glanced out of the window to reassure herself. Then, armed with the oven cloth, she removed the bread, tipped the bulging loaves out of their tins and tapped each one smartly on the bottom before setting them to cool on a wire tray. 'Shan't be able to bake again for a while,' she said, almost to herself.

'So, you'll be all right?'

'Fine. I'm expecting the District Nurse to look in sometime. She said she would, on her way by. Just to check progress. But I don't suppose anything will happen before tonight.' She laughed. 'I'll soon let you know if it does, don't worry.'

'In that case Daisy'll beat you to it. It looks like any moment with her.' I smiled and patted her tummy before walking to the back door. 'I'm going to take Donald to see her. He'll like to see a calf born.'

'Well don't let him get too close. You know how quick he is.'

I knew that only too well.

By now I had been at Maywood for five years. When I had bought the farm I was a twenty-one year old bachelor, fresh from an apprenticeship on large farms, and I had persuaded my Mother to move house and come to live with me. She was then sixty, the mother of five children, and she had reared us in the comparative comfort of a country vicarage. And when Father died she had moved to a large semi in Dulwich to complete our upbringing.

At first it had been a hard time for her at Maywood, straight from a warm house with all mod. cons. to a lonely farmhouse with a brick-floored kitchen, a single cold tap over the sink and an old black kitchener that billowed smoke whenever the wind was in the east. To say nothing of a jerry under the bed or a shivering trot across the backyard to the privy. But she threw herself into making it a home. Later we had our mod. cons. installed and they made life easier. She bubbled with joy at the good times, was stoical in the bad, took an interest in all the animals and tried to love the sows.

Then I got married and the original plan was for Olive to continue with her nursing. It was a part of her bargain at my proposal of marriage. She was a farmer's daughter herself. She had lived on margarine and mushrooms and rabbits as a child in the hard Thirties, and had sworn never to make the mistake of marrying a farmer. Now she was in love with one. And just after she had passed her nursing finals as well. She was really a State Registered Nurse at last, brimming with dedication and able to command the full salary after the pittance paid during training. The full salary of eight pounds, seventeen shillings and sixpence a month, all found. What madness to give up such riches after all the hard years of training; all the inspired devotion to the calling in exchange for a farmer husband. But to continue nursing meant she had to stay on living in at the Nurses' Home. Go on being a prisoner. In by ten, ruled by sisters who were spinsters and who frowned on the new regulations, spawned by the war, that actually allowed a nurse to get married and continue working. And the Nurses' Home was twenty-five miles away from Maywood. There were only two days off in ten. Anyway money wasn't everything. Love was.

So Mother laughed and made ready to welcome her into the farmhouse after the honeymoon. She told me to get on and decorate the bedroom that overlooked the garden, into the flowing branches of the cherry tree. She suggested pink for a blushing bride. And as she prepared to take a back seat I am sure she reminded herself sternly that jealousy and interfering criticism were sins.

Of course, sometimes those early days were not easy. It would have been a miracle if they were. Mother was happy-go-lucky, scooting through housework and cooking hit or miss. She always tried to do her best and if things went right for her she laughed and said: 'Hurrah!' If not she sighed, then smiled: 'Better luck next time.'

Olive was methodical, thorough, and determined to learn the arts of cooking and housekeeping. Only Mother's ways had nothing whatsoever to do with what was written in the books she consulted. So often there was exasperation. Sometimes, in the quiet of the pink bedroom, there were sobs. And how do you mediate between two women you love in two different ways? But it was only in the beginning, only until sighs turned to smiles, only until the bond developed between them that was to brim with love over the years to come.

Soon came the afternoon when Olive went to the cowshed to fetch a jug of milk fresh from the cows. I was elsewhere feeding the pigs. Pete and Bert, the teenage brothers who worked on the farm, had their heads buried in cows' bellies, gazing down into their buckets and unaware of her arrival.

Bert offered some information to his elder brother: 'I reckon her's going to have a baby, then.'

Olive paused on her way to the dairy. What woman could resist dawdling to hear more of such tantalising gossip? Had one of Bert's girl friends succeeded in commanding his serious attention, prevailed upon him at last to advance beyond the French kisses for which he always claimed to be famous among the local girls? Or had the remark she had just heard been a question, perhaps a reply to an earlier admission by Pete of a complication in his relationship with his steady girl friend, Rose? Whatever it was, she waited out of sight, eavesdropping in the dairy doorway.

She told me later that it seemed an age as the boys went on milking in silence. The cows closed their eyes, chewed their cud and weren't a bit interested. Just as she was thinking the topic was finished, that she had walked in on a final remark, Pete asked: 'Who?'

A few tense moments later, Bert replied: 'Who d'you think? Her, silly. Her indoors.'

'Who? Olive?'

'Course. Who else?'

'Aye Maybe.' And Pete dismissed the subject and continued milking, apparently lost in his own thoughts again.

Olive filled the jug silently and stole from the cowshed. In no time at all she found me. 'How did he know?' she asked, urgently. 'I'm still not absolutely sure myself.'

I laughed and put my arm round her. 'You know Bert. He always likes to be first with any news and I suppose he thought it was about time to make a guess. Most girls seem to have a baby about a year after they're married, and lots of 'em much sooner than that, as you well know. I expect he thought you're overdue and has been busy counting off the months on his

12

fingers.' She laughed and I pulled her to me and kissed her. 'I'm glad, I'm delighted, I don't care who knows, who guesses. As soon as you're sure I'll blab it to everybody I know!'

And when I did tell Pete and Bert, trying hard to sound matter-of-fact and hide my glee, Pete just nodded and went on with his work. But Bert grinned across at his brother: 'Told yer so, now didn't I?'

It was after Donald was born that Mother decided it was time to make a move from Maywood. She always waited for God to show her the way and about two months later He brought it to her notice that there was a cottage for sale, overlooking the green in the next village. It was the ideal place for her, close to all amenities, within her means, somewhere where she could set up home again as the centre of her family and large enough for her to welcome visiting grandchildren, who were now arriving in the world thick and fast.

We looked over the cottage together. Jessamine Cottage it was called and it had two tall chimneys, one at each end of the roof. 'Just like two arms raised in prayer,' she said, with satisfaction, as we stood and stared at if from across the green. That seemed to clinch it for her.

Donald was on the other side of the yard, busily absorbed in his favourite game of drilling the chickens. He was three now, tall for his age, thin because he never stopped still long enough to put on any weight and with a mop of very fair hair. He had his mother's dark brown eyes, together with her perseverance and determination that things should be done in an orderly manner.

I had a motley flock of chickens on the farm. They were Rhode Island Red crossed with Light Sussex mostly — at least they had started as that when old Mrs P.P. had hatched out the first brood. She was a solitary old hen who had been left behind when I bought the farm. All her mates had departed at the farm sale together with the hen house. So she had taken up residence in the disused privy across the backyard, sitting on the seat to hatch out a huge clutch of eggs. Then she escorted this new generation of Maywood chicks around the farmyard with much clucking and scratching as she introduced them to all the titbits to be found in the horse dung in the dark stable, along the

13

mangers in the cowshed, in the bright straw littering the stack-plat, or in the heaving depths of a decaying cowpat. As soon as they were able to fend for themselves she wanted no more to do with them. They were banished to find their own roosts along the beams in the cartshed at night, to amuse themselves during the day while she returned to her position as boss of the backyard and with first refusal on any scraps emanating from the kitchen. She was old and dilapidated even then and alas, one morning I missed her patrolling the backyard with her slow, measured steps. I found her in the privy, hunched up in the corner, where she had died in her sleep.

But her offspring thrived. The hens sought out secret nests to lay their eggs and then gave the game away by cackling, so that we always knew where to look. The cockerels preened themselves, learnt to crow and chevied their sisters into incestuous relationships. So one by one they provided us with roast dinners and I bought two dandy red cocks to satisfy the hens, and introduce new blood into eggs that remained hidden long enough to be hatched out.

Now there were twenty-five hens of various ages roaming around the farm and they adored Donald because he was always feeding them. As soon as he had learnt to walk he had gone trotting out into the yard. And this had perplexed the passing hens. They had never come across a lurching infant before and immediately assumed that he was some new breed of cock bearing down on them. So they stopped and squatted, expecting the inevitable copulation, and instead found themselves clasped in a tight embrace and lifted off their feet to squeals of delight. And strangely they submitted to this treatment without so much as a squawk or the flap of a wing. Donald could fool them every time. As he grew older he took note when I scattered corn and soon demanded that he should be allowed to feed them.

As the months passed and he became more adventurous, so the chickens became the most important things in his life. Toys were all right if he was forced to stay indoors. Even then he preferred the company of our two golden retrievers, Sadie, and her son, Pat, who followed him everywhere and flopped down to watch his play. But he couldn't lug them about like he could the chickens. If he grabbed at them to play some part in a game, they just rolled over, slapped their tails against the floor and

14

pawed at him to rub their tummies. That was very dull. So he escaped outdoors whenever he could.

By then he had acquired a little seaside bucket and with this he would go tearing off to the corn store at the back of the cow-shed, with the dogs in hot pursuit. There they would watch him up-end a pail from the nearby dairy to stand on to lift the latch of the corn store door, fill his bucket, shut the door, replace the pail and race back to the yard, calling 'Coop, coop, coop, coop,' as he went.

Chickens would appear from all directions, heads forward, bodies swaying and wings flapping in a bid to be first, while the cocks came long-striding, like a race between two red-faced gentlemen in plus-fours.

Donald would wait until they were all grouped round him, red eyes flashing and pecking at each other. And the dogs watched from afar, sitting bolt upright, quivering a little with jealousy, longing to join in but knowing full well that chicken-chasing was forbidden when anyone was looking. Once he was sure there were no more late arrivals, he would slowly trickle out a long line of corn right across the yard. Now some chickens are greedier than others, bullies, bosses of the pecking order. And Donald had no time for these. It had to be fair shares for all. So the bosses were picked up and banished to far corners of the farm-yard, where they would be released to lose valuable eating time in the mad dash back to the line-out. Persistent offenders were dealt with more severely; incarcerated in the stable until they had the presence of mind to fly out over the half-heck door; locked in the privy, sentenced to varying lengths of loss of eating time. Sometimes they were forgotten altogether in an emergency. So Olive and I were in the habit of opening the privy door in passing, just in case there was a prisoner whose release was overdue.

But on one occasion there was an offender whose greed had evidently demanded the ultimate deterrent. I didn't know about it at the time. Not until several hours later when we came to do the milking and I rolled a churn into the dairy to stand it under the milk cooler. As I lifted the lid I happened to glance inside. Which was fortunate, because there was a chicken squatting in the bottom, gasping in the last of the air. It blinked up at me and cocked its head towards the sudden light of freedom.

15

Feeding time was any time Donald felt like playing with the chickens. They were marvellous playmates, always willing to come running at his call, ever ready to submit to his decisions over forfeits. But in the end I had to limit the number of times he filled up at the corn store. The chickens had started to give up foraging. They began sitting around like bloated vultures at a kill and even Donald paused long enough to realise they were losing interest in the game. So he spent more time on egg hunts instead, visiting all the known nests, clutching two eggs at a time and running full tilt to hand them over to his mother in the kitchen. And when all known supplies were exhausted he searched for more, diving under mangers, squeezing into the more inaccessible places while the dogs went berserk, convinced that it was now either rabbits or rats he was after and offering their advice with loud sniffings and high-pitched yaps.

Now he was with his line of chickens as I came out of the house. His little yellow bucket was tucked firmly in the crook of his arm, the corn being severely rationed as he patrolled the line adding a little more here and there before deciding who should be captured. He was too busy to notice my approach.

Sadie did and she came ambling over, swaying her bottom from side to side, her tail sweeping, glad of an excuse to desert her post. She was beginning to look matronly, five years old now and with two large litters behind her, of which Pat was the pick of the first and the one we had saved for ourselves when the others had been sold. But mother and son were so different from each other in temperament they could have been unrelated.

The experts say of golden retrievers that only one in five is suitable for training on as a gun dog. I'm quite sure neither Sadie nor Pat would have qualified. If they did have one trait in common it was that they were both soppy fools. But Sadie was much more inquisitive and more the farm dog. She always had to know what was going on and seemed to sleep with half an eye open. She was the first to bark before anyone else had heard the baker's van, or even the clatter of Stivvy Wild's travelling shop. She seemed to know if I had phoned for the artificial inseminator and would appear and amble out to the lane to await his arrival minutes before I heard his car. She was always the first out to greet anybody. Then she would wander off and leave them severely alone. I always felt sure she would have welcomed a

16

burglar in the same way. And she kept tabs on what was going on on the farm as well; if the cows were grazing in a new field; if the sows had got out and where they had wandered off to; where I was going. She would follow me at a distance if she thought I was off to visit the sheep because she fancied herself as a bit of a sheepdog — just because she had noticed long ago that they all ran into a bunch and stamped their feet if she gave a bark or two in the gateway. She knew very well she should keep her mouth shut and not disturb the sheep when I wanted to walk through them. But she could never resist the temptation and afterwards she always looked across to me with her ears flat, knowing I would swear at her and order her back to the farmyard.

But where Sadie was fickle, Pat was faithful. He was the fiercely devoted one, who had spent hours under Donald's pram when it was outside. Sometimes Sadie had joined him, but she soon tired of guard duty, yawning, stretching and moving off to find something more interesting to do. And when Donald had grown out of his pram and started to run off on his own, Pat didn't know what to do for the best. Olive was his first love. She had reared him, fed him and fussed over him when all his brothers and sisters had been sold, and Sadie had only snapped at him when all he had wanted was a bit of comforting. It was Olive's slippers he had chewed in gratitude, she who had scolded him, then cuddled him, and later introduced him to Donald soon after he was born. And as Olive and the baby were always together there was no problem. He could sit upright beside the nursing chair and watch the nappy changing, even daring a quick lick on the baby's bottom if the opportunity arose; drool beneath the high chair at meal times, gazing up at this delightful new provider of sticky delicacies; roll before him on the floor when he started to crawl, offering tummy to be pummelled, ears to be pulled, eyes to be scratched — anything in the ecstasy of attention. And at the first tentative steps he had been on hand to offer support with a solid back at just the right height; later to give shrieking rides that were far more fun than on any old rocking horse.

All that had been indoors, with Olive close by. As far as Pat was concerned Donald was still part of her and he could infiltrate nicely between them. Even when the pram used to be out in the garden, under the big cherry tree that grew on the lawn, he could lie beside it and still hear her bustling about if he kept an ear cocked. Life had been nicely organised for him.

This all changed when Donald had started to venture into the farmyard. Pat had found himself uncertain as to where his loyalty lay. At first he had crouched outside the back door, head between paws watching, ears flicking forward and then back to the sounds in the kitchen as he tried to keep his attention on two places at once. There was a pond across the yard and if Donald started to head for this Olive would come flying out of the door. Then Pat could yap with delight and take off to round Donald up so that they could all three be together again. After a few such sorties Pat learnt to bark a warning and would head off on his own when Donald left the chickens and started towards the pond, sometimes staggering under the weight of a hen and evidently determined to see if she could swim like the ducks.

The ducks were a mystery to him, always launching themselves out of reach before he could get near, swimming off with deep-throated protests, pursued by their husband, Sinbad the Sailor, squeaking after them with his silly falsetto. And even if Donald surprised them well away from the pond, the ducks never dawdled or submitted like the silly hens. They beat off out of range, flapping their wings and trying to fly in their haste.

Sinbad had ten wives and he was exceedingly strict with them. They were drab, brown Khaki-Cambells, well camouflaged against the earthy hues of the farmyard. But he was easily distinguishable with the silky green sheen on his black head, the smart white flecks on his feathers and the kiss-curl that stood up proudly at the base of his shiny back. While the ducks sometimes tended to look bedraggled with the heavy burden of laying, Sinbad always kept himself immaculate. Yet, although he spent a great deal of time on his personal toilet, his bright eyes were always on the lookout for possible danger. Even when his head was buried under a wing, his whole attention seemingly concentrated on the finest titivating with his quivering bill, he was always ready for the playful charge from a passing dog, or the blundering advance of a litter of piglets, not in the least particular where they snuffled to in journeys of constant discovery. He even seemed to know when Ditty, the kitten, was silently shaping up for an attack, waggling her backside and hoping to catch at

18

least one duck in her scampering charge. He was ready for her too, as well as the rushing attack from Donald, ever determined to get his hands on one of them at last. Then Sinbad was always the first to flounder to the safety of the pond, squeaking to his wives to follow his example, anxiously twitching his tail as he swam in circles and pouncing on any latecomer with a flurry of water and importance. Sinbad always admonished a dilatory wife with a severe sexual assault.

As Donald had grown, learnt to respect the danger of the pond, moved out of sight of the kitchen window into stable, cartshed or cowshed, so Pat decided it was his duty to go with him. And so did Sadie, but only if she had got nothing better to do.

I greeted the bitch as she came up to me, taking her head into my hands and rubbing her ears. She sat on her haunches, groaned with approval and looked smug. And when I stood up and my hands left her, she rolled her eyes and bared her teeth in a satisfied grin, which was really a request for me to continue fondling her.

'Come on, Donald,' I called, 'let's go and see Daisy. She's going to have a calf.'

I took his bucket and placed it out of harm's way on a wall. I held his hand and together we started off into the lane. The dogs trotted off purposefully in front of us, tails and ears alert, glad of some action at last.

'No, you two! You can't come,' I called them back. 'Dogs and calving cows don't mix.'

Pat understood immediately. He stopped, looked round and rolled the whites of his eyes as he waited for us to catch up. Sadie pretended I hadn't meant her. She kept going, hurrying faster if anything.

'Sadie! You heard! Go *home*!' I shouted at her.

Donald copied me. 'Pat! Home!' He grabbed him by the collar, heaved him round and pushed him rudely down the lane. Poor old Pat, I felt sorry for him. He slunk off with his tail between his legs, giving a despairing backward glance as though he was guilty of sheep worrying at the very least.

Eventually Sadie obeyed. But she only pretended to go home, finding smells in the ditch to delay her while she kept an eye on our progress. I knew Pat would go to find Olive. If the door was open he'd go tail-waving into the kitchen, brush a cold nose up under her skirt so that she'd cry: 'Pat, don't *do* that!' Then he'd flop on the floor with a loud sigh, put his head between his paws and follow her every movement with his eyes. But Sadie would slink after us, keeping her distance and hoping we wouldn't notice as she insinuated herself into our company again. I knew I would have to keep my eye on her because Daisy certainly would not allow her in the meadow.

As we started across the meadow one by one the cows watched our progress. We weren't worth more than a short stare just now. The grass had flushed with recent rain and it was only their second day in this meadow. They had to fill up while the going was good. There was time enough to sit and stare at passers-by once first stomachs were full and the dreamy round of cud-chewing began.

Donald knew all the cows by name. He had learnt them almost as soon as he could talk, from the days when Olive had carried him into the cowshed at milking time, pointing to them one by one while he repeated the names after her. There were ten cows altogether and they had responded to this roll call with just an acknowledgment from long ears while they went on chewing, or a single revolution of white-edged eyes. Only sometimes there was the rattle of a chain and a head turned round to stare. And this produced a cry of delight, which was answered by a lazy curl of the tail.

Yet it had taken them a long time to make up their minds about Donald. When they had first seen him on his own two feet, he had come trotting up the lane just as they were coming out of the cowshed. Those in front had stopped dead. Those following had cannoned into them, suddenly forgetting the fragrance of grass on the wind. Their heads had gone down and they had shuffled into a blowing line. What was this strange little creature? He smelt human and yet he was no bigger than the dog behind him. And faced with this formidable line of staring mountains Donald's confidence had deserted him and he had returned crying to the backyard, leaving Pat to bark furiously at the cows. They had tossed their heads and gone on their way. As if it was their fault!

After that they had got used to him from afar, staring over hedges as he played in the yard, taking note when he started to venture into the cowshed on his own, listening to his shrill orders as he helped to drive them back to the meadow. So now he was just one of the gang.

Daisy was in the far corner. She watched us come towards her and when we were close she turned away. Already the first membrane was oozing from her, still unbroken and filled with liquid. She stopped, raised her tail and strained. But it was only a half-hearted attempt.

Donald said: 'I can see a balloon.' He was leaning forward, hands on his knees.

'That's the calf coming,' I explained. 'Soon the balloon'll burst and then you'll see two small feet pushing out.'

'Will the balloon go bang?' he asked anxiously. He was not too keen on bursting balloons. He had been nervous of sudden bangs ever since the tractor had backfired and woken him with a start in his pram in the garden.

I laughed and ran my fingers through his hair. 'No, you won't even hear it. It's only a bag full of water with the calf inside. It just goes plop.'

He watched intently for a little longer. But when Daisy showed no more signs of getting on with the job he lost interest.

He stood up and looked around. 'I can see Lotty. She's looking at us. She wants to come and see Daisy have her calf.'

'I expect she does. Old Lotty always wants to know what's going on.'

Lotty was the first cow I'd had at Maywood. Most of the cows were young, ones I had reared on the farm and who had now taken the place of my original herd. But four of the old brigade still remained, those that had been the best milkers and therefore the last to bow out to the new generation. Besides Lotty and Daisy, there was the white cow, Popsi, with her pink-rimmed eyes and sweeping eyelashes and unassuming Bluebell, who took her rôle in life as a milk-producer more seriously than any cow I've known. She kept herself to herself, grazed a little apart from the others and chewed her cud more intently. She even kept her heats as refined as possible, limiting herself to a modest jump or two and certainly never letting herself go with the randy abandon that Lotty enjoyed on such occasions.

But Lotty was showing her age now. I felt a small stab of sorrow every time I looked at her. As she stared at us, blades of grass still hanging from her jaws, the tall curving horns that had kept her the boss cow over all newcomers, she looked as arrogant as ever. But age-rings adorned her horns like heirlooms on a dowager's fingers, her body sagged and her bones stared. And she wasn't in calf. She should have been heavy in calf by now. But month after month she had returned, flinging herself on the other cows quite shamelessly, bellowing when we tied her in the shed to await the inseminator and costing me another twenty-five bob each time he came. As each month had gone by I had told myself fiercely she would have to go if she did not get in calf. Yet each time she had returned and I'd given her another month's grace. At least she was still milking quite well. That was my excuse for putting off the evil day. But soon new heifers would be calving and I would need her place in the cowshed. There wasn't enough food to keep unproductive animals on my small mixed farm. So I knew I could not delay the phone call for the cattle lorry much longer. We would have to load old Lotty up and send her off to Ashford market, to join the sorry band of barreners destined to fill the next week's meat pies.

Daisy gave a low moan and I turned to her again. Her tail was waving violently. The membrane ruptured so that the liquid gushed down over her udder and the whisps of her tail caught it and flicked it into the air. Now she was straining in earnest.

'Look, Donald!' I pointed. 'Now you can see the calf's feet. See? Just pushing out now.'

He nodded, bending forward with his hands on his knees again and staring with his mouth open.

'You keep watching,' I urged him. 'Soon it'll be born. Soon it'll come out with a rush.'

Daisy turned round and stared at the sound of my voice. She strutted on a few paces. She didn't need any comments from me, thank you.

But I said: 'Come on now, old girl. One big push and it's all over.'

Which is just what she did, squatting as she pushed so that the calf dived downwards in its shiny sheath, landing gently on its outstretched feet. It was poised there for a moment, its hind legs still caught in the tangle of membrane coming from the cow. And as she straightened up it all came away and flopped to the ground with a shudder and a rush of water. Immediately Daisy turned to the calf, thrusting her head forward with a moan of pleasure, rasping it with her tongue as it shook its head and snuffled to free its face from the clinging membrane.

'There!' I exclaimed, 'did you see? That's how a calf's born. Wasn't that a lovely sight? And look at its eyes, open and blinking already to see its mummy.'

Donald looked at it without speaking, nodding quickly because I had sounded excited. It was another new sight, just another of all the new things that filled the days of a three-year-old and he took it in his stride. But I was glad he had seen it all the same. He could learn things naturally as he grew up, not be faced with all the secret puzzling that I could remember experiencing.

Daisy was licking at the calf haphazardly, like cows always do. They never seem to concentrate on the places that matter, quite content to bowl it about with a strong lick along its back, another under the belly, repeating the same places while the calf splutters, shakes its head and longs to be free of the sticky sheath clogging its nostrils and veiling its eyes.

I told Donald to stay where he was as I walked the few paces to the calf. Daisy paused and watched as I brushed my hand down the calf's face to clean it. It was small, dainty, brown like Daisy but with a white triangle on its forehead and it blinked up at me with long, curling lashes. It seemed to be trying to focus out of the dark blue pools of its eyes. I felt a thrill of pleasure, sure it was a heifer and ran my hand into the slimy white folds between the hind legs to make certain. No, there was no bunched up little scrotum, just four tiny teats. One day she would have a white udder like her mother.

'Well done, Daisy! There's a clever old cow.' She shoved her tongue up one nostril in acknowledgment of my congratulations. The difference between a heifer or a bull calf was the difference between an animal to become a cow herself, or thirty shillings to go for veal next market day, which is all bull calves from dairy breeds were worth. It was a good job the cows could not understand my reaction to the birth of their calves; why sometimes it provoked smiles and congratulations, at others just; 'You silly old sod, another bloody bull calf.'

Already the calf was struggling to her feet. I helped her up. She stood unsteadily, seemingly trying to balance on the tips of still translucent hooves. Daisy took a step forward and raked a

23

long lick under the scraggy chin, knocking her over again. For a second the calf looked bewildered, floppy eared. Then she was lurching up again, bundling forward into Daisy's dewlap.

'See, Donald?' I called. 'A heifer! We'll be able to keep this calf. Perhaps you can feed her later on.'

'I want to stroke it,' he said, starting forward.

I picked him up, quickly. 'In a minute, wait a minute. Just wait till Daisy's sure she's standing up properly.'

She was an old cow. She had always been quiet with her calves and never seemed to miss them once they were shut away from her to be reared on their own. But there was just a chance she would object if Donald rushed forward to clasp the calf. So I stood him down quietly and in a moment he chuckled as he reached forward to touch the calf.

Strangely Daisy turned away and strutted off. She seemed to have lost interest. She lowed quietly, not turning her head and calling to the calf, but looking straight ahead, more as though she was talking to herself. The calf gave a skip and bumped into Donald, catching him off balance so that he sat back firmly on the grass.

I picked him up quickly, before he could howl, carrying him away, laughing to make a joke of it and walking towards the hedge.

In a moment a destraction made him forget his fright. He pointed, holding his finger close to his nose. 'I can see Sadie.'

She was just visible through the hawthorn hedge, sitting upright. Daisy must have smelt her. That was why she had moved away and lowed. Except she'd moved in the other direction. If she had smelt Sadie she would have walked towards the hedge to sort her out. Or had some trick breeze wafted her scent in from further along the hedge? Whatever the explanation, Sadie would have to go home.

She saw I had spotted her. Her ears went back and her tail swished guiltily.

'You crafty devil,' I growled. 'Just *had* to see what was going on, didn't you? Home! Go on, home!'

'Home, Sadie!' Donald copied my tone from his perch on my arm.

Her ears shot forward, her head cocked to one side. Her tail beat with more confidence as she tried to brazen it out. With a

24

child on my arm and a hedge between us she knew there was nothing I could do to enforce my commands. Oh well, I would have to take Donald home now anyway and come back for Daisy and her calf. Sadie would follow and we would meet in the lane — except she would keep her distance at first, just in case I was still thinking of aiming my boot at her backside to help her home. That was the trouble with Sadie. She was such an excellent mind-reader that she always had the last laugh.

As I started for home Donald was looking back over my shoulder. 'Daisy's lying down now,' he informed me.

'I expect she's tired.' I carried on walking, peering through the hedge to make sure Sadie was coming. There was just a chance she would stay behind. She knew a new calf was soon followed by a pile of placenta and she was partial to a chew at that if nobody was looking. But she was keeping pace with us on the other side of the hedge.

'Lotty's talking to Daisy's calf now,' Donald told me. 'Look!' He laughed. 'The calf's running aside Lotty now.'

I spun round, just as Lotty was about to inform the calf that she wasn't her mum. She had swung round with a great flurry of hooves and tail and was snorting a warning. The bemused calf stopped in mid-stagger, trying to decide where the welcome warm udder was to be found. And, strangely, Daisy was lying down several yards away, her back towards them and only her ears turned back to catch the sounds, unconcerned that Lotty was considering hoicking her calf into the next field, possibly even the next world.

'Lotty, you great bully!' I roared. I dumped Donald on his feet and rushed at her. She shook her head, turned and took off, raising her tail and kicking up her hind legs like a heifer in spring grass. 'You ... you devil,' I fumed after her. 'Pick somebody your own size. It's no good, you'll just have to go.'

I turned back. 'Come on, Daisy,' I called. 'Why don't you look after your calf? What's the matter with you? Get up and give her a drink.' I put my hands on the calf's back and gently pushed her in front of me.

But Daisy was on her side now. Her belly was heaving upwards. She had already calved, and yet ...

'Look, Donald! It's twins. Daisy's going to have twins!'

The sows had ten, twelve, sometimes more piglets at a time.

25

Often the sheep had triplets. But I had never had a cow give birth to twins before and I celebrated by picking Donald up and hugging him. He looked at me with concern as he drew away. A cuddle was something to be suffered with a good grace at bedtime. But not in the middle of a field when there was so much else going on.

So I released him down and he stood beside me to watch the next calf being born. And while it floundered out and shook for a breath of the new world, the first calf fidgeted beside us, sucking at my finger, spitting it out, skipping, wobbling and bunting to have another go.

In a moment Daisy was on her feet again, reaching out to the new calf with her long tongue. And it was another heifer, almost like the first with her brown coat and the white triangle on her forehead. Only now the white on the udder extended in a splash along her belly and ended in the brown of the shrivelled little dewlap.

I pushed the first calf towards her mother. She welcomed it with a sniff and a lick. Now she was quite willing to give her whole attention to her offspring. They wobbled around her, nosing into her — the udder must be around here somewhere. The first calf found it. Already the milk was weeping from the tight teats. She fastened on to one and Daisy shifted in the beginnings of a kick, only to let her foot fall back gently to the ground. She twisted round and licked the calf's now wriggling tail. Soon the second calf joined her sister and they stood side by side shakily sucking, now missing a teat, now grabbing it again while the milk trickled in a constant stream and sprayed the brown faces when they bunted in the wrong direction. Daisy looked at me and blinked slowly. From her expression you would have thought she produced twins every time.

On the way home we named them Primrose and Prunella. Without hesitation Donald came up with Primrose when I asked him for names, because Primrose the cow was the heroine in one of his story books. Then he trotted off to peer through the hedge to make sure Sadie was coming. So that left me wracking my brain for another flower beginning with P that would sound right together. And the little purple prunella was the best I could think of, the flower the old folk called Clumsy Carpenter's Herb because it was said to be a fine healer of cuts.

26

Then I said: 'Won't Mummy be surprised? She won't believe Daisy's had twins when we tell her.'

'I want to tell her. Let me tell her.' He hurried ahead. At the gate he stopped, fidgeting for me to open it. As he squeezed through, he said: 'P'raps Mummy'll have two babies as well.' The idea sent him speeding ahead because just recently he had become very interested in his mother's condition. Up to a week ago he had seemed not to notice in spite of all our talk of another baby. Then Olive had pushed back her chair from the breakfast table and sighed as she made the effort to stand up. And Donald had given her a searching stare: 'Crumbs, Mummy, you've had a big breakfast.'

That night Olive gave birth. But not before the baking was all finished, with the bread cool in the bin and the cakes and the buns glowing in their own tins — enough to last a week and more. The kitchen table was scrubbed with sweat and sighing and: 'No, let me do it, of course I can manage, thanks.' The house was cleaned through and notes were left in strategic spots to guide Mother through the days' tasks when she arrived to take charge.

There was a large walk-in pantry off the kitchen, that used to be the old dairy. Here, too, it was well documented with 'Dog Food' followed by how much each should have, and 'Wine Fermenting — Don't Move', and 'Use cracked eggs for cooking' because she sold all the sound ones. Once I'd had free range in here, sprawling over the shelves with cow medicines, udder ointments, horse oils, healing salves and bottles with large black teats for feeding lambs. Now they were all set neatly together in a corner and labelled simply 'David's Stuff'.

After tea Donald was put to bed, still full of chatter about calves instead of chickens and convinced that the morning would bring both a new brother and a sister. Olive bent to kiss him goodnight, saying: 'Yes, yes, we'll see. But I'm sure it'll be just one or the other.' His arms were round her neck, his cheek against hers. Suddenly she was on her knees, her face buried in the pillow, her knuckles whitening in a grip on the bed head as the first pains went through her.

By the time the pains were coming close together the night had come. The midwife arrived. Together they went upstairs and

I followed them into the bedroom, unrecognisable now in anti-septic correctness, with the bassinet waiting expectantly beside the bed, delicately draped in a pleated skirt of organdie.

Everything was so clean and tidy that I entered uncertainly, conscious of my rough hands and working clothes, and the few stray cow hairs embedded in my trousers. A frozen stare from the midwife emphasised the fact that from now on it was women's work and I crept away, banished to the sitting room below to join the dogs; to sit and listen; to wait and wonder.

The boards creaked above the black beams in the ceiling. It sounded as though they were both pacing the room. Faint voices talked and were silent, talked again. Then they stopped altogether and the boards no longer creaked. Now I knew the real meaning of a pregnant silence.

The dogs had lost interest. They had greeted the midwife with a certain amount of suspicion for visiting at such a late hour and had padded after her to the foot of the stairs. But they were not allowed upstairs and when I came down they were sitting side by side staring upwards, waiting for an explanation at this strange break in routine. Now Sadie had decided it was not worth losing any more sleep over and had stretched right out on the floor with a loud sigh and soon her feet were twitching as she re-lived some escapade. Pat was almost asleep, his head between his paws, his eyes tight shut, only now and then an ear moved and he opened half an eye. He just couldn't drop off to sleep properly until he knew why Olive had gone upstairs with that stranger, and why she hadn't come down.

Now came stern words from the midwife. They were orders, shouted orders. They came again, drowning a cry of desperation. And then there was silence again. It seemed an age before it was broken by the first thin cry.

Pat pricked up his ears and looked at me.

'It's a baby, Pat,' I cried. I knelt on the floor and grabbed his head, holding it close as I gazed into his eyes. 'Another baby,' but now my voice croaked and I found tears in my eyes.

I stood up quickly and Pat followed me to the foot of the stairs. He sat down with his chin on the bottom stair as he watched me go up.

In the bedroom the midwife smiled at me. She pointed to the bed. The baby was tiny, perfect, like a doll with red cheeks, wide

28

eyes and a tuft of black hair, lying in her mother's arms.

Olive was breathing fast. She gave a tired smile. 'Well,' she gasped, 'don't just stand there.' She caught her breath again and smiled down at the baby. 'Here she is, here's our little Cherry.'

In the morning Donald charged in, clasping a large red tractor. He ran to the bassinet, peered into it and held the tractor just above her face. 'See, Baby? Tractor!' We held our breath while he waited for a reply — some sign from Cherry that she realised she had arrived on a farm and was prepared to discuss tractors. But she slept on and we breathed again when he hauled the tractor back and sent it clattering across the floor.

Only he didn't give up that easily. At breakfast time he drew up a chair and laid a place for his new sister, adding three cows and a pig beside it for her to play with.

2

IT WAS SADIE'S and Pat's custom to greet each new day with a tour of inspection of the farm and animals as though they had been away for a week. Not that they would stir from their baskets under the kitchen table until Olive arrived down to cook breakfast. They would watch me earlier, opening half an eye as I made a cup of tea in the five o'clock morning and deciding it was too early for respectable dogs to stir. And when I went out of the back door to start milking, they would squeeze their eyes tight shut and sigh loudly to forestall any idea I might have of calling them out after me.

That was the routine. When Olive did turf them out they would stroll away stretching and spend a long time sniffing about the yard and the verges of the lane, selecting the exact spots to pee. Then a good sniff all over the farm was important to them, for when a dog takes a walk he is like a man reading his morning newspaper. To him each smell is an item of news, and to a country dog the tangled verges and the thick hedge bottoms of a country lane, the dusty corners of a cowshed, the dark reaches of a bullock lodge and the rustling rick bottoms are their *Times* and *Mirror* rolled into one. There is news of mice, rats, rabbits, pheasants, as well as of other dogs or stray cats that could well be worth an exhilarating chase.

Sadie and Pat always started by rounding the pond, often cutting off Sinbad and his wives as they made their morning advance on the back door in single file, to await Olive's appearance with their breakfast. The ducks were her special favourites and she always insisted on feeding and looking after them. And Sadie could never resist nosing out of her way to make the ducks break rank, even if she knew Olive was going to shout at her from the kitchen window. She wouldn't chase them, but just made sure they waddled in disarray with loud protesting quacks before she caught up with Pat. Then it was off under the rails of the bullock lodge to the calf pens for a quick sniff at the noses of the calves as they snuffled over the low walls awaiting the morning milk. And from there, through into the covered yard of yearlings and an inspection under the long manger because sometimes they were lucky enough to put up a rat. But always it was a quick skedaddle out again when the bolder heifers started towards them, wanting a boisterous game of chasing round and round in the clogging straw.

Off then for a quick visit to the pig meadow, pausing for a squelch round the edge of the midden on the way because the rich smell always excited them, and they would stand side by side at the gateway beyond the pigsties staring through at Skinny and Fatso, the two old sows. But they never ventured inside the meadow. Only sometimes the sows weren't there because they liked to break out and stroll around the farmyard themselves. And if the dogs bumped into them unexpectedly they would pretend they hadn't seen them, look the other way and veer off as though something more interesting needed their immediate attention. They had long since discovered that there was no way you could get the better of a sow. Not even of Martha and Mary, the two gilts I was rearing to take the old sows' places. At one time, when they were weaners, the dogs had been friendly with them and there had been some exciting games chasing them. But now the gilts had grown large and solid so that Sadie and Pat found they had to look up to them. And these days the gilts seldom ran, but walked ponderously, and stared menacingly, daring the dogs to start something. All the same, it was always part of the morning ritual to call by the pig meadow just for a short stare and a low growl.

Then it was on through the stack-plat for a rummage round the ricks in case a stray cat was patiently waiting for mice or rats to emerge. Sometimes Henry, the old tom cat, had girl friends visiting and they liked to prowl the stack-plat, looking for a square meal before sleeping off a night of love in the silence of the oast house just across the lane. So the dogs circled each rick in turn, snorting into the hay and straw before coming out into the lane again and hurrying down to the cowshed to catch the end of the milking. They came in panting, tongues lolling, and would greet each of us in turn. And if old Henry happened to be around, back on the farm again after one of his sex-seeking safaris, scowling and meowing for milk, the dogs would bundle into him, bowl him over, lick his balls and generally let him know they were quite glad to see him again.

And when the milking was finished and the early morning chores done, the dogs would follow me down to the house and in for breakfast, to sit around looking smug and behaving as though they, too, had been up since dawn and done their share in the running of the farm.

Only it was all different on the morning after Cherry was born. Suddenly Sadie and Pat found their routine shattered. Olive never appeared in the kitchen to turn them out and they were in no mood to take orders and explanations from me. They were already thoroughly perplexed at being disturbed when I ushered out the midwife in the deep watches of the night. They had both heaved themselves out of their baskets and sniffed her suspiciously. Now I was preparing to cook breakfast and ordering them outside. However they did agree to amble across the yard for a pee, but only because they were bursting, and then they were back again, yapping to come in and even ignoring Sinbad and his harem filing past on their breakfast parade.

Donald finished laying the place at table for Cherry and rushed to let the dogs in. Pat barged by first, gave him a lick in passing, carried out a rapid search of the kitchen and pantry and went through to the foot of the stairs. There he plonked himself down with a loud sigh and gazed upwards with his chin on a stair. And there he stayed during the ten days of Olive's confinement, only leaving his post when Nature called or if Donald really insisted in dragging him away to play. Even then he opted out of the games almost immediately and returned to the stairs, to be there when Olive should return down them and into his life again.

Sadie wasn't so bothered and she was the first to get wind of Mother, tilting her head to listen and then agitating to be let

32

out. She bounded into the yard and sat upright by the gate, rigid and expectant.

And in a few moments Mother came swooping in on her old bike, heralding her arrival with a 'Coo-ee!' and scattering Sinbad's solemn procession.

'Whoopsey! Sorry, Sinbad!' she called, above the scraping of inefficient brakes and indignant quacks, and with a skid or two from her foot she completed her stop. Her cheeks were bright red, her white hair flying for freedom around her woolly beret and at sixty-five she was still as fond of a cycle ride as she had ever been.

She carried her belongings in a paper carrier bag bulging from the bicycle basket, strapped drunkenly to the handlebars, and it threatened to topple out on to the yard as she flung her bike against the fence. She grappled with Sadie's prancing welcome, wrapped her arms around Donald when he ran to her and laughed up at me.

'So glad everything went all right. Lovely to have a baby girl. But Cherry, what a strange name. Never mind, now you've got a pigeon pair.' She gave her gay little laugh and ruffled her hand through Donald's hair. 'Come along, you must show me your new sister. I simply flew here as soon as I knew.'

I had telephoned her with the news. We had arranged for Olive's own mother to come, but just two days previously she had been taken ill and so my mother had agreed to take over.

In no time at all there was chaos in the kitchen as Mother became established. She always came in like a flurry of autumn leaves, hat on a chair, scarf on the floor, coat hurled across the table, handbag dumped anywhere handy and the inevitable carrier bag of bits and pieces, that always seemed to travel with her, cast idly aside and spilling its contents like a broken-open parcel. And when she had hurried upstairs to greet Olive, lifted Cherry from the bassinet, cuddled her and crooned over her around the room and popped her back again in a tangle of long nightie, she was soon downstairs and high busy starting on the washing, poking and stoking the fire and wondering aloud what to cook.

'*What* a good idea!' she declared, as she spotted Olive's strategically placed aids to housekeeping, 'Now I'll know just where to find everything.' She screwed up her eyes as she tried to read one of the instructions, then banged her hands against her sides and looked around her. 'Come along now, Donald, use your sharp eyes to help me find my specs. I *know* they're here somewhere.'

When she found them: 'Ah! Here they are, lost in the wretched lining of my overcoat pocket as usual,' she moved from place to place, reading each notice aloud, committing them to memory and resolving to do things Olive's way.

Not that there was any chance of that, although she did try. Instead she became thoroughly confused, could never remember what each notice said nor lay her hands on her specs right away to read it. So before the end of the first day she had reverted to her own slap-happy methods and in a way it was just as well that Olive was safely out of sight, sound and smell or she would never have managed to stick out the regulation ten days of 'laying-up'.

As it was, Donald kept his mother on tenterhooks with fleeting visits to the bedroom and garbled accounts of goings-on in the kitchen, and my visits were spent in cover-up explanations, assuring her that Mother was managing splendidly, telling her to lie back and make the most of the rest and the room service, enjoy the baby and not to worry or she would lose her milk.

Joyously Mother arrived every morning in time to cook the breakfast, after her three-mile ride over from Jessamine Cottage. And equally joyously Donald greeted her, looking forward to yet another exciting day in the entertaining company of his granny. He followed her everywhere, in and out of the kitchen, up and down the stairs, and seized on idle moments to lead her around the farmyard and bring her up to date with a constant chatter of the latest news of birds and beasts. Whatever she did he watched carefully, forever telling her: 'Mummy doesn't do it like that.' And when, almost every morning at breakfast, smoke curled upwards filling the kitchen with the tell-tale smell: 'Quick, Granny! The toast's burning *again!*' With a peal of laughter he would scramble from his chair, knife in hand: 'Let me help! Let me help you scrape the black bits into the sink!'

He pulled up a chair to stand on and they worked hard side by side, laughing. And Donald always looked up at her with a wicked grin: 'I wonder if Mummy'll know?'

'I wonder!'

When it was done: 'I'll take it up to her. Let me, Granny. But I *won't tell* her.'

But we always heard him giggle before he reached the top of the stairs. And when he came down again he was laughing. 'She knew! She knew! She said Granny wouldn't be Granny if we didn't have scraped toast for breakfast.'

Yet I don't know what we would have done without her. She slaved away at the sink, sloshing her way through the endless stream of nappies, always some soaking, or some being rinsed, or sometimes some getting mixed with potato peelings by mistake. But at the end of each day, by the time she rode off home, all the work was done, with the kitchen neat and tidy once more and still glowing with love left behind.

One morning, a few weeks after Cherry was born and life in the house was back to normal, I noticed a strange dog breezing down the lane as I left the cowshed during the morning milking. It was a fox terrier type, but smaller, white with brown blotches and looking as though he had Jack Russell blood in him. He was only skimming through the news, nipping along, now and then stopping for just a moment, running mostly on three paws and carrying a hind leg, as a terrier will when his mind is on something special. He was coming down from the top road, the one that led to the village two miles away and beside which a few lone houses straggled. Perhaps he came from one of these but I could not recollect having seen him before. Somehow he did not give the impression of being a country dog at all. A pheasant rose with a shriek and a wild flapping, beating its way into the wood behind the farm buildings as though a dozen foxes were after it. Sadie and Pat would have leapt into joyous pursuit, quite fruitless, but returning well pleased with themselves, grinning and with tongues lolling. But the terrier hardly noticed. Obviously he had weightier matters on his mind. He flattened his ears, hugged his bum with his tail and continued on his three-legged way towards me.

Sadie and Pat were still indoors so he had the lane to himself. He reverted to all fours as he passed me, casting me a sly glance and running crab-wise as though he was expecting me to swear at him. Suddenly he stopped, his ears pricked, his tail erect. Here was the item of news that interested him. You could keep

35

all your accounts of pheasants, partridges, rabbits and rats for here, among broad smells of cows and passing pigs, was real Page Three material. Here was news of a bitch. And he searched diligently through the grass with a delicate, heady sniff here, a snort and half a sneeze there and further on a long, serious study of a special patch while his docked tail thrust upwards, beating like a metronome. And so that there should be no misunderstanding that he was interested he left his calling card in half a dozen places before he was satisfied. Then he stiffened, threw out his little chest and scratched into the grass with four rigid legs and an important look on his face. He trotted past me again, still crab-wise but arrogantly now, and he only paused for an occasional sniff and a pee to mark his passing before he was out of sight.

This was the first of what soon became a regular morning visit.

'Who does he belong to?' I asked Pete, while we were milking.

He eased his greasy beret up his forehead. 'Buggered if I know. I ain't seen 'im before. Randy little sod by the looks o' him. All the same them terriers be. Prick's all 'em think about. Prick and rats.' He smiled, showing large, even teeth and his brown eyes flashed with fun.

'He comes down from the top road,' I said, 'but I thought I knew all the dogs along there.'

'He comes from the village, most like.' This suggestion came from Bert. He spoke as he came out of the dairy at the far end of the cowshed.

'Two miles?' I laughed. 'Sounds a long way to me for his little legs.'

'It ain't far if 'ees after a bit.' Bert defended his suggestion.

'You speak for yourself,' Pete chided him.

'Cor, bugger me! You're a one to talk!' Bert shuffled his cap, spat in the gutter and clanked off with a bucket and cluster to fix the machine on Bluebell.

The two brothers had worked at Maywood ever since I had bought the farm five years previously. Pete was now twenty-two and Bert was twenty and they both still lived at home with their parents in a cottage on the brow of the hill. Sometimes I wondered when they would get married and leave home. Selfishly I hoped they wouldn't because it would probably mean they

36

would leave the farm as well, off in search of work where a cottage went with the job. They both had girl friends. Pete had been going with his Rose ever since I had known him, while Bert tended to play the field. But while there was the inevitable chat about girls, neither of them ever talked seriously of marriage.

At one time I thought Pete would be sure to get married soon. Rose was the only girl friend he'd ever had and Bert often insisted: 'Why, he were fiddlin' after 'er even in school.' And in the early days Pete used to get fidgety and anxious to be off work sharp on time. Sometimes, if a delay was unavoidable, perhaps with a sick animal needing extra attention, or a calving cow, or at haymaking and harvest times, Rose would cycle out from the village to seek him out and find out why he was late for their date. But gradually she seemed to take second place while Pete stodged on in what were fast becoming his set ways. He seemed to love the animals more.

Rose was an attractive girl, in a nicely rounded way, and I often chided Pete that he would lose her to another young ram if he continued to stand her up too often. 'Go on,' I would say to him, if we were late at work, 'I can manage now. You go on home to your tea or we'll have Rose down here looking for you again.'

'Her don't mind. Her'll wait.'

'One day she won't. One day some other smartie pants will charm her off you.'

'Sod 'er then. Her wouldn't be no good to I if that happened, now would 'er?'

But Rose adored Pete and seemed quite content to string along at his beck and call. And Pete was sure of her. Already he had the old countryman's belief that a woman was God's gift to man, that she should know her place and be prepared to be taken for granted. Even when Rose did come looking for him, propping her bike against the cowshed wall, stepping shyly through the mud and standing at a discreet distance when she found us, Pete never even acknowledged her arrival. I would smile at her, dressed for her date and reeking of cologne, say hello and tell her that Pete was just coming. He would carry on working, without even a glance in her direction, and insist on staying to help me finish. And when he did leave with her, his beret thrust down on his head in stern determination, I never ever heard them talk.

Once I asked him about his off-hand manner with her. He smiled and looked embarrassed – as he always did when the topic of conversation had nothing to do with the farm. And while he thought of a reply he removed his beret, scratched his thick black hair, kicked at a stone and jammed his beret back on again.

But before he got around to saying anything, Bert chipped in with his opinion: ' 'Tis same as the old chaps down the pub allus say.' He cleared his throat in imitation and frowned in mock seriousness. 'If yer wants a woman to stay by yer, then you've to keep 'er well stuffed and poorly shod.'

Bert was never short of an opinion on anything. Although he was more quick-witted he did not have the staying power of Pete, nor the reliability, nor quite the dedication to the job. He wasn't a clock watcher, but he was always careful to be off on time and leave his elder brother to cope if something needed finishing. That is not to say he wasn't a good worker. He was, and during the plodding hours in the hop garden, each of us working his way down a row, skimming off the crowns of the roots in the clogging clay of early spring, or parting and training the tangled shoots in the fitful April sun, it was always Bert who reached the end of his row first, lolling against a pole and rolling himself a fag while he chided us for being slow-coaches.

And Bert liked to know what was going on. Where Pete was content to discuss the milk yields of the cows, the price of a pocket of hops, how to increase the average number of piglets in a litter – or to report if blacksmith Boney Jackson had been cursing the decline in the number of cart horses, or Fred Cummins holding the floor on a new strain of wheat, Bert took an interest in the wider world beyond the farm and village. Sometimes he took the bus to Ashford on his day off. And the next day we would have his opinions on such diverse subjects as the new models of cars now starting to reach the streets after the war, the plot of the Western he had seen at the Odeon, the vital statistics of the usherette and usually an unlikely, blow by blow account of a meeting with 'one of they London girls wot's come to live in Ashford'. And Bert read a newspaper too, every Sunday. So during Monday morning milkings he would treat us to a quick rundown of world events and a detailed description of the latest sex scandal, which had the cows fidgeting and shaking their heads in disbelief – unless it was because we were late feeding them as we listened to Berts' graphic descriptions.

Bert took an interest in my life as well. He seldom asked a direct personal question but would glean information by discussion, suggestion, or asking my advice. I'd had a girl friend called Jean before I met Olive. During my first year at Maywood this bewitching blonde pitched up on the farm one winter's evening and I fell in love with her at first sight. She was in the Women's Land Army, had been given the job of a peripatetic rat-catcher and fell in love with me too, as we plunged around the farm looking for rats and found the soft couch of hay in the corner of the cowshed. And Pete and Bert followed the wooing with little comment as it progressed through the bright spring and into the dreamy summer evenings. They were still teenagers and I was in my early twenties and on the swoony road to marriage. There was nothing remarkable about that. So when I returned from a visit to see Jean, coasting down the lane on my bike in time for the afternoon milking, and breezed into the cowshed to announce that she and I had become engaged, they accepted the news with wise nods. Eventually Pete said: 'That's nice,' because some remark seemed called for. Bert just grunted his agreement.

Then came The Row, the irreconcilable clash of ideas that shattered the dream Jean and I shared. And afterwards the dragging nights, the fitful sleep, the sinking mornings as consciousness returned. And the long silences in the heaving work of the days, while I grovelled in my misery and the boys talked together in undertones, as though there had been a death in the family. Even the cows seemed to sense the despondency, shuffling uncomfortably as they missed the laughing chatter and the hearty bursts of swearing.

Finally it was Bert who probed the hidden depths of my misery. Then he was sixteen and from beneath a cow, busily milking, he suddenly remarked: 'Glad I ain't got a reg'lar girl friend.' He waited for some response to this opening gambit. As neither Pete nor I offered any reply, he went on: 'Casual girls, that's what I has. Love's 'em and leaves 'em, I do.'

'Bloody liar,' Pete muttered, 'you ain't never had a girl.'

Bert finished his cow, stood up and banged the milking stool against the wall with a clatter. 'Who says?'

'I do.' Pete had his head in Lotty's flank and was gazing into his bucket and the milk frothing there. 'Why, you'm only a bloody kid. You ain't hardly finished shitting yellow.'

Bert was quick to notice my smile. 'I've kissed plenty of girls,' he bragged, looking at me and obviously waiting for some observation.

'Have you now,' I said, 'I hope they enjoyed it.'

'Of course.' He sniffed and wiped his nose with the back of a milk-sticky hand. 'I knows how ter use me tongue an' all. They likes that. But when they starts groanin' and lookin' goofy, I leaves 'em. I don't want 'em getting serious. That ain't no good if you gets serious back 'cos they can bugger orf two-timin'.'

I knew this was a question. I had never explained the reason for my break with Jean. It wasn't any of their business. And yet they had known her quite well, had laughed and joked with her on her visits to the farm, especially when she joined in with hay-making, corn harvest and hop-picking. Like me they had been expecting her to become a permanent part of the farm. Perhaps it was time I talked about it. Certainly I did not want them assuming that Jean had found someone else. So I said: 'Jean didn't push off with anyone else, if that's what you're thinking.'

Bert was fair skinned and freckled and he blushed as he started towards the dairy with his full bucket of milk. Pete was still milking, and from three cows along he surprised me by asking: 'Then why?'

I finished milking, stood up and carried the bucket and stool to the wall behind the cows. I put them down and leant back against the wall. 'We had an argument, a real row all about priorities. I said that when you were a farmer it could be a twenty-four-hour-a-day job, that first and foremost you were wedded to your farm and your animals. Not a very tactful thing to say to a fiancée, I suppose. But then, I said it in a sort of joking way. She knew I meant it though and she flared. She said she certainly wasn't going to play second fiddle to a load of cows and pigs and sheep, and if that's how I felt about it I could whistle for a wife. *She* wasn't going to marry me.' I shrugged and picked up the bucket. Bert was standing with his mouth open, half on his way back from the dairy. 'So that's it really,' I went on, 'now you know. It's over. Finished. Kaput.'

They were silent as I went to the dairy to empty the milk. I was glad I had told them. It helped to dilute it, this sickening solution sloshing around in my brain, seeping into every thought so that I was unable to set my mind clearly on anything else. Of course Jean and I had tried to simmer down, to argue round it, to make up in a voluptuary of tears and tenderness. We went on meeting for a time but the easy agreement had gone, the lovely telepathy clouded in hidden thoughts until we were only uttering pleasantries and afraid of speaking our minds. So we agreed to part. Just for three months, we said, to test our feelings for each other. Yet we both knew it was really for keeps because the magic had gone and uneasiness and uncertainty had replaced it. In a way I felt relief. But that did not lighten the drab cloud in which I walked, wrapping gloom around those with whom I came in contact.

Especially my Mother. She and I lived alone together at Maywood then and she had been preparing herself to welcome a daughter-in-law into the house with her usual enthusiasm and Christian charity. And when she felt the gloom, and asked about it, I shouted at her that it was finished, that love was a con. She looked sad, put her arm in mine, tried to help, although she knew that sympathy sometimes only turns a knife in the wound. As usual, she fell back on God. Perhaps it was not His will that Jean and I got married and had I thought about that? No, no, what the hell had God got to do with it? As far as I was concerned a disaster had befallen me and if that was God's will then He was a God of calamity and not a God of love. So she sighed and turned away because to her God was everything and it gave her pain to hear blasphemy. And then I was sorry and kissed her, wrapped myself more tightly in my cloak of sadness and we never mentioned Jean again.

It seemed like an eternity, but a week or two later I was beginning to get over it. After I told the boys, it cleared the air. In a few days conversation was more or less back to normal. But Bert was still concerned for my welfare. He had therapeutic advice to offer: 'You'll have to try the heifer market in Tenterden,' he suggested, and I knew he was referring to the occasional dances that were held in the Town Hall a few miles away.

These dances were more select than the usual village hops. They were advertised in the local paper. And bills were posted around the place with GRAND DANCE in large red letters. You had to buy a ticket and it cost half a crown against the shilling tossed into the saucer at the door, which bought admission to a village hop. The Grand Dance boasted a buffet, some fish-paste sandwiches, rock buns and a cup of tea at half time, card tables for tête-à-têtes between dances, and red crêpe paper round the white bakelite lampshades to add a touch of intimacy. And as well as a Master of Ceremonies in a dinner jacket and a five-piece band, it also attracted the daughters of local farmers, auctioneers and other important people, so that for two shillings and sixpence a bachelor could cast his net over the available talent from a fairly wide area.

I have never been much of a dancer. But I enjoyed trying out my few self-taught steps, and in the years before I bought Maywood, when I was learning the trade as a farm worker on other farms, I used to go to the Saturday night dances. There was always a dance in one village or another and after meeting with like-minded friends at the nearest pub, and loosening up there for an hour or so, we would wander across to the village hall to inspect the weekly offering of wallflowers and join the fray.

One Saturday I had been working overtime all afternoon. At that time I was a shepherd's mate on a large farm in Worcestershire. We had plenty of sheep to keep us busy but the day before the boss had bought a new flock of ewes. He said they were a bargain, but when they arrived many of them were limping with foot rot. So with the old shepherd grumbling and cursing the previous shepherd, continually referring to him as 'that bleedin' limb o' Satan', we spent the whole day catching the ewes one by one, sitting them up between our thighs while we pared their hooves and dressed them with a mixture of saltpetre and Stockholm tar. It was wearying work, wading into the steaming sheep, grabbing the lame ones, hauling them out and heaving them upright. But when we finished, brushing the odd sheep tick from our clothes and straining aching backs, there was still time for a wash to remove the clinging smell of tar and foot rot and to change into Saturday night gear.

After a few reviving beers at the pub I was ready for the

42

dance. It was lively and in particular there was a tall girl, with black hair and eyes as dark as deep water. She reminded me of my mental picture of Minnehaha. What is more, she was a marvellous mover. Usually my style of dancing was a quick trot down the sides of the floor and a sort of shuffle round the corners. But this Minnehaha really seemed to have 'heart and hand that moved together, feet that ran on willing errands', so that I was tempted into some daring and elaborate steps that took us cannoning across the floor and brought laughter to her eyes and sweat to my brow. I was doing fine. We were dancing together all evening. Already I had found out where she lived and had been accepted as her escort for the cycle ride home. I couldn't go wrong.

We were nearing the end of the dance. I held her daringly close. Her head was on my shoulder while we drifted as one in a convention-defying forerunner of the modern-day smooch. Suddenly I felt her grip tighten. I responded by squeezing her closer to me. This was my night. Slowly her head left my shoulder, drawing backwards. I looked into her face, searching into her eyes for the soft look of longing I expected to see. But her eyes were wide, staring, not looking into mine but fixed on the side of my neck instead.

Slowly, firmly, still staring at my neck she pushed me away from her. She gave a strange gasp and swallowed to find her voice: 'Ooh — err! You've got an 'orrid thing crawlin' up yer neck!' And she dropped me and fled, leaving me standing like a leper in the middle of the dance floor.

I put my hand to my neck and my fingers touched a sheep tick, casually journeying upwards from under my collar, hoping to hide in my hair while it paused in its search for the lost sheep's fleece.

It caused a laugh among the sons of the soil present, but it ruined my chances. Minnehaha shied away. She wouldn't even listen to my explanation and she covered her lovely eyes as I held out my hand towards her to show her the harmless little tick crawling across my palm. But I suppose I couldn't really blame her for changing her mind and refusing to let me take her home.

Since I had come to Maywood I had not done any dancing. I had not even patronised the local village hops. But a month or so after Bert had mentioned it, I bought a ticket for the Grand Dance at Tenterden.

And it was there that I met Olive. She was off her guard, immersed in the last hectic swot for her State Registered Nurse finals but on a visit home for her two days off in ten. Friends had persuaded her to relax for an evening, to put aside her books and accompany them to the Grand Dance. Poor girl, little did she know what a fatal move that would prove to be.

3

THE LITTLE TERRIER continued to come by on his regular morning walks. His routine never varied and it soon became obvious that he had a one-track mind. Perhaps he kept tabs on several bitches, I don't know. But if he did, Sadie must have been the first on his morning list because he always trotted by during milking and seemed to be working to a fairly tight schedule. He never dawdled and only loitered long enough to read the sex signals, leave news of his own continuing interest and push off back the way he had come. He never seemed anxious to hang around on the chance of meeting Sadie; to have a word to her face to face, or nose to tail, to size her up and tell her of his undying love. So it was rather like a pen friendship. Only, I suppose, they were really pee pals.

But he must have known all about Pat by now and perhaps he thought discretion to be the better part of valour. Certainly he was no match for the golden retrievers and this was proved one morning when he was late arriving and they were already out in the yard. We had named our importuning visitor, Randy, and he came sidling down the lane, scarcely stopping to pick up any scents en route and making straight for the spot where Sadie always left her greetings. Only this time she saw him coming when he was still a hundred yards off. From her reaction it was quite obvious that Randy in person bore no resemblance to the fellow who had been leaving such stirring messages for her each morning. She stared at this little white runt and growled menacingly. Which alerted Pat and brought him trotting out of the yard, growling importantly and with his hackles rising. And in a sudden spurt of speed both dogs took off together, feet scrabbling, tails flying and barking with impatience.

Randy hesitated, trying to make up his mind whether he ought to wait for formal introductions. But it did not take him long to decide that that could be bloody and away he went, ears flat and tail down as he made the most of the sixty-yard start still remaining to him. And Sadie and Pat let him go, breaking off the chase to rummage after another scent. He wasn't worth chasing when they knew they could not catch him.

Perhaps it was this fright that made Randy act as he did a few weeks later. He still kept coming as before. I was surprised. But evidently he reckoned he had put in too much groundwork to give up now, only his approach was more wary. His pauses were longer on his way down the lane. He must have sensed Sadie's approaching heat and this gave him the courage to persevere.

Now a bitch takes a good week telling all her friends about it before she is ready to entertain callers. I had been wondering how Randy would behave when the great day arrived, when his patience was rewarded and he read the first definite news for which he had been waiting. Poor little chap, I knew he was in for a bitter disappointment because I always shut Sadie away during the vital days. But it would be interesting to see whether he stuck around, was bold enough to stand his ground and to stake his claim during the heady days of anticipation and foreplay.

However, I was not prepared for the way he did act. He came down the lane as usual, but the nearer he came the faster he came, throwing caution into the winds of the scent that was already in his nostrils. And when he reached the spot he scurried around, his tail going mad as he made quite, quite certain. He never even stopped for a pee, still less for a scratch in the grass. Instead he took off as though the devil was in him and disappeared off up the lane as fast as his little legs could carry him.

'Did you see that?' I called out to Pete as Randy fled from our sight. 'What d'you make of that? All these weeks of waiting and now he's scared stiff of the real thing.'

Pete scratched his head through his beret. 'Buggered if I know. Ain't never seen a dog run away from the scent of a bitch, that I ain't.'

46

'Nor me.' I shrugged and turned back into the cowshed to get on with the work.

Half an hour later the milking and the morning feeding jobs were finished. The milk churns had to be wheeled up to the top road in a hand cart to await collection by the milk lorry. Bert was preparing to set off with them.

As he trundled them out into the lane he stopped and called back to us: 'Hey! Here comes Randy again. Christ! He's brought his bloody mates with 'im an' all!'

The urgency in his voice made us bundle out into the lane. Randy was in the lead, tail up, chest out, trotting as fast as dignity would allow. And behind him straggled a motley gang of dogs, tails waving, eyes glinting, tongues slobbering; snuffling and scuffling as they advanced on the farm; into the hedgerows and out again, catching each and every scent on the way; pausing, peeing, getting left behind and racing to catch up as it gradually dawned on them that what Randy had been bragging about all along was really true.

'Bug-ger me!' Pete jammed his hands on to his hips. 'Where the hell did 'ee find that lot?'

There must have been a dozen dogs, ranging from a large, ungainly Airedale, that kept over-running little Randy so that he was continually losing dignity as he was forced to scurry from beneath the tangle of paws to keep in the lead, through mongrels of all sizes and colours to a shifty-eyed sheepdog bringing up the rear, belly down, slinking and weaving. From the expressions on the mongrels' faces there was no doubt they were out for a day's enjoyment – two days, three days, as long as it took. But the sheepdog kept glancing behind him as though listening for a call to heel, unable to tear himself away from work completely in the pursuit of sex. He salved his conscience by following the dogs as though they were a flock of sheep in his charge.

'That big 'un's the doctor's dog, I'll lay,' Bert declared. 'And that pug-faced lookin' thing, 'ee comes from the pub. Aye, down the village that's where that Randy's been. Down there and fetched 'em all up 'ere.'

'Well they can all go back again.' I waved my arms, shouting. 'Go on, the lot of you. Home! Home!' There was just a chance they would obey.

Pete and Bert joined in and for a moment the dogs fetched up

47

in a ragged, panting heap, ears cocked and heads tilted as they tried to make up their minds about us. Randy was looking perplexed, as though he was sure his gang was still relying on him for a lead. He stared at us while the Airedale towered over him. Then he gave a sharp little bark, and his ears shot back and he glanced round him as though expecting to be set upon for useless leadership.

But the sound brought Sadie swaggering out of the yard beyond us. For a moment she stood in the middle of the lane, slowly moving her tail as she took in the scene. She seemed uncertain how to behave in the face of so many admirers. But when Pat appeared behind her, the pack was galvanised into action. A dog there already? That would never do! And they charged past us, growling, snarling, really uttering the most foul language in the presence of a lady.

I started after them, expecting terrible carnage. Poor Pat, already thoughts of sticks and buckets of cold water were going through my head as I worked out how I was going to rescue him.

Suddenly, as though on an order, all the dogs stopped when they were three or four yards away. They stood around, hackles up, eyes revolving, ears askew to catch sounds from any direction. It was a tense moment. One false move and I knew there would be a free-for-all and more than likely Pat would be at the bottom of it. Only Sadie was looking pleasantly amused. Her head was up, her nose twitching and she was holding her tail slightly to one side, gently moving the tip to waft her scent and tantalise.

I moved cautiously among them: 'Now then, boys, don't start anything. She's not ready yet. Not worth losing any skin over. Go on, off you all go. Home!'

It seemed to take the immediate heat out of the situation. Probably Sadie's scent sank well in and temporarily took their minds off battle. One by one they began cautiously circling and here and there a tail started to wag in joyful anticipation. If I could just get Pat out of harm's way I would be happy. Sadie would not come to any harm and I could deal with her later.

But Pat was no coward awaiting rescue from this pack of strangers. His hackles were higher than any, his teeth bared and his growl deep and continuous as he prepared to take on all comers in defence of his mother. She was also his preserve. Randy wasn't the only one who had been following the signs,

48

and the fact that Sadie was his mother made no difference to Pat's desire to have her away himself.

I had never seen such a wicked look on his face as he eyed the dogs strutting before him. 'Go on in, Pat,' I said, sternly pointing across the yard to the back door. 'Home! Home!'

He ignored me and continued growling. I dared not catch him by the collar and drag him away, not because he would have bitten me but because I knew it would only spark off an attack as the other dogs sensed an advantage.

As I pointed the back door opened and Olive looked out. 'Whatever's going on?'

At the sound of her voice Pat's ears flicked backwards momentarily although he was still snarling 'Quick!' I shouted, 'Call Pat! Call him in before he gets chewed to pieces.'

She called. Pat's ears flicked again and now his eyes swivelled as he tried to decide what to do. He had never disobeyed her when he knew she could see him. And yet, and yet, how could he possibly turn tail and leave Sadie to a gang-bang?

Olive called again, more sternly now. And Pat knew hesitation was fatal when you were squaring for a dog fight. If you relaxed your menacing posture for a moment you were a gonner. So he did the only thing he could and his ears went back, his tail down and he backed slowly towards the house, fiercely assuring his adversaries that he would be back in just a moment to sort them out. When he was nearly home, Donald escaped past Olive, hurried into the yard and grabbed him by the collar to drag him to safety.

Meanwhile Sadie was behaving like the belle of all the balls. She was the centre of a ragged, yelping circle and displaying her charms by striking various poses. From ears back, eyes swivelling and legs straddled, she would spring right round to sit primly on her haunches when the more adventurous sniffed at her tail. Then there was a delicate nose-sniffing session with the Airedale, erect and tail wagging, while Pug Face approached hopefully from behind her right ear and the sheepdog sneaked in for a furtive lick. And as he hadn't got time to hang around all day, he dared a quick clasp at her sloping back.

Immediately she sprang round with a snarl at such presumption. Which set Airedale on Pug Face and sparked off a series of side scraps among the watching mongrels, while a

49

couple of other dogs paired off and jumped about on one another in happy anticipation.

Strangely Randy kept a very low profile. As instigator and original leader of the expedition I expected him to be right there in the forefront. But he just hurried about in the background, busily wagging his tail, sniffing, matching every dog's pee, watching, panting, yapping his encouragement as the big boys tried their luck. So I decided that he must have long since come to terms with his stature, and once he knew the bitch was out of his class he was content to get his thrills as a voyeur.

While I had been rescuing Pat, Pete and Bert had been arming themselves with pebbles. Now, one by one, they were picking off the dogs with laughter and deadly accuracy. But instead of driving them away it only increased the pandemonium. As each dog was hit he swung round with a yap, lost his concentration and was straightway set upon by his neighbour.

Through it all Sadie posed and pranced and yapped, working herself up into a delirium, revelling in all the sudden, snarling attention. She was utterly oblivious to my shouted calls to heel, my orders for her to return indoors, the dire threats of punishment for disobedience that I hurled at her as a wanton bitch.

In the end I got her away and dragged her indoors, with Pete and Bert fighting a rearguard action, spraying pebbles like machine-gun bullets, while the dogs that were hit in vital parts howled off in hurt pride and the others barked after them. They disappeared in disarray, some this way, some that, and it seemed as though they had decided to slink off home to lick their wounds. But Randy remained. So did Pug Face from the pub, and a long-legged poodle that had arrived late and seemed to be making more headway with Sadie than any of the others. And these three positioned themselves around the farm, the vanguard of a howling vigil that was to last for days.

On an afternoon of blustery wind a week later, Mother came cycling down the lane. She looked more windswept than usual as she free-wheeled into the yard and scooted to a stop. For cycling she usually wore her dark blue woollen beret with the bobble on top, because it was the only one of her many hats that would really stay put when jammed down over her unruly hair. It was one of what she called her 'scrub' hats. She had 'hightum' hats, 'tightum' hats and 'scrub' hats. Hightum hats always started as new hats, bought especially for weddings, or going to church on festivals, or perhaps because she happened to spy a bargain at the sales. And as they were ousted by newer models, so they became 'tightum' hats, suitable for attending the Mothers' Union meetings, to which she travelled far and wide giving holy talks, or for going to church on ordinary Sundays, or travelling on the bus to Ashford. And finally tightum sank to scrub, shoved on for shopping, or a quick sprint to early service on a mid-week saint's day, or digging the garden in winter, even for a cycle ride if the beret was nowhere to be found.

But when they were used for cycling, these wide-brim creations had to be nailed in place with horrific hat pins, or they were apt to fly off when picking up speed on a downhill run. Hat pins that passed right through hat and hair and out again at various angles so that one day, as she went pedalling by, an old parishioner was heard to remark: 'There goes Mrs Creaton again, off to church wearing her Crown of Thorns.'

Quite often her beret disappeared for days, hiding under an armchair, snarled in sagging springs — 'I can't *think* how it can have got there!' — or perhaps just stuffed into the pocket of her gardening coat and forgotten. And once Guffy, her old Scottie, borrowed it and carried it off to his basket as a comforter and buried it among his belongings, where it stayed for a week before she thought to extend her search through his tatty blankets.

This afternoon the beret had been mislaid again because she was wearing a quite unsuitable model with a wavy brim, that tended to snap down in a head wind and obscure her vision. The heads and points of the hat pins sprouted from it, but even so the hat was sadly askew. She looked dishevelled and lacked her usual confidence.

I crossed the yard to greet her: 'Good grief! You look as though you've come here across country!'

'I nearly did. I landed in the ditch.' She laughed, ruefully.

'Going too fast again, I suppose,' I teased her. I looked her over, carefully. 'But you haven't hurt yourself, have you?'

She propped her bike against the fence and sighed. 'No. Mercifully not. It was that wretched old Stivvy Wild. *What* a turn he gave me, driving his rackety van all over the road as usual. I do wish he'd look where he's going instead of turning talking to Reuben all the time. And I'm sure he can't see properly through all those clouds of pipe smoke either.'

Stivvy Wild and his brother, Reuben, owned a travelling shop in which they swayed through the country lanes, calling on outlying farms and cottages. They came to Maywood once a fortnight and had left only a few minutes earlier.

'That's the trouble with old Stivvy,' I agreed, 'he always drives as though the lanes belong to him. He never expects to meet anything. Nor do you, come to that.'

Mother frowned and jabbed me with her elbow. 'Rubbish! I always look where I'm going. But I'm sure he never saw me. I had to scoot on to the side to miss him and of course I toppled into the ditch.'

'You wait till I see him again,' I threatened. 'I'll tell him you're considering prosecuting him for dangerous driving.'

'No, darling,' she said, quickly. 'Don't be hasty now. There's no damage done. Least said, soonest mended.'

She still harboured bitter memories of a court appearance. Years before, when we were children, she used to drive a Morris Oxford with hasty prayers and hopefulness. And once she left it parked on a slope in town and hurried off about her business. While she was gone, the old car rolled off gently on its own and ended up half sitting in a horse trough. The policeman took his notes, nodded as she stoutly maintained she had remembered to apply the handbrake, and promptly prosecuted her.

And the local paper ran banner headlines:

WINGHAM WOMAN FINED
ASKED TO PLEAD SAID SHE
"DIDN'T FEEL GUILTY"

She pulled at her hat to straighten it. Then she unbuttoned her coat. An expanse of vest was showing between jumper and skirt. She laughed: 'Oh dear, just look at the state of me. My body and soul are parting company again.' She wriggled about with her clothing and then she brightened. 'There! That's it. Now I'm good as new.' She turned and kissed me. 'Well now, how are you?'

There was a shout from Donald as he spotted her. He was in the top yard, by the calf pens, talking to the twins Primrose and

Prunella because now he spent nearly as much time playing with them as he did with the chickens.

He came running down past the pond. Pat followed him, lolloping behind, veering slightly out of his way to disturb some preening ducks and send them scurrying into the pond. 'Granny! Granny! Sadie's in the privy,' he told her breathlessly, as he hurled himself into her arms and she bent down to kiss him.

'Dearie me. Poor Sadie! What a funny place to put her.' She laughed, assuming that Sadie was suffering imprisonment in the cause of one of his games. And Sadie had heard her arrival and was beside herself, loudly demanding to be released. She was devoted to Mother because she had reared her as a puppy and had spoiled her lovingly.

'Don't you think it's time we let her out?' Mother went on.

'No! Daddy put her in the privy. Daddy put her there 'cos she's ON HEAT.'

'And don't you dare let her out,' I said. 'She's got admirers lurking around everywhere.'

'Poor dear,' Mother sighed, 'she does sound unhappy. Never mind, perhaps I can talk to her later.' She held Donald's hand. 'Now, let's go in and find Mummy. And I'm longing to see little Cherry again. Can you show her to me?'

After tea Sadie was still pleading to be released from the privy. Cherry was kicking and gurgling on Olive's lap. Donald was building an elaborate farmyard on the hearthrug and explaining every move to Cherry as he darted about fetching the various pieces. Pat had wedged himself between Olive's feet and a pen of pigs. He was lying like a lion with his head above his paws, his eyes darting to show that he was trying to follow all that was going on, while his ears gave the game away, twitching ceaselessly to prove that his real concern was for Sadie.

Mother sat over the fire, warming her hands and flexing her fingers. She looked across at me with a frown. 'It *does* seem cruel to shut Sadie up like that. Are you sure she can't come in — just for a little while?'

I laughed. 'What about Pat?'

'But she's his mother. I'm sure he wouldn't bother her.'

'Don't you believe it! She's still a bitch on heat.'

'Oh dear! I wish you wouldn't be so explicit.'

Olive said quickly: 'P'raps Pat could go into the office for a time. Give Sadie a chance to come in and say hello to Granny.'

So it was agreed and Pat was banished to the office, giving me a desperate look as I shut the door on him.

Sadie came panting into the living room, greeting everybody twice with a cold nose and a slobber. She returned to Mother's embrace once more before flopping down on the hearthrug with a sigh, knocking over a whole line of fencing and squashing a herd of cows.

'Sadie! Come *off! Mummy*, look what Sadie's done.' Donald grabbed her by the collar with both hands and lugged her backwards. She rolled on to her back, grinning and pawing at him to rub her tummy.

Now Pat started whining from the office. At first it was a peevish request for release. Soon it developed into a howl, poignant with grief and frustration. It was a sound we had never heard him utter before.

'Pat's *crying*.' Donald looked up, horrified. In a flash he was across the room and had opened the office door. Pat came hurrying out and never even stopped to thank him.

'No! Pat!' Olive and I screamed together. I jumped from my chair to grab him and Olive nearly shot Cherry on to the floor as she started up. Donald hurriedly stuck two fingers in his mouth, sucking at them with concern at the sudden turmoil he had caused.

'Naughty Pat,' Mother scolded him, while Sadie was the only one who took no notice. Instead of leaping up lustfully she remained where she was, grinning and waving her paws in the air. 'I don't believe it,' I said, as I looked down at her. I was holding Pat in the corner and he sat back on his haunches, quivering.

'She knows he's her son,' Mother said, primly. 'Of course she's not interested. I'm sure it'll be all right if you just leave him there in the corner. Poor Pat, he just wants to be one of the family circle too, don't you, darling?'

Now that the excitement had subsided, Donald forgot his concern and came over to stroke Pat as I let go of him, ordering him to stay where he was.

For the next hour the wretched Pat passed through purgatory. He stood up, he sat down. He whimpered and he shuffled about on his bottom. If he moved a step forward Donald ordered

54

him back and he would lie down with a forlorn stare. We tried shutting him back in the office but his howls were worse to bear than his frustration. So he returned to his corner while the object of his desire lay stretched out in front of the fire, snoring and ignoring him, worn out with her own long hours of importuning.

For Pat, bedtime was a merciful release. When Olive stood up to put the children to bed, and Mother followed her upstairs to join in the bathtime fun, Pat went to the foot of the stairs and lay down with his chin on the bottom step. Now, at last, he was back to routine. He could concentrate on following the sounds above and forget his frustration. It was the place he always went to when Olive was upstairs.

So I took the opportunity of returning Sadie to her basket in the disused privy. It was the only safe place for her, with the door bolted top and bottom. None of the farm buildings were dog-proof and anyway the privy served as quite a comfortable kennel.

'Bad luck, old girl,' I commiserated with her as I locked her in. 'Can't let you have any more pups, not after the way the last lot nearly drove you scatty.' She had had ten, reared the lot and they had milked her into a skeleton. But it was not so much that as the fits she had started to suffer from after the pups were weaned. Alarming fits when she writhed on the ground, jerking, scrabbling with her paws, urinating, frothing and yapping. And as she started to come out of one she would walk in a daze, unseeing, bumping into things, frothing at the mouth, grinding her teeth and staring with glazed eyes. Now she had put on weight again, was almost back to her old self, but even now a sudden excitement sometimes sparked off a fit. 'Keep her in the dark and give her these sedatives,' the vet said. But that was always after a frightening fit was finished. And I could not keep the dog sedated all the time.

But at least I could stop her having any more pups and the privy was as dark a place as any to dampen her days of libido.

By the time Mother was ready to leave for home, bashing the lights on her bike into life, refusing my offer as escort with: 'Gracious me, I'm not an imbecile', and had wavered off up the dark lane, the nightly courting chorus began. A howl from the

55

echoing wood beyond the pig meadow, another from the orchard, staccato barks from somewhere in the direction of the cowshed, Randy and his gang were tuning up for another frustrating night of fights and fruitless endeavour.

4

PRIMROSE AND PRUNELLA grew fast. In a somewhat complicated statement, Pete declared: 'Calves be all the same, they do either do, or else they do go back. But these two, bugger me they do do.'

We had taken them away from Daisy on the same day that they were born. It always seemed unkind at the time and some cows felt the loss of their calves more keenly than others. Lotty, for instance, in the days before she became barren, used to moo non-stop for a good twelve hours, calling us all the names she could lay her lungs to for parting her from her calf. But she was always pretty vocal about everything and she looked at us so aggressively that it dulled much of the sympathy we felt for her. So we just shouted back at her to shut up. Bluebell was just the opposite. She was so obliging, so quiet and unassuming that I always expected her to accept the loss of her calf with stoicism, to understand that it was taken away from her for her own good, so that she could forget it before she became fond of it. Her grief could be really touching, make me feel a heel because she seemed to be pleading with plaintive moos. Some cows just shouted the odds across the yard from the cowshed to the calf pens; a non-stop answering service to the calf's lonely enquiries. But Bluebell was selective. She would be quiet and I'd think; good, she's forgotten at last. I would feel relieved. But as I walked into the cowshed she would turn round, prick her ears, hoping to see me bringing the calf back. And when she did not see it, that was when she would low with desperate sadness.

They say horses are the intelligent ones, that they can communicate with man above all farm animals. But a cow comes a very close second and can often convey her feelings with absolute clarity. In fact, a farmer I once worked for, a man of means and many years spent close to animals, organised his own crude IQ test among his livestock. And the cow won, the sow came second and the cart horse only just scraped in with a place.

If you keep cows for a living, you have to instil in them a single-minded desire to put the maximum amount of milk in the bucket. You cannot allow them the luxury of loving a calf, of harbouring thoughts of saving back enough milk to provide it with a generous slurp when it comes bunting for a drink. A cow can hold back milk at will. And the more often she holds it back the sooner she will go dry, or end up only producing enough for her calf; or get mastitis. The farmer has to be cruel to be kind to his bank overdraft. And the cruelty of quickly snatching a calf away means the kindness of short-lived sorrow.

Anyway, Daisy never cared a hoot about losing her calf. Not even when she had twins to pine for. At first we kept them in a pen together and came to them with pails containing the thick yellow colostrum, warm from their mother and seething with antibodies. It can be a rough-and-tumble teaching a calf to drink from a bucket. Milk comes from soft teats temptingly swinging from a warm and reassuring udder. Any new-born calf knows you have to look upwards for it, to bunt about in the softness until your tongue curls round the teat and you can suck it into your mouth. It is definitely not the same when you are offered a couple of horny fingers to suck while your head is pushed downwards into a clinical, clanking bucket. You can smell the milk all right, but any fool calf knows it's not down there. And it does not smell quite right either. Instead of the comfortable surrounding smell of hot hide there is a nasty niff of disinfectant. So you spit out the boring fingers, jerk to thrust your head upwards, clip the rim of the bucket, feel the milk splash into your face and hear a gruff voice swear at you. Then the fingers are there again and this time your mouth is plunged into the milk so that it slops up and gurgles into your nostrils. You blow it out but now the warmth is all around, milk is flowing into your funnelled tongue and you suck at it eagerly. Suddenly it does not matter any more about the strange-smelling bucket, or that

the milk is coming from the wrong direction. You can't get it down you fast enough. When it is finished you bunt the bucket searching for more.

So Primrose and Prunella soon learnt to drink from buckets. The warm, comforting bulk of Daisy was not even a memory to cry for. They were so tiny, and as they stood so close together and seemed to want one another, we kept them together in one pen. We fed them twice a day with Daisy's milk, only two pints each for the first few feeds because they were so small. But gradually we increased the feeds to three pints, and then to four, until each calf was eagerly consuming the full amount of a gallon a day.

They soon learnt to recognise the sounds as milking got under way across in the cowshed. They stood up and stretched luxuriously — a sight full of health and contentment which I loved to see. Side by side they waited, straining to see over the door in the dwarf wall, their absurdly long ears moving to catch every sound, the white triangles shining in their matching brown heads. Sometimes, if they thought there was an unnecessary delay, perhaps even that they had been forgotten, they shouted reminders across the yard in strangely deep voices. When the milk arrived it was finished in a flash. Then came the rattling battle as they chased the handfuls of calf nuts thrown into the empty buckets, pulverising them into a soggy mess as they learnt that nuts had to be chewed, not sucked. All too soon the excitement was over and they were left facing each other with drop-eared stares. Now the only thing left to do was to have a nose at the soft meadow hay in the little rack, to curl out a tongue and try a few strands, to wind them back and swallow in one chewing movement.

One day we had to part them. Donald had been to pay them a visit and he came running to find me. 'Primrose is eating Prunella's ear. She's got it *all* in her mouth.'

When I went to check on his report I discovered that it was by no means a one-sided attack. While Primrose was sucking her ear, Prunella was seeing what sustenance was to be had from sucking her sisters' navel. Calves do tend to cross suckle and that was why we usually kept them in separate pens. Now the twins had to be parted until they were weaned. But we put them in adjacent pens and at least they could see one another between the bars of the dividing hurdle. And they never strayed very far from each other. When they came to lie down they always kept close together with just the hurdle between their shining brown coats.

The calf pens were at one end of the bullock lodge, which took up one side of the top yard at right angles to the cowshed. Thus the calves were able to graduate from their individual pens when they were weaned and join the other young stock in the main part of the shed. A passage divided the calf pens from the rest of the shed and from this a door led through the back wall into the stack-plat beyond. It made the feeding of hay and the carrying of bedding straw easy.

It was also a popular short-cut for Donald and the dogs. He had just discovered how useful string was, and all the games that could be played with it. There was plenty of it lying about, short lengths of binder twine cut from the sheaves at threshing time and from the bolts of bedding straw in the untidy stack behind the bullock lodge. String hung in tempting little skeins from nails on dusty beams, or clung in tufts in the hedge around the stack-plat, or was draped over fences or bundled together in old apple boxes. Nobody ever threw string away because it might come in useful sometime. It seldom did, until Donald found a use for it. He gathered handfuls of it and ran off to find someone to knot the pieces together for him into long and interesting lengths.

Bert was always willing to oblige. 'Let's have it 'ere then, Moses Maggot, I'll join it up for yer.' Ever since Donald had started trotting round the farm on his own Bert had called him Moses Maggot. At that time the *Daily Mail* had just started a strip cartoon about a strange little dwarf, with big eyes and a bald head, who was always popping up with diabolical ideas. Bert followed his exploits. But I think it was the name that tickled his fancy as much as the similarity to Donald's stature and activity.

Donald would hand him a bunch of string. 'Make a long, long, long piece, Bert,' he would say, excitedly.

Bert loved an excuse to rest from his labours. Soon Donald was hurrying off with yards of the wretched string bulging from his pockets and trailing behind him. He could not tie a knot as such, but he had a way of twisting the ends in tangles round door posts, threading them through anything handy, working and weaving so that familiar, hurry-through doorways became barred with complicated cats' cradles into which I rushed and became enmeshed. Or I would be toiling down from the stack-plat, lost under a pitchfork-load of hay, then falling forward with my feet snared in string, which was stretching unseen between the spokes of a waggon wheel and the tines of the hay turner. Of course I would swear. I would shout at him when I found him later and he'd look agitated and suck his fingers because he had not consciously set up booby traps. It was just that he loved playing with string. But as he could never unravel his own handiwork, sometimes the farmyard looked as though it had been overrun by an army of giant spiders weaving webs in binder twine. We really needed pangas to progress from place to place.

The chickens were roped in, literally, to join the new string craze. Suddenly it was more fun to tether a greedy hen than to shut her in the privy. I would come across them, forgotten and skulking in dark corners, all the flight gone out of them with their legs trussed in twine. They had submitted to Donald's ministrations in silence. Yet as soon as I came to the rescue, picked one up to cut her free, she would screech at the top of her voice and fix me with a beady eye as though it was all my fault.

Of course Sadie and Pat were fair game. They would watch him at work, sitting upright beside him as he busied himself diligently at a doorway. Sooner or later it was bound to occur to him to join the dogs together. I only saw the final fling which resulted. But I could well imagine them sitting there, panting and vying with each other to be the closer to him, thoroughly approving of all the attention as he fiddled with their collars, threading the string in and out as he bound them together. And then innocently calling them after him as he hurried off in search of more string. By the time I saw them they had forgotten all their manners. They were snarling and swearing at one another, thoroughly fed up with each other's company, each blaming the other for hanging on while Pat was trying to make for the kitchen to tell Olive of his troubles, and Sadie didn't care where she went so long as it was away from Pat. I captured them and cut them loose. Then I lectured

61

Donald sternly on the dangers of tying dogs and chickens up with string.

It never occurred to me to mention calves as well. A week or two later we were working in the hop garden on a grey winter's day. As usual Bert had finished his row first and was gazing down to the farmyard. Suddenly he called: 'Them bloody calves be out.'

'Never!' I stood up, searching for them. If he had said pigs I would have believed him without question. They were apt to roam at will and paid scant attention to hedges or fences. But the calves were about the only animals which always stayed where we put them. Yet now I could plainly see the twins taking off with tails high through the stack-plat. There was no sign of any of the other young stock so I hoped the rest were still safely yarded.

It was a nuisance. As usual we were behind with the repetitive work in the hop garden. But Pete and Bert downed tools and set off in good heart. There was nothing like a fast animal chase to relieve the monotony.

The calves were entering the lane by the time we reached them. They stopped, standing side by side and looking perplexed, wondering at the hard feeling under their hooves after the soft straw of their pens. And from each of them trailed a long piece of string with the ends wound several times around their necks.

'Donald!' I yelled. 'Where are you?'

He appeared from behind the hay rick. His knitted beret was askew, his coat unbuttoned and one leg of his dungarees was no longer safely tucked inside his wellie. The dogs panted past him, anxious to get on with the chase.

'Did you let the twins out?' I tried to sound nice.

'They wanted to go for a walk.' He replied, innocently.

Bert laughed. 'What's up, Moses Maggot, couldn't yer hold 'em?'

I rounded on him. 'It's your fault. You keep knotting up all that blasted string for him.'

Pete was approaching the calves, cautiously and with his arms outstretched. 'C'mon, me beauties. Let's be havin' yer. Back yer go.'

Just to show willing, Sadie barked. And away the calves went, a startled spurt at first, but scared into top speed by the un-accustomed hammering of their hooves on the hard road. They were nearly six months old by now and calves of that age really can move. Especially if they have been confined to a pen and are suddenly faced with freedom. So they were well on their way up the lane to the boys' cottage before we had ourselves orga-nised and the dogs under control.

I should have noticed that the garden gate into the lane was open as we hurried by to drive the calves back. Olive was at work in the garden. It was her great joy. She hurried through housework to save a precious hour or two which could be spent toiling over her plants, or re-enforcing the surrounding hedge against marauding pigs. I ought to have noticed the gate because the dogs both scooted through it, thoroughly unnerved by the names we had called them for starting after the calves up the lane. Now they had taken refuge beneath Cherry's pram, which was parked on the path and from where she could keep an eye on her mother. She greeted the dogs' arrival with a cry of delight and flung a doll down for them to share. And Donald ran through the gate into the garden too, obviously anxious to get to his mother first with his version of how the calves had got out.

In time we surrounded the calves and started to drive them homewards, Bert walking in front and calling them while Pete and I brought up the rear. If only Sadie had minded her own business! But just as the calves were almost abreast of the garden gate she decided to stroll out into the lane to check on our progress. Bert had gone on ahead and when she saw the calves bearing down on her she felt duty bound to bark. Which sent them scurrying into the garden, tails up and with renewed en-thusiasm after the restful walk back down the lane.

They raced full speed across the lawn, swerving round the cherry tree, leaping line abreast into the herbaceous border and pounding through the Mrs Sinkin pinks, churning up clods of clay in a crazy slalom through staked plants, ripping through the roses, circling into the carefully-planned young shrubbery and charging headlong into the vegetable patch. The pace slackened as they clattered through the sprouts and now they stopped, suddenly struck by the strong smell of crushed leaves and stems, snorting steam from their nostrils as they stretched out tongues to sample this new delicacy.

Olive watched their progress, fork raised above her head and struck dumb with horror. She advanced towards them, breathing rapidly: 'Oh, oh, how could you! You, you . . .'

The twins did not wait to hear her get the words out. They retreated, backing away, heads down and blowing defiance, before swerving off again in a quick dash back to the shrubbery. They stopped short when they saw that we were now facing them.

Olive followed them, fork still raised. 'Oh, Primrose, no! That's my best Cytisis Kewenis you're standing on!'

Donald called out: 'That's not Primrose, that's Prunella. Silly Mummy.' He laughed. He had been laughing all through at the calves' antics, jumping up and down beside the pram while Cherry chortled.

Bert cackled: 'Moses Maggot knows all right. 'Ee knows one from 'tother.'

'Prunella then!' Olive cried, brandishing her fork and afraid to use it. 'Go on with you. David! *Do* something, don't just stand there laughing.'

The calves decided to surrender. They were worn out. The tour of inspection through the garden left them gasping and they offered no resistance when the boys put their arms around their necks to lead them off.

'Oh well, not much damage done, fortunately.' I tried to sound nonchalant, averting my eyes from the sharp hoofprints and squashed plants as I prepared to follow them out of the garden.

'You always say that.' Olive hurried around, sympathising with wounded shrubs, straightening stakes and hacking at the deeper hoofprints. 'You said it last spring as well when the cows broke in and ate off all the daffodil blooms.'

'Oh. Did I?' I paused, jabbing my heel to conceal some rather nasty skid marks across the lawn before she noticed them.

'You know you did. Then you joked about it. You told Donald to watch and see if the daffodils turned the milk nice and yellow.'

'They didn't, did they, Donald?'

But he was not listening. He had started off behind the calves and Cherry was shouting after him because she no longer had his attention. Pat stood up from under the pram and decided to stroll across to console Olive. Foolishly he took a short cut.

'Keep to the *path*, Pat. At least I thought *you'd* learnt to keep out of the flower beds.'

But he kept going. Even so she stroked him when he reached her.

I stopped by Cherry's pram and ogled her. 'Poor Mummy. The naughty calves have spoilt her nice garden. Did you see your two beauties running through the garden?'

She offered me a doll without a word. When I reached to take it, she threw it over the side of the pram for me to retrieve.

As I bent down to pick it up I caught Olive's eye. She gave me the beginnings of a smile.

Her smile widened at the sound of demanding quacks, and a moment later the ducks filed round the side of the house and into the garden.

'It must be teatime,' I said, glad of a better opportunity to draw attention away from the damage done by the calves.

Olive looked round. She made no move to shoo the ducks out of the garden. Instead, she called to them: 'All right! All right! But you'll just have to wait a bit till I've cleared up this mess.'

Chickens in the garden sent her searching for clods of earth to hurl at them, underarm and inaccurately, but with enough abuse and bursting shrapnel to send them squawking away before they had a chance to scratch out seeds or lay bare the roots of delicate plants. Yet she always maintained the ducks did no damage. Certainly they kept to the paths when they ambled in to find her and remind her it was feeding time.

The ducks had their special gap into the garden where the bottom of a spile was broken off in the wicket gate leading from the yard. It was a gap they had used since they were squeaking yellow ducklings, hurrying to escape when the inquisitive dogs had cut off their route to the pond. The opening was too small for the dogs to squeeze through, too small even for the puniest piglet. Yet after they had grown full size the ducks had a way of waddling up to it, sinking to their bellies and squeezing through one after the other, each long neck in the queue threading through after the twitching tail in front. There was never any jostling to steal a march on each other and the only agitated one among them was Sinbad. He hated the indignity of slithering through the gap in the gate.

Although Sinbad usually led the procession in search of Olive at feeding time, he was always last through if they drew a blank at the back door and went searching for her in the garden. As soon as his wives started through, following each other in silent agreement, he faffed around behind them squeaking out orders which were ignored. Because he had arrived on the farm fully grown he had not been brought up to this acrobatic exercise. In fact, for the first two weeks after he had arrived, a splendidly attired suitor adept at constant consummation, he was completely flummoxed by the escape hole into the garden which his brides negotiated with such ease. He would hurry up and down thrusting his shiny green head through gaps in the spiles, scowling with fierce black eyes after the bustling bottoms and ordering them to return, in a voice quite drowned by the raucous chorus as the ducks advanced on Olive. I often laughed at Nature's joke of reversing the vocal chords of ducks and drakes. She made the drake such a gaudy, demanding fellow, gave him the power of rapid chase and violent rape, and then cut him down to size by bestowing upon him the voice of a eunuch.

Now Sinbad was bringing up the rear as the ducks threaded their way through the garden. He kept up a constant commentary but mostly the females were silent. Only now and then one of them croaked a reminder at Olive as they milled around, and for a moment or two the others all backed her up with deafening rejoinders of: 'Here-here. Here-here. Here-here.' And each time the ducks all shouted together, Cherry clapped her hands and shrieked with laughter.

Finally Olive jammed her fork in the ground. 'Oh dear! I suppose I'll have to down tools and feed you lot. No peace for the wicked.' She looked across at me beside the pram. 'Wheel Cherry round after me, will you? She'll scream if she's left here on her own. Come on, ducks! You may be obsessed with punctuality, but at least you know how to behave and don't go around wrecking the place.'

Outside the back door I lifted Cherry from her pram and held her while Olive mixed up the duck food. A saucepan of scraps simmered on the back of the Rayburn and she poured this into the corn meal and stodged it about with a wooden spoon. The ducks always got the best. A nice hot supper to go to bed on. They padded about in the yard waiting and three chickens got wind of the steaming smell and advanced on the back door.

66

Immediately Sinbad took off after them, head stretched forward and grabbing a billful of tail feathers from the last to take flight. He returned puffed with victory, feathers sticking to his bill and his own tail twitching violently as he swaggered through the ducks, asking them if they had all noticed him.

But they only had eyes for Olive just then, beady eyes on craning necks. And they followed her full tilt as she led the way to the duck house. It was a simple wooden shed with a door inland and a trap leading directly on to the pond.

She fed them inside, away from thieving chickens, and they scurried in after her, shovelling up the food from the low trough with eager bills. And every now and then one would flop out of the trap door on to the pond, guzzling at the water to help the sticky food down before hurrying back inside for more, often colliding with another one on her way out. I held Cherry close to the water and pointed to them. She gave fat chuckles each time a duck appeared.

Olive came out and shut the door behind her. 'Now you won't forget to shut the trap when they're all in after milking, will you? We always lose eggs when you do.'

I smiled. 'As if I ever forget!' But sometimes I did. And apart from the danger of a dawn-roaming fox grabbing a duck, we lost eggs because they swam off and laid them in the pond. The ducks always laid first thing in the morning, so by keeping them shut in until after breakfast we were sure of the full number of the blue-green, greasy-shelled eggs — rich, dark-yolked eggs, the finest for cooking and custard.

'Well, that's that.' Olive held out her arms for Cherry. 'Send Donald in when you see him. *Don't* let him hang around all through milking because then he comes in too tired to eat his tea.'

5

Lotty must have realised her days at Maywood really were numbered. I had told her often enough, threatening her with the meat pie market every time she misbehaved, or was particularly uppity with new heifers entering the cowshed for the first time. She still came on bulling, regular to the day and as brazen about it as ever. But now I had given up getting the inseminator to her.

Offering her one last chance we drove her down to Farmer Dunnell's bull at Frogs' Hole, just in case the thrill of a natural mating would do the trick. He had a strapping young Sussex bull, an eager and efficient performer and not in the least put off when faced with a cow old enough to be his great grandmother. Dunnell was usually a man of few words, but he shook his head sadly when I paid him the seven shillings and sixpenny fee. 'You're wasting yer time there, my lad, that you be. Wasting yer time and money. Her'll never have another calf to lay tongue to 'er tits. Out 'er, my lad, out 'er. Keep yer stalls full of young 'uns, if yer want my advice. No farmer ever made money hanging on to the old 'uns jest because 'ees grown fond of 'em.'

This stab of truth from a large and successful farmer hurt. I felt foolish as we drove Lotty home. She would definitely have to go if she did not hold this time. But at least I had not lost money on her yet. She was still giving two gallons a day so she was more than paying her way. But only just.

Now little Lotty was due to calve shortly. She was one of Lotty's daughters and all along I had planned for her to take her mother's place in the cowshed as soon as she calved. So there was no time like the present to make the switch. After all, Little Lotty needed a few days to get used to the sounds and the routine in the cowshed before she calved. We would introduce her to her new life just as soon as we got home. The old cow would have to stay on her own. We could milk her out by hand in a spare stall in the stable.

Lotty was banished to spend her days awaiting sentence in the field with the old carthorse, Colonel. He was a pensioner, definitely a part-time worker now, and by all the rules of efficient farming he should have gone clobbering off to the knacker yard ages ago. But I always felt duty bound to supply him with his board and lodging for as long as need be. It had been an unwritten part of the bargain when I bought Maywood. Old Checky, the previous owner, had insisted that the ancient carthorse stayed on the farm, assuring me that I would always find him useful and that he would earn his keep. In the early days Checky had been a regular visitor to the farm because he had only retired to the village and could not get Maywood out of his system. He usually had a word or two to say to Colonel in passing and the old horse would nod his head and blow down his nostrils in reply. But nowadays Checky hardly ever came to the farm, except to do the hop-drying each year. He had grown too stiff for the cycle ride up and down the two valleys from the village. Apart from his annual stint in the oast house, we only ever saw him on the rare occasions when he prevailed on his son-in-law to drive him slowly down the lane. And then it was only a quick stop, just time for him to ease himself out of the car, roll a fag, pop it in the yellow hole in his white moustache, light up and blow sparks as he asked about the farm. But before he climbed back into the car, Checky would ask: 'And ol' Colonel? Still orlright, eh?' When I nodded, he would smile: 'Gawd, bugger me. That ol' horse'll outlive I yet.' And his laugh would send another shower of sparks from his fag.

Colonel stamped his way into everyone's heart. It was no longer the bargain with Checky that made me keep him on. But we still made him work now and then. Although Pete and Bert were always quick to start the tractor up at the slightest excuse, there were times when it was much more convenient and economical to use Colonel. With light carting jobs, for instance. The tractor started on petrol and ran on paraffin once the engine was warm, and it was a performance to keep stopping it and starting it again with the starting handle.

Most times the old horse would stand quietly between the shafts, munching away at a pile of hay while the cart was loaded, and then trundling off with a fart and a swish of his stumpy tail to wherever the load had to go. But you had to remember to bribe him with the best hay or he would take off in search of it, pulling the half loaded cart behind him and leaving you swearing beside the midden. He had a mind of his own and would only work when he felt like it. Even then he always left you with the impression that he was just doing you a favour these days and did not expect to be put upon. If you piled a load too high; if you forgot to give him a rest between rows, harrowing in the hop garden; if you hurried him to get a job finished because it was milking time, then he would stop, lay back his ears, turn his head to face you and give you a withering stare from between his blinkers.

We knew his ways, and he knew ours, and there was not much he didn't understand when any of us talked to him, about day-to-day farming affairs.

It took Olive a long time to learn to love him. She just could not bring herself to forgive him for the gruelling afternoon he had given her in the hayfield soon after we were married. She wanted to help and the hay needed turning. There was a seat on the hay turner, and reins on the harness, and Colonel knew just where to walk between the rows to fluff the hay up in the warm sunshine. But he was not used to female commands, and the gentle taps with the stick were a joke compared with the stern punishment he expected for slacking. The only way Olive was able to get him to go was to dismount, grab him by the bridle and drag him round and round the field, determined to finish the job she had started, recalcitrant horse or no. And all through the sweating afternoon she'd had the feeling that Colonel was laughing at her behind her heaving back.

She never felt much love for him after that, until the day when he happened to be standing in the yard outside the kitchen window, harnessed in the cart. I had left him standing there while I went indoors to answer the phone. Olive was busy in the kitchen and Donald was playing outside. Soon she glanced out of the window. She felt her heart leap and she stifled a cry. Donald was bending between Colonel's front legs, tugging at a fetlock, trying to get him to raise a heavy hoof as he must have seen me do at some time or another. Through force of habit at this signal, from years and years of visits to the blacksmith, Colonel lifted his foot and Donald clasped it with both arms. Now a carthorse seldom puts his foot down gently and he won't hold it up on his own. As soon as you leave go of it, clonk down it goes and never mind if your toe happens to be in the way. And to Olive, as she crept to the rescue, terrified that Colonel might move if she called out or went too fast, his hoof and gleaming shoe seemed half as big as Donald as he struggled to hold it and peer underneath.

Suddenly he had seen all there was to see. He let go of it and gazed up into the strange sky of a horse's belly instead. Colonel held his foot up motionless. But his head went down and his ears cocked as he looked at this busy little lad still standing under his poised hoof. Then Donald backed out. Slowly Colonel lowered his foot. But now, very gently but quite firmly, the old horse gripped Donald's coat in his worn teeth, pulled him forward and dumped him with a snort and a rattle of his bit. 'There! Let that be a lesson to you.'

Thoroughly scared Donald flew into Olive's arms. And I came out of the kitchen door just as she carried him back to Colonel. She flung her arm round his head, put her cheek against his and patted his neck. He nodded his head and rubbed his snout into her shoulder. He liked a bit of fussing. And I think he was glad to make friends with her at last.

He was standing looking over the hedge into the lane as we drove Lotty back from Dunnell's bull. We called it Colonel's field because it was the only one where he would stay put. He loved to roam, to visit neighbours' hay ricks and could find the weak spot around most meadows to kick his way out. So, after a series of humiliating visits to retrieve him from neighbouring farms, I had surrounded his field with an electric fence. And this kept him in, so long as he sensed the current pulsating through the single strand of thin wire. As the field was opposite the farm buildings he was quite happy to live there. He could keep his eye on what was happening, and for the cold winter nights it was only a short step across the lane to his warm stall in the stable.

He was dozing as we approached down the lane. His ears flopped and his head was nodding down to the hedgetop. Now and then he jerked his head up and his eyes half opened as he tried to stay awake to see what was going on. But both his sight and his hearing were failing so that we were really quite close to him before he noticed us. Then his ears shot forward and his lips quivered in a whispered neigh that started as a rumble from deep in his chest. He just wanted us to know that, of course, he had watched us coming all the way down the lane.

Lotty bellowed at him as she went by. And she bellowed again at us when we turned her into the field with him and refused to let her join the other cows. She stood just inside the gateway, her feet firmly in the mud and refusing to budge to allow Pete room to shut the gate.

He smacked her smartly on the rump. 'Go on in there, you ol' bugger. Go on in the old folks' field.'

She shook her head to show she had not heard this insult and stodged off into the field. Colonel ignored her. He stayed by the hedge and continued his doze.

That same afternoon we drove Little Lotty into the cowshed to join the big girls. We ushered her in quietly and just inside the doorway she stopped dead. She rolled her eyes, blew through her nostrils and her front feet remained fixed to the concrete as I grabbed her tail and tried to urge her forward. Strange things had been happening to her lately. There was this calf thumping about in her belly. The little udder, that had always been tucked up neatly out of sight, had swelled alarmingly and she felt it against her legs as she walked. Now she was being urged into this unfamiliar shed. It was full of the cows that had delighted in bossing her around whenever the heifers had grazed in the same meadow. The shed was dark, full of echoes of new sounds and where was the wide sky?

'Go *on*, silly sod. Those cows won't hurt you. They're all chained up. They're not even looking at you. They're waiting for corn. Go *on*. There's some corn for you too. Can't you smell it?'

She took a few steps forward, Pete close to her neck and guiding her towards the empty stall. 'Come on, come on,' he urged her, 'and *don't* trip over the dung channel.'

She put a foot into it, lowering her head and blowing at the spare space beyond it. With an exaggerated skip she tried to leap over it, landed with her back feet in it and her head peering into the manger. There was corn waiting there to tempt her in and she blew at it cautiously in case it was another trick.

Pete eased up beside her, running his hand along her back. 'What you want ter go an' do that for, yer silly ol' fool?' He glanced back at me. 'Allus do's that, don't 'em? Every bloody time us brings a new 'un in 'er has ter go arse over tip in the dung channel.'

While she was busy with the corn he reached over her neck for the chain. Without a click to alarm her he unhooked it and stealthily fastened the two ends round her. She felt it bite into the folds of her skin as she stretched forward after the corn and for a moment she shook her head and swished her tail in annoyance. But it was not worth really bothering about. This unexpected meal of corn was worth the strange surroundings and unaccustomed restriction. Soon she had licked up every last crumb and was looking around cheerfully for more.

It took me a day or two to get used to seeing her standing there in Lotty's place. She was not unlike her mother, with the same upright horns and similar brown and white markings. But, of course, she was rounded with youth and with her neat, budding udder. And she lacked Lotty's presence. When she looked up she did not hold her head in the same commanding way, casting her eyes over all that went on, like a school ma'am at assembly. I missed that penetrating stare whenever I walked into the cowshed.

Apart from getting a heifer used to her new surroundings before she calved down, we liked to have her attend every milking so that we could 'steam her up'. This was one of those jolly farming expressions with no literal meaning. It referred to the feeding of corn in gradually increasing amounts until the cow, or heifer, was eating the optimum amount for her milk yield by the time she calved. Another expression I always liked referred to keeping a 'flying herd'. Cows with wings? It was a favourite trick question if a townsman happened to be applying for a job, perhaps boasting of experience he did not possess as he hankered after a dream of idyllic life, or a country cottage at three bob a

73

week. 'Oh yes, and have you ever worked with a flying herd?' the prospective employer would ask. And it only meant a dairy herd where no calves were reared and all replacements bought in fresh calved instead.

So we 'steamed up' Little Lotty and whoever fed her made a point of handling her as she ate her corn. He ran his hand down under her tail, into the silky folds of her swelling udder, down and round and revolving over her thickening teats. They were sensitive, tingling, and she moved irritably, flashing her tail and shuffling her feet while she tried to concentrate on the delicious corn, the sudden bonanza that kept coming her way and must be eaten with all speed in case it disappeared as miraculously as it came.

Soon she was keen to walk into the cowshed. She learnt which was her stall after only two days and ambled into it and waited to be tied up like an old timer. Now she hardly flinched when the milking-machine engine started up and throbbed away from beyond the dairy. She became used to the hissing through the pipe above her head, the clanking of the buckets and the throbbing of the pulsators. But she kept her head erect, her ears flicking, her eyes revolving, following the progress of the corn bin and awaiting her turn. Soon, too, she became used to the hand on her udder, even the firm pressure when fingers held her teats to prepare her for the clasp of the milking machine.

It was a fortnight after she took her mother's place in the cowshed when we noticed she was ready to calve down. We drove her into the loose box we kept as a maternity wing-cum-sick bay. It had a half-heck door and as Pete bolted the lower part and left her she poked her head over it and stared after him with astonishment.

He turned and looked back at her. 'Get on with it, then,' he called, 'don't look at me. 'Tis gorne dinner time and us wants you all finished and done with by knocking orf time, mind.'

I laughed. 'You're hopeful. You know they always wait 'til it's dark as a rule.'

'I'll lay 'er won't be that long.' He mounted his bike and rode off with a grin to his dinner.

But when the day's work was finished Little Lotty was still staring over the loose-box door. Apart from some angry tail swishing, and one or two exaggerated attempts to pee when

74

strange pains gripped her, she showed no inclination to start calving in earnest.

'I'll, come back and looker 'er later, if you like,' Pete offered, as he prepared to go home. He seemed disappointed that she had not calved as soon as he had predicted.

'Not courting tonight, then?'

He looked down and tested the brakes on his bike, for somewhere to look. 'Yea. But that don't matter. Her's only comin' up home. I can easily pop down.'

'What? And leave Rose on her own?'

Bert drifted up, slow pedalling his bike. He jabbed one foot on the lane to keep his balance. "Ee always leaves 'er on 'er own. Sits by the fire 'ee does and 'er stops in the kitchen gassin' to Mum.'

I smiled 'Oh dear. They sound just like an old married couple already.'

Pete kicked at the pedal of his bike and sent it spinning. 'T'ain't like that. Anyway, Bert, what d'you know about it? You'm allus orf out sniffin' after skirt. Least you *say* you are. But you never seem to land one. You ain't never ever brought one home yet, not with all yer braggin' '.

'Huh!' Bert sniffed. 'I got better things to do with 'em than bring 'em home and sit 'em in the kitchen ter talk sweet nothings. Anyway, I'm orf home for me tea. You coming? 'Night, Gaffer.' He rode off, whistling tunelessly.

'Goodnight, Bert,' I called after him. 'Mind what you're up to. If you can't, then remember the date.' It was a stock joke, not even worth a reply.

'I'll looker Little Lotty if you like,' Pete persisted. 'T'ain't no trouble, honest it ain't.'

'No, I can manage. It's easy for me to keep an eye on her. Anyway, I'm sure she'll calve okay. I can always come up for you if I need you.'

We left it at that. I thought he looked a little disappointed as he rode away. For a second I felt as though he did not really trust me to look after the heifer. I remembered that he had been present when she was born. It was he who had called her Little Lotty because she had such similar markings. Maybe that was why he wanted to see her have her own calf. I shrugged as I started to walk indoors. Oh well, there was nothing to stop him looking in on the heifer later if he wished.

After tea I went out again to check on her progress. But as I walked towards the loose box, swinging the hurricane lamp, I saw her eyes glinting at me as I approached. And when I looked over the door she backed away, shuffled round in the straw and flicked her tail. She seemed to be no further advanced than before.

So I left it until eight o'clock before I went to see her again. Now, as I approached the loose box, I could see a yellow glow lighting up the doorway. So Pete had come down after all and I smiled as I walked.

I was still several yards away when I heard a girl's voice, clear as starlight on a frosty night. 'I'm so proud of you, Pete,' Rose exclaimed.

I stopped. Perhaps I should not have done. It's deceitful to eavesdrop. But I could not help myself. All the years these two had been courting I had never heard them say more than a few words at a stretch to each other.

'There you are! A heifer an' calf.' Pete sounded pleased with himself. And I felt glad that Little Lotty had obviously calved all right.

'Ain't it sweet! I didn't think you was going ter get it out with all that pulling.'

I heard Pete spit. 'You have ter know how. 'Course, I brought Little Lotty into the world too, yer know.'

'I know you did. I remember when you told me.' Silence. Then she said: 'I can remember all the things you've ever told me, Pete.'

It was time I moved. His reply was low and inaudible as I coughed and shuffled my feet. I looked over the door and they were standing with their backs to me, arms around each other and they had not heard me. They were lost together, gazing down at the calf while Little Lotty rasped it with her tongue. Pete had his jacket off, his sleeves rolled high from helping with the calf and one bare arm was hooked round Rose's neck. Even as I looked he pulled her roughly to him and she folded herself willingly against him as he bent to kiss her.

Hell, I couldn't let them know I had seen them. I would feel as embarrassed as they were sure to be.

I crept back to the corner where the loose box came into

76

view. 'Hello! Is that you in there, Pete?' He could not help but hear that.

As I walked forward again his face appeared over the door. He was beaming into the swinging light of the hurricane lamp. 'Her's calved. Just got it away, I have. Her needed a bit of help.'

'Well done.' I reached the door and he swung it open. 'Why! Hello, Rose! So he brought you down to help too, did he?'

'Her ain't never see'd a cow calve,' Pete explained, quickly. 'Thought 'er ud like to come along o' me and see, I did. Just in case we was in time for Little Lotty's calf, like. Lucky it happened jest right.'

'Just right,' Rose repeated. 'Ain't 'ee lovely?' She bent down and held her hand out to the calf.

When she stood up again I held the lamp towards her face. 'Rose, *you're* lovely! You look lovelier than ever tonight.' And she did. Her cheeks were glowing and her eyes full of sparkles from the kiss.

She giggled and turned away. 'Go on with you. You'm always teasing me.'

I laughed and Pete joined in. Little Lotty stared at us and lowed seriously.

'Afraid it's a bull calf,' Pete said. 'Pity. Nice if 'er could've had a heifer. I'd uv liked that. Then p'raps I could've helped *her* calve as well one day.'

Rose said: 'Pete had to pull and pull to get 'im out.'

'Yes, sometimes they don't come easy.' I could remember times when we had almost given up and three of us pulling with ropes attached to the calf. That had been with the first calves by artificial insemination; semen from giant bulls on small cows. Now, with the second generation it was easier.

'So Pete said,' Rose went on. 'But I didn't know it was that hard. Still, I ain't seen nothing born before. Only when our ol' cat had kittens. Had 'em in the drawer, 'er did. Just sort of licked 'em out easy. Purring all the time, too. So I'm glad I seen this calf born.' She laughed. 'My friends won't believe me when I tells 'em tomorrow.'

I had never heard her talk so enthusiastically before. I looked at Pete. 'We'll have her working on the farm yet, instead of scrubbing sheets in that old laundry.'

But he was not going to be drawn. Too much conversation

77

with a woman was bad form. 'Reckon I better give Little Lotty some bran. I got some all ready. Just got to mix in a bit o' hot watter from the dairy boiler. Then us can get the calf away while 'er's eating.'

He was in charge. We usually gave a cow a hot bran mash when she calved, for medicinal purposes and 'ter help 'er inside outside', as Bert always said. Now Pete had remembered to get it all ready beforehand. I would have only thought about it after the calf was born.

Rose wasn't going to risk being left alone with me and she skipped after him as he disappeared with a lamp. I heard her chattering to him all the way to the dairy.

Little Lotty kept her eye on me while I waited. As the calf moved so she shuffled about being very protective. Every time it bunted at her belly looking for the udder, she swung round and nosed at it and licked it spasmodically. She seemed uncertain of what she had produced, as though she must not let it out of her sight until she had quite made up her mind about it.

'Come on, gal, get some o' this down yer.' Pete came back in, rattling the handle of the bucket and the bran was steaming.

Little Lotty watched him go to the manger in the corner. Her ears shot forward, but she hesitated about walking away from her calf.

'Come *on*, what ails yer?' Pete offered her a smell of the bucket. Then she came forward when he tipped the bran into the manger.

And as soon as her back was turned I lifted up the calf, one arm under its neck, the other under its bum. I clasped it against me and stole off with it like a thief in the night.

When I returned from putting it in a pen, Pete was still trying to explain to Rose why a cow could not keep her calf. So I left them to it, perhaps to find a love nest in the darkness.

And by the time I reached the back door, paused to take a last look up into the starry sky, Little Lotty started to mourn the loss of her first born.

6

COLONEL AND LOTTY were uncomfortable bedfellows. They shared the stable by night, the field by day and never had a good word to say to one another. The trouble was that they had both been used to having their own way. They were both bosses and neither was prepared to yield to the other. Open a gate and Lotty had always been first through, either to the cowshed or to a change of pasture. Sometimes there was a challenge from an uppity heifer, but it seldom needed more than a gesture with her horns and she was queening her way through in the lead again.

But Colonel was used to strolling down towards the gate about tea time. He liked to look over it and watch us at work across in the farmyard as we set about the evening chores. And now and then he would neigh quietly, only it was more of a series of discreet little coughs, just to remind us that it would soon be dusk and he was still there, waiting to be let through to the stable.

So there was bound to be a clash when the gate was opened and they both tried to go through at once. Colonel was already there watching me with interest as I approached. As the gate opened inwards he always stodged back a step or two and then moved into a clumsy *chassé* through the mud to be in a position to plod through as soon as the gate was opened wide enough. Lotty was a few yards behind, coming forward and tossing her horns as I started to open the gate, looking surprised that Colonel ignored her warning as he *chasséd* in front of her.

'Watch out, Colonel,' I said, 'ladies first.'

He continued with his manoeuvre. I must be daft if I thought he was going to give way to a mere cow. It seemed inevitable that Lotty's horn would gouge his bum.

'*No*, Lotty, you vicious sod!'

Even as I shouted, Colonel became aware of the danger to his person. Suddenly he flattened his ears, bared the yellow stubs of his teeth, swung around through the mud and lunged at Lotty's shoulder.

She was taken by surprise, so horrified as she was forced into ungainly evasive action that she uttered the long, low moan of submission, the same sound she had so often extracted with such glee from others.

It sounded so strange coming from her that I laughed. 'Serves you right, mate. Nothing like a dose of your own medicine at last.'

Colonel pushed past me on his way to the stable. He had already forgotten about the stupid cow and his ears were pricked and his head high as he thought about the hay which would be waiting in the rack. He just gave Lotty a contemptuous swish of his tail. And if looks could kill, the stare she gave him in return would have crumpled his legs and sent him crashing to the ground.

She paused before she followed, trying to regain her dignity, still thoroughly perplexed by the unexpected attack. Whoever heard of coming in head high and using teeth? She shook her head and walked past me. She should have known better. That was the sort of foul play to be expected from a horse.

In the stable you could have cut the atmosphere with a knife. There was a partition between them. Colonel could just see over it if he raised his head and Lotty, being shorter, could only catch fleeting glimpses of him. So she shook her head and bashed her horns against the wooden partition whenever she thought he was looking.

'Keep still, Lotty, for Chrissake!' I milked her in there by hand. She was fidgety anyway because she was used to the steady suction of the milking machine and my forearms ached through lack of practice. It hardly seemed worth the bother. Better to dry her off altogether. But milk was my main income. Every drop was precious and if Lotty did hold to Dunnell's bull I knew I could rely on a steady two gallons a day from her for the next six months. Then I could dry her off and when she started to bag up for the next calf I could sell her as a down-calver. She would fetch more like that than as a barrener for meat pies. Sometimes the calf-rearers liked to buy old cows close to calving and use them for multiple suckling. It could prove cheaper than buying expensive powdered and fortified calf milk. It was healthier too because the calves were less likely to get the scours. And it would mean a longer lease of life for Lotty. I dreamed away as I milked her while she bashed out threats to Colonel on the partition. And he swished his tail and fired off anxious little farts because she would not let him settle down to a good steady munch at the hay.

Altogether it was a trying time for both of them. Out in the broad meadow they could not even agree to differ. We threw them some sticks of kale during the mornings on our way back from driving the cows to strip-graze the kale behind the electric fence. And they churned about changing places, each believing the other had a better piece, Colonel charging in with his ears back, Lotty lumbering off with a stalk hanging from her jaws, swinging round and hoicking at him as she chewed, but always missing because she was scared to get within range of his teeth.

It was all the more trying for Lotty because she was used to selecting the pick of the crop. At one time we used to cut the kale by hand and cart it down to the cowshed to feed. And that was a wet and shivering job. So when it became fashionable to graze cows across a field in strips, by the regular advancing of an electric fence, I became a keen follower of the trend. It was an easy enough operation in a pasture field. I had lashed out on the latest design in metal stakes, each with a footplate above the sharp tip so that it was easy to stamp it into the ground, and the top was curled like a pig's tail and insulated with a plastic sleeve to take the wire. No messing about with clumsy porcelain insulators like those on the stakes surrounding Colonel's field. In a pasture field it only took a matter of minutes to shift the fence forward by the required number of yards into the uneaten grass. And, of course, it made for much more efficient use of valuable pasture. Left unrestricted cows roam everywhere, propelled by the fond belief that the grass will taste even better a few yards further on. And as they roam so they shit, loosely and lavishly, and foul nearly as much grass as they actually eat. But grazing to an electric fence their heads face into grass that is sweet and new and vice versa with their tails.

But the strip-grazing of kale was not quite so simple. The crop was taller than the stakes. It was nearly always wringing wet so there were several thousand chances to one that a stem would short circuit the wire somewhere along the line. Photographs in the farming press made it look so easy. You just moved the fence forward to the face of the uneaten kale and there was a picture of a line of cows, neatly kneeling on their front knees with their heads under the wire while they gently helped themselves to kale.

Nothing would be simpler, I told the boys, and showed them the pictures in *The Farmers' Weekly*. And my cows were no fools. They soon got the hang of dropping to their knees and reaching under the wire until it was within an ace of sizzling the hairs on the backs of their necks. Only they lacked the manners of the pedigree cows in the pictures. My lot wound hungry tongues around the juicy stems, yanked them forward in a disgraceful display of greed so that soon the wire went dead as stalks lolled against it. Of course they knew in an instant. It was a mug's game eating on your knees when the whole field lay temptingly before you and the wire no longer bit back if you happened to touch it. So off they all went, plunging about happily in the kale, kicking their heels and roaring as it developed into a huge game of hide and seek.

As we dashed about in the crop, getting soaked to the skin trying to drive them out, Colonel would come plodding in to join them. The fence around his field was linked in the same circuit and it never took him long to discover that the wire was dead. Naturally the commotion two fields away aroused his interest and he knew a short-cut to get there. And certainly we could have done without him because he always blundered into the trailing wire hooking it firmly round his back leg and dragging it after him into the kale, ripping out the stakes and leaving a tangle that took us hours to unravel.

But we soon learnt the technique for coping with a tall crop. It meant a trip along the fence with a bagging hook, lopping the stems in half so that they could be pulled through without fouling the wire.

Yet you could never be sure that the current was passing

82

along the fence full strength, or not. It only needed a stray twig from the hedge around Colonel's field to touch it, or a leaf of kale, and much of the current would drain away leaving the fence useless. There was a gadget for testing the current. I should have bought one. But as I had already overspent on the fence it seemed to me to be an unnecessary luxury. A quick grab at the wire would soon tell us if the six volts were pulsating through full strength, or not.

Only the trouble was we were all scared to touch it in cold blood, as it were. An unexpected shock bit for a split second but never hurt. But actually to gaze on the wire and deliberately grab it required a courage that none of us possessed. So we tested the wire crudely by tickling it with a dry stick to see if we felt a tingle. But it never gave much idea of the true strength.

Until Donald happened by one day as we were setting up the fence for the next stint in the kale. We finished and he followed me as I walked to the corner of the field to connect the fence to the live wire coming up from Colonel's field. The connector was a simple spring clip affair with a nice thick wadge of rubber round it so that it could be handled without getting a shock. And when I had made the connection I began the tentative tickling with a dry stick.

'What are you doing, Daddy?'

'Seeing if the wire's working.'

'Why don't you hold it? I always hold it when I go to see Colonel 'cos you know he breaks out if it's not working.' And just to prove he was no storyteller he grabbed the wire and held it. I watched, speechless, as his little arm shook to the shudder each time the current surged along the wire. He smiled, broadly. 'Yes, it's working.' Then he nodded, gravely, 'I can feel it working all right.'

I feared my first born was abnormal, perhaps that he would develop into a masochist. So I was relieved when I happened to mention it to other farmers in passing. Not only were they all as cowardly as I when it came to grabbing an electric fence deliberately, but there also seemed to be several little sons and grandsons running around who just loved to clutch the wretched things.

Lotty had come on heat so many times that I could recognise

the very earliest signs. So when I heard her low quietly as I walked past the stable one morning I knew she wasn't bidding good morning to Colonel.

When I went in to milk her she looked round quickly. Her head was high, her expression haughty and when I tossed some corn into the manger she was only half interested. She swished her tail as I milked her and only let me have half the usual amount.

'So that's it, eh?' I muttered, with my head buried in her belly as I squeezed at the empty teats. 'Not even Dunnell's lusty young bull could ring the bell again? Sad, sad, but there it is. I thought as much. Now you've really got to go.'

When I stood up she rolled an eye at me and lowed. 'If you mean what I think you mean, the answer's no.' I threw the milking stool down in the corner. 'There's no more trips up the lane to Dunnell's bull for you, my gal.'

But she never took no for an answer. When I turned her into the field after breakfast she importuned loudly from over the gate.

Whether it was this that got on Colonel's nerves and forced him into a wild kick at the electric fence, and so out through the hedge, or whether it was Lotty lunging off in search of a mate that caused the twisted wire and the yawning gap, there was no knowing. But halfway through the morning there was a frantic call from Olive at the back door. 'Colonel's out! He's marching off up the lane.'

'Then turn him *back*!' I was cutting out hay in the stack-plat at the other end of the farmyard.

'I can't! Cherry's on the pot.' She had reached the interesting stage of crawling off it and emptying the contents on the floor if she got half a chance.

'Oh *hell*.' I jammed the hay knife in the stack and slid down the ladder. As I reached the ground I noticed that Lotty was no longer bawling. Out in the lane I could see Colonel plodding up the hill, his head going up and down as he made maximum speed without actually trotting. By the way he was going it seemed obvious he had already made up his mind where he was off to.

Over the lane I climbed up on the gate and searched the field. There was no sign of Lotty — only the gap in the hedge that marked her passing. Of course it was she who had broken out first. I should have kept her shut up in the stable. I ought to have realised that the quick stab from the electric fence would prove no deterrent when thoughts of a day of leaping enjoyment were surging through her old head.

'*Pete!*' I cupped my hands and shouted towards the hop garden. When I heard his answering shout, I called: 'Can you see Lotty? She's got out!' If she was making for the other cows he was bound to see her.

'No! Her ain't 'ere!'

That could only mean she had preceded Colonel up the lane. And that way led up past the boys' cottage and on down the hill and up again to Dunnell's farm. Of course! She knew the way and if we would not take her she would go on her own to help herself to the bull.

I yelled to the boys to come. But they were already on their way at this fine excuse for leaving the boring work of shaving the bark from new hop poles, and the awkward job of sharpening the thick and curving ends with an axe.

As they came into sight, I called: 'Quick! Grab your bikes! Get by Colonel and drive him back, Bert. Pete, you get after Lotty. She must be halfway to Dunnell's by now. I'll follow as soon as I've unearthed my bike.'

It was in the woodshed and I knew I would have to pump up a tyre. Why did I always leave undone those things I ought to have done? As I ran to the woodshed I cursed the lack of time in each day for all that had to be done. And I mouthed choice obscenities for animals that broke out and caused a loss of what time there was.

When I reached the woodshed there was Olive's bike, all polished and pumped up, proudly propped up on its stand while mine lay where I had flung it down on the pile of logs. How did she always manage to be so neat and tidy? She had masses to do with the old house and the children, no electricity and no gadgets, and yet she even found time to polish her bike. But I was sure she would not mind if I borrowed it. After all, it was in a good cause.

Donald and the dogs has sensed action. They had already started up the lane by the time I swept out on Olive's bike.

'No. You can't come. Take the dogs back. Home! Home!' I

wobbled past them, pointing fiercely behind me. They would only make matters worse and Donald would slow me down.

'I want to come *with* you.'

'You can't!' I rode on, feeling rotten. So I called back: 'You guard the gate. Stop Colonel going into the yard when he comes back.' But when I looked round he had already turned back and was running towards the house. I hoped he didn't let on about the bike.

As I pedalled past the boys' cottage I heard shouts coming from behind it, where there was a tiny smallholding. Their father, old Jack, kept a few chickens, pigs and a cow called Polly and by the sound of things all the living creatures there were on the run. I could see the boys' bikes in a heap just inside the garden gate, so I circled back in the lane, dismounted and propped up Olive's bike carefully on the verge.

There was a small track leading past the back of the cottage and the way into the smallholding gave off this. As I hurried along, drawn by the shouts and sounds, I startled a tethered goat, attentively observing the goings-on in the smallholding through a hole she had eaten in the bottom of the hedge. She spun round as she heard me and it is strange how you can suddenly see a likeness to a person in an animal he keeps. As this goat lowered her head and watched me pass, she had the furtive look of old Jack.

The gate was open and I hurried through. For a moment I stood and gaped, unsure of which way to go first because everything was busy. At the back of the cottage the boys' mother, the buxom Mildred, was screaming words I was surprised she even knew as she hauled at a sadly sagging line of washing. But I could understand her grief because there, amidst the encircling, stick-waving boys, their coat-flapping father, the flying chickens, the escaping sow and her litter of pigs, Lotty and Polly were joyfully leaping upon one another.

Evidently they were enjoying simultaneous heats, and to celebrate the occasion Polly had chosen to adorn her horns with one of Mildred's flannel nighties, while Lotty was riding her, sporting a pair of Jack's corduroy trousers, firmly hooked on a horn with the legs saucily draping over one eye.

Even as I joined in to help part the cows Polly re-arranged her nightie. It was her turn on top, and as she swung round

86

from beneath Lotty and prepared to mount, she tossed her head, sending the nightie floating backwards as a long haired woman would throw back hair from her eyes. Now only one sleeve clutched a horn and soon the rest of the garment slid from her shoulders and became entangled in her prancing feet. There was no doubt it would have to be washed again. Yet even as the thought crossed my mind there was a horrified shriek from Mildred as Polly mounted and the nightie was rent in two.

Now the top half was high in the air, flying from her horn like a tattered flag of truce, while the skirt was trampled unceremoniously into the mud by the excited gyrations of Lotty's feet. The cows were facing me now and while the flag waved wildly above, Lotty stared at me with lustful eyes, one gleaming and unashamed, the other peering out from between Jack's trouser legs.

The cows had formed such an intense relationship that it took much swearing and belabouring with sticks before we managed to part them. And while Jack drove Polly off to simmer down in her stall the rest of us prevented Lotty from following her.

Mildred walked sadly over from her washing line. She pulled the remnants of her nightie from the mud and sighed as she gazed after the rest of it, disappearing into the shed and still firmly fixed on Polly's horn. She seemed deflated. She had used up all her considerable vocabulary of swear words and it hadn't done any good. 'Don't reckon I'll be able ter stitch these bleedin' bits together, that I don't.'

'Bloody ol' thing were wore out anyway, by the look on't,' Pete observed, gruffly.

'Aye,' Bert agreed, 'time you 'ad a new 'un.'

Mildred shook her head sadly at her unsympathetic sons. 'Can't buy warm flannel nighties like this nowadays. Afore the war I bought that, afore the war when things was made proper.'

'I'll get my missus to buy you another one,' I offered, 'next time we go to Ashford.' It was the least I could do. She gave me a glimmer of a smile and I felt slightly less guilty about the disruption of her washing line and the damage Lotty had caused.

Jack shambled back from tying up Polly, carrying the top part of the nightie carefully in his hand. He always had a clay pipe in his mouth and now it gurgled and pulled down his lower lip. I had not seen him for several weeks because he never stirred far from the cottage these days. At one time he had been a regular visitor at Maywood, helping out at the busy times and often offering useless advice. Not that he had ever been more than just another pair of hands and his sons used to chide him mercilessly for his slowness. So gradually he had stopped coming. We found we could manage without him anyway.

He took his pipe from his mouth and spat. 'What about me trousers?' He looked up at Lotty as we held her at bay.

They were still firmly pierced on her high horn, just as she had spiked them during her back-tingling charge along the hanging washing.

I moved forward to see if I could dislodge them. But she backed away, throwing up her head so that the trousers flopped right across her face. She shook her head to stare past them. Finders keepers.

I said: 'We'll have to wait 'til we tie her up back home. Pete can bring them back. I don't think they're much damaged.' The horn had pierced them by the waist band. It was only a little hole. It wouldn't show under a jacket or a pullover. 'Come on, you two!' I hit the ground with my stick. 'Let's get this old sod home before she gets up to any more mischief.'

'Hell! Where's Colonel?' I had forgotten all about him in the excitement.

Pete looked around him. 'He *was* 'ere.'

The smallholding was gradually returning to normal. Hens were scratching for grubs where the cows had broken the turf, cockerels were preening and strutting and the sow flopped down with a loud grunt to feed her family. And in the far corner two geese and a gander were advancing on the hay rick, heads down and hissing.

'There 'ee be, the ol' bugger.' Bert pointed. We could just see his swishing tail as the old horse helped himself behind the hay rick.

Bert went to fetch him, and with Pete walking in front and me behind we started to drive Lotty home.

She had quietened down and started off sedately. The trousers hung limply now, like the bedraggled scarf of a reveller returning home. Behind me Bert brought up the rear, leading Colonel by the forelock and he was walking quietly, well pleased with him-

88

self because he had not tasted stolen hay in months.

If the tethered goat had kept quiet I am sure we should have reached home without trouble. But she was grazing in the hedge on Lotty's blind side, obscured from her view by the dangling trousers. And just as she drew near, the goat decided to pass the time of day with a piercing bleat. Now Lotty had never come across a goat before and the sound startled her. She shuffled round to face her, saw the furtive look, watched the wagging beard, snorted at the strong smell and needed time to think.

The goat was not used to being stared at. She stamped her foot and bleated again.

I thought Lotty was going to charge. To impale Jack's goat on her other horn really would add injury to insult. I ran towards her with my stick raised: 'Go on, you misbegotten quadruped! Get on with you! You've done enough damage for one day.'

She backed away down the track, still snorting threats at the evil-smelling goat. And I hurried her along heedlessly, only concerned to get her away from the goat, staring at her lowered head and the trailing trousers and not caring where she was backing to.

Pete's shout came too late. The fool should have seen it coming sooner because a backing cow is apt to swing off suddenly in any direction. And it only took her a few horrible, grinding seconds to topple Olive's bike and stumble over it.

By the time she had extricated herself from the spokes that persisted in wrapping themselves around her hooves, the polished, perfect bike was a write-off. While I looked down at it, speechless, Pete picked it up.

He shook his head sadly as he tried to set it up on its buckled wheels. Then he looked up at me quickly and with his mouth open. 'This ain't your bike. It's . . .'

'I know. Don't tell me.'

'Oh Christ!'

Before I reached home with it, lugging it over my shoulder, I knew I would have to buy Olive a new one. That was one new lady's bike, one new lady's flannel nightie and, to be fair, I supposed one new pair of gent's corduroy trousers. But they were only things, and borrowed though it was, money could replace them. Yet it could never really buy back the damage done to the goodwill of neighbours, never remove the nasty feeling you experienced when someone else's stock ate your grass, or your hay, or caused havoc on your farm. Nor could it compensate for the misery I felt at having to see sorrow in Olive's eyes when I told her.

So I blamed Lotty as she swayed down the lane in front of me. It was all her fault. And as soon as I had made my peace in the kitchen, I stormed through to the telephone to book her in with the barreners.

7

I HAD A motor car called Cob. It was a pre-war Austin Ten with
a brown body, smart black mudguards and the registered number
COB 903. Hence the name.

I bought it soon after I met Olive. I had been trying to con-
vince myself for ages that I needed a car for the farm. So when
I discovered that this delicious, dark-eyed nurse lived and worked
out of cycle range, that courting her was limited to two fleeting
evenings in ten, and that even then it meant a twelve-mile cycle
ride there and back to her home, I hesitated no longer. On a
visit to Maidstone I saw Cob, shining under his sixty-pound
price tag and I snapped him up. Second-hand cars were scarce
after the war and you could not afford to hang about making up
your mind.

I drove him home with great pride. There is something about
the feel of your very first second-hand car that makes it seem
like a Rolls — until you begin to become more intimately ac-
quainted after a few miles. Even then, if the salesman has done
his job properly, you are only too willing to turn a deaf ear to
suspicious sounds; to blame the Council for the rough roads
when the steering wheel judders in your hands; and, of course,
it is just a side wind when the car seems to have a penchant for
wandering across the road. But still, I suppose your attitude is
the same with most new things upon which you've really set your
heart. It is like the first besotted days of a love affair.

Pete and Bert were suitably impressed. They had been expecting me, and at the first sound of Cob coming down the lane,

they left their work and were there to greet me. They piled in, Pete in front, Bert behind, and we all went off for a drive.

The lane past Maywood was narrow and from the top of the rise by the boys' cottage it plunged in hedge-bound steepness, a thrilling, curving downhill which levelled out past Frog's Hole Farm and then shot upwards, tunnelling through hedgerows again until it broke into the sky at the junction where the pillar box stood strapped to a post in the grass triangle at the top. It was a fine feeling on a bike. We all knew it well. Riding down with Mother there was always competition to gain the maximum speed on the downhill run, to hurtle up towards the pillar box and see who could get the nearer before the steepness forced you to dismount. Now, together with the boys in Cob, we rattled down like a roller-coaster, skimming the verges, flashing past Frog's Hole with Bert shouting and waving to a dazed Farmer Dunnell, while Pete kept urging me to 'give it to 'er, then', as we forged up towards the pillar box and I scraped my way down through the gears until Cob, gasping, reached the top.

'Bugger me! That were better'n a bike ride,' Pete declared, with a wide grin.

'Aye,' Bert agreed, enthusiastically, 'turn round and let 'er 'ave it again.'

Evidently Farmer Dunnell had been unable to believe his eyes. A car passing by along the lane was rare, worth a stare. But had it actually been that hair-brained young lot from Maywood shooting by at such speed? Since when did young Creaton have a car? At any rate, he must have decided to walk out into the lane and gaze up the hill after us to satisfy his curiosity. He was a big man, vast corduroy breeches and a barrel belly, and there he was when we came plunging down again, firmly facing us and taking up half the lane.

'Give 'im a hoot!' Pete shouted.

'Out the way, yer silly ol' sod!' Bert screamed.

For a moment the big man hesitated as it slowly dawned on him that we really were coming back down again. I was on the point of braking when he leapt to the side and crucified himself on the gate as we tore by.

'Silly ol' bugger!' Pete shook his fist. 'Bloody nigh stopped our run up the hill, yer did.'

But as Cob crawled up the last few yards of the hill, and

then gathered speed again on the slope down to Maywood, I felt a twinge of shame at my rude rush past our startled neighbour. And I decided that it would be advisable to use the other route out of the farm for a few days, to give him time to calm down. Only I need not have worried. I met him in the village the very next day. He gave me one of his rare smiles and told me to make sure I sounded the hooter to warn him next time because he was not so young as he used to be.

Back at the farm, Pete asked: 'Where you goin' ter keep the ol' car?' He was standing beside Cob, running his fingers lovingly along the shining roof.

'Here, in the yard, I suppose. It's as good a place as any.'

'Pity ter leave 'im out in the weather, ain't it? T'will take all the shine orf of 'im.'

'Well, there's nowhere else. Only the cartshed and that would mean turning out implements and littering the place with them.'

Bert sniffed and suggested: 'What about the cowshed?'

'Can't keep 'im in there.' Pete sounded horrified.

'Why not? There's room on that wide concrete just inside the double doors. Be a good place, that it would.'

'It'd get covered in shit. Flies all acrost there the shit do.'

'So?' Bert was belligerent. 'What's a bit o' shit? Soon wash orf.'

In fact, that is just where Cob did end up — but only on those damp and misty nights when leaving him out in the open meant that he refused to start in the morning. In the cosy company of the cows he had a centrally-heated garage and was never any trouble to start, even on the mistiest of mornings. Only Pete was right. When the cows tended to be loose, perhaps after an extra dollop of frosty kale, poor old Cob really did get plastered. I think we spent nearly as much time washing him down in the morning as we did trying to start him if he had spent the night outside.

And there was another thing that happened to him through sleeping in the cowshed. Because he was there handy, and had to be started up and moved out of the way anyway, he was soon pressed into service as a milk cart. Usually we sweated the half mile up the hill to the top road hauling a hand cart, to carry the full churns to the stand where the milk lorry stopped to pick them up. It was always a race against time. Officially the lorry was meant to come by at half past seven and if you missed it, bad luck, because it never waited. Often it didn't pitch up until gone ten, sometimes even later in the summer and that was a curse. The milk sat in the sun getting hotter and hotter and the next day it was returned — sour. On those days only the pigs were delighted. And the ducks, because they got a basinful as well and gorged themselves silly, staggered about with distended crops and ended up with the squitters, usually all across the back yard sending Olive berserk with bucket and broom.

Anyway, we soon found that we could balance the churns in Cob's boot, and provided we remembered to rope them on, all was well. They made the old car sag somewhat and the steering was light going uphill. But officially he was a farm car, drawing extra coupons for rationed petrol, so it was only right he should pull his weight.

The first time I took Olive out in him, Cob disgraced himself and nearly caused the end of our blossoming friendship. It was raining, which was a pity because it spoilt the gleam which I had burnished into the ageing panels. Never mind, it was really something to go courting in a car and I swept into the entrance of the Nurses' Home with a rich and satisfying scrunch on the gravel. And she was waiting already, smiling, slim and lovely in a new red dress that must have cost a fortune in clothing coupons.

Away we went, bouncing along empty roads, swaying round corners in the sagging bucket seats, everything purring and the gear lever rattling merrily between us. Soon we were on a side road. I was steering with one hand while the other had crept round her shoulder. She was leaning towards me, as close as the gear lever would allow and I was on the point of suggesting that we pulled in for a while to admire the view. The lane was rough. There were wide puddles and Cob splashed gaily into one with all four wheels. Olive drew a sharp breath and cringed away with a shudder as a fountain of cold water shot up under her skirt from the hole where the gear lever went through.

It was a disaster. I pulled in profuse with apologies. So sorry. There should have been a rubber collar there under the circle in the carpet to block the hole. Sorry again. God, you can actually see the road down through there! Can't think why I'd never noticed and blocked it up. All my fault. Was she all right? Obviously not. She sat awkwardly on the seat, dabbing herself with a tiny hanky and all I could find to offer her was a dirty old duster. Until I remembered my own handkerchief was clean. When I pulled it out and gave it to her she smiled. Soon she was laughing and I loved her some more because she had a sense of humour.

You needed understanding when travelling in Cob. Sometimes he suffered from severe bouts of coughing. There was never any warning. He would be bowling along with evident enjoyment when suddenly the paroxysm would grip him, causing him to leap about in stops and starts, each surge forward less enthusiastic than the last until all he could do was splutter and stop with a gasp and a final report from the exhaust. The strange thing was that he never acted up like this when I was alone with him. It was nearly always when Olive was with me and once his fit was so violent that the passenger seat shot backwards and sent her sprawling. So it seemed to me that it was really attention-seeking on the old car's part. When he stopped I had to get out, lift first one side of the bonnet and then the other, fiddle with the leads, tickle the carburettor and generally fuss over him for a few minutes before he would agree to start again.

He even let me down on the way to my wedding. There had been the usual last minute rush, trying to get everything organised so that Pete and Bert could manage on their own during the week I would be away honeymooning. And then the struggle into the morning dress which I had been persuaded into hiring, much against my will because I could have spent the money to better purpose on honeymoon. So we were late already as we set out, my best man in similar attire beside me, Mother in a new 'hightum' hat and other finery on the back seat, and Pete and Bert all set to wave goodbye but staring in open-mouthed disbelief as I doffed a topper to them.

The church was seven miles away and Cob set off as though he was determined to get there on time. But three miles out, on the loneliest stretch of road, he decided to have one of his coughing fits and stopped to get his breath back.

'Oh *dear*,' sighed Mother from the back seat. 'I *knew* we should have hired a car.'

95

I got out and lifted the bonnet. It was trying to snow and one or two very large flakes drifted down and disappeared with faint hisses on the hot engine. 'Bloody car, what's the matter with you?' I pulled back the sleeves of the morning coat, the snow white cuffs of my shirt and leant towards the engine gingerly.

My best man joined me. He was a city dweller and looked anxiously up and down the deserted road. 'I say, old boy, you'll get yourself filthy. No chance of a garage anywhere handy, I suppose?'

'Not around these parts.' I was tinkering with the engine, trying to look as though I knew what I was doing. 'Damn car, you would choose today of all days, wouldn't you?'

My best man peered over my shoulder. 'Have you found the trouble?' He lived among the swirl of modern motor cars. How could I explain that this old car would only start again when it was good and ready? At least I hoped it would. Then, like delayed shock, the awful possibility that perhaps it wouldn't crept over me and I found myself starting to sweat in spite of the snow. I fiddled feverishly with carburettor, distributor, leads and plugs while I had visions of a church full of restless relatives with Olive waiting patiently in the porch.

'Hurry up, darling, we'll be late.' Mother was half out of the car. 'It's really not done to arrive at the church after the bride, you know.'

'Hell! As if I didn't know that,' I snapped.

But in his own good time Cob started up and moved off as sweetly as though nothing had happened. Now we really were late and I thrashed the car mercilessly in an effort to arrive before the bridal party. Olive would not be late. Two thirty meant two thirty so far as she was concerned. So I was surprised to see no sign of her when I slithered to a stop outside the church at twenty-five to three.

Only I need not have worried and hurried. It just proved that I did not know my bride as well as I thought I did. But she knew me, and she knew Cob, so had planned accordingly. As my route to the church followed the main road in sight of her house, she had posted a bridesmaid as look-out in a window with a view. And only after I was reported to be safely by did she set her own procession in motion.

96

Anyway, Cob's cough was cured soon after we returned from honeymoon. He had taken us down to Devon, touring from place to place, running perfectly and enjoying the journey as much as we did. So much so that he did not want to head back for home and he shuddered to a stop in Paignton High Street. He decided to take his time recovering. Traffic began to build up but I tried to ignore it, until I saw the black boots out of the corner of my eye. 'Yes, Officer, I'll move it along. Into the next side street? Yes.' And I summoned my bride in her honeymoon finery and for better or for worse she helped me push. After that I made a solemn promise that I would have the car over-hauled.

It was Ebenezer Jarcomb who cured Cob. He was an old man who lived in the next village, one of those rare beings who could cope with any repair from the faulty knotting mechanism of a reaper-binder to a twisted horse plough, from the knocking big ends of a Fordson tractor to the fine tuning of Colonel Claremont's Rolls Royce. He worked from a World War One ex-army hut up a lane behind his house and the way to it was strewn with a few old cars, farm implements of all kinds, some deep in undergrowth, some dumped recently, some bought for spares at sales, others just left there with 'see to it for us some-time, Ebby. Shan't be wantin' it afore next haying.'

Ebby must have been nearing seventy. He was also bent and riddled with rheumatism. It made me ache just to see him move. Yet once he had his mind on a job he could ease himself under a car, or crawl over an implement with the ease of the Hunchback of Notre Dame swinging on his bells. At least I always supposed it was sheer concentration and the obvious love of his work that allowed him to forget his pains, until he let me into his secret.

I explained about Cob. I ran the engine and he listened. 'Right you are.' He straightened up with a grimace. 'Leave 'un with me. I'll set 'un up for 'e good as new. Decoke. P'raps new rings but I'll see 'bout that when I gets to 'em. Clean out that ol' petrol tank for 'e too. Some shit in there, I'll lay. Allus is with you farmers. Comes of tippin' in bits and pieces o' petrol out o' cans.' He closed the bonnet and turned away slowly. 'About a week. Let 'e have it in about a week if so be I be spared.'

'The old rheumatism playing you up again?' I asked with sympathy.

97

' 'Tis this darn weather. Rain ain't no good for me screwmatics.'

'I'm sure it's not. You'll have to look after yourself. Don't know what we'd do without you.'

He laughed. 'Lord luv us, I knows how to look atter meself. I'll soon give 'un a bit o' physiking. I knows how to tune up me ol' screwmatics when they'm bad.'

'Really? Horse oils or ironing with brown paper?' I laughed.

He hobbled towards the door, beckoning me to follow. 'You come along o' me.' And I followed him round to the back of the shed where young stinging nettles were growing in profusion. Without a word he bent down painfully and grabbed a handful. Suddenly he slipped his braces from his shoulders, his trousers dropped to his ankles and he started to lash his legs and thighs with the nettles. He wore no underpants and even as I stared at him, my mouth open like an idiot, he flicked up the tail of his shirt, slapped the nettles over his scrawny bum and then shoved them up his back as far as he could reach.

He threw the nettles down with a sigh of pleasure, pulled up his trousers, tucked in his shirt and flicked his braces back over his shoulder. He seemed to be moving more easily already. 'Ah! Ha-ha!' He smiled, broadly. 'That do set I up proper. Nature's own cure, that be. Folks say nettles be weeds. But they ain't, you know. Not to me, they ain't. I beats away the pain wi' 'em. *And* I eats 'em too. Poached egg on boiled nettles, nothin' like it to clean the blood. And I don't throw the watter away neither. That be good for rubbin' into me joints nights, if I wakes up wi' the screwmatics.'

So I left Cob with him. Just over a week later I had a message to say the car was ready. And when I drove him home it seemed as though old Cob had been born again. He zipped along almost as though he too had a bunch of young stinging nettles stuffed in his tank.

8

THE LORRY CAME for Lotty soon after seven in the morning. Cattle lorry drivers have little patience at the best of times, still less on their first journey on a busy market day. There was no chance of a fond farewell as we bundled the old cow out of the stable and up the ribbed ramp into the lorry. She went easily, without protest. So I did think it was hard on her when the driver landed two hefty thwacks on her hide as she disappeared into the depths of the lorry.

'Poor old Lotty,' Olive said, when I told her over breakfast. 'What a cruel send off for her. It's bad enough just packing her off because she's no use any more.'

'You women! You're too sentimental. We can't *be* sentimental, you know that. We've got to earn a living out of the creatures somehow.'

She smiled as she wiped a beard of porridge from Cherry's face. 'Listen to your father talking! Tough Daddy, hiding his feelings again.'

'Well, Lotty's gone now, anyway. She'll be in the market by now, bossing all the other cows in the pen, I dare say.' I stood up. 'And it's time we were off too, if we're all going to Ashford today. How long are you going to be?' I started to clear the table.

'Not long. Even less time if you don't try and hurry me. You get changed and take Donald with you outside.'

Donald was off in a flash at this mercifully quick release from the table. He hated waiting for permission to get down. He

99

fidgeted in his chair because there were always a dozen things to do more interesting than eating.

I called to him: 'Come on, we'll go and load up Cob'.

Olive looked round, quickly. 'Load the car? What with?'

I should have kept my mouth shut and presented her with a fait accompli. 'Well, you see, there's Little Lotty's bull calf...'

'Oh no! Why ever didn't you send it on the lorry?'

'I forgot. At least the lorry came so early I only remembered after Lotty was loaded. And the driver was in such a foul temper I couldn't very well ask him to wait. Particularly as we're going in the car anyway and we have to justify it's use as a farm car. Besides, anybody would think it's the first time we've carried a calf in the car.'

She sighed and resumed her work. 'I don't know! It really does take the fun out of a trip to town when a calf licks the back of your neck all the way there.'

'Never mind, Mummy, I'll hold it very tight.' At least Donald was all for the idea. It would liven up an otherwise dull journey for him.

'And what about Granny?' Olive continued, as I opened the back door. 'I suppose you've forgotten we arranged to call by and take her with us as well.'

I had. 'There'll still be room. At least Granny and Donald between them should be able to stop the calf from licking your neck.'

It was a bit of a squash. But many a farmer carried a calf to market in the back of his car – in those days before the practice was made illegal. The trick was to pop the calf into a cow cake bag and tie the end under its neck so that just its head protruded. Sometimes they struggled a bit at first, but they soon got used to it and usually curled up quite comfortably on the floor of the car, often even on the back seat and admiring the passing scene through the window. To my way of thinking it was a far more pleasant ride to market for a calf than being bundled together with other bawling passengers in a cubby hole of a cattle lorry, lurching and jostling round corners, standing calves treading and shitting on sitting ones.

But busy-bodies, roaming the market with nothing better to do, tut-tutted at farmers hauling calves shrouded in sacking from cars. They lobbied MPs and protested to the RSPCA.

Anyway, Little Lotty's calf had a lovely ride to market. Mother sat with his head on her lap while the rest of him was swathed in sacking. She stroked his face and spoke soothingly to him because she knew he was a bull calf destined for the veal market. 'Never mind, little man, I'm glad you don't know anything about it.'

Donald shoved his fingers in the calf's mouth. 'Look, Granny, he likes that!'

Only then the calf got excited and bunted because he thought fingers meant milk. And he struggled in his sacking and for a moment there was turmoil in the back of the car. Which startled Donald and sent him cringing to the corner of the seat, leaving his granny to wrestle with the calf. And Cherry stood in the safety of Olive's lap on the front seat, laughing merrily at granny's contortions as she soothed the calf and persuaded it to calm down.

I dropped them off in the town, pulled Cherry's push cart from the boot and saw them off to the shops. 'Meet you at the Copper Kettle at one.'

'Lunch is going to be my treat,' Mother declared, firmly.

Donald was pulling her hand. 'I'm going to help Mummy choose her new bike. Come on Granny.'

'And don't forget Mildred's nightie,' I called after Olive.

'All right, but you'll have to buy Jack's trousers.' Her reply ricocheted off passers-by between us. They stared curiously as I climbed back into the car, where the calf was busy steaming up a window and nosing patterns on the glass.

It was a slow job driving into the market. Many farmers still found it cheaper, or more convenient, to continue to employ drovers to take their stock to market on the hoof, rather than rely on the vagaries of the cattle lorries. So the roads converging on the market filled with flocks of steaming, bleating sheep and herds of wild-eyed bullocks, through which cars struggled, some with trailers where bulging nets encased a sow with shining snout raised, a lonely bawling calf, or a bumptious load of porkers or perhaps a single, sad-eyed ram.

And the drovers plied their trade as though the motor car, the lorry and the omnibus had no place in the town. They were stern old men, some in long brown smocks and worn gaiters that squeaked on their hob-nailed boots; others in caps, collarless shirts and neckerchiefs, and corduroy trousers hitched up below the knees with binder twine. They raised heavy sticks and made gruff noises that had no human translation; only their dogs understood, weaving, snarling, barking, biting. Bullocks bashed cars and sheep shed wool on bumpers while the drovers plodded by, and if they bothered to catch your eye they scowled at you as though you had no right to be there. Perhaps they knew their job was dying. Yet there can have been little joy in it, even at the best of times, plodding here with bullocks, agreeing a rate and off somewhere else behind a flock of sheep, rain down your collar, wind in your face, shit spattering on your shoes; no continuity with the animals you followed, no constructive purpose, just the job of an ageing errand boy. Perhaps that was why drovers never looked happy. Their only joy was spitting on the shillings they received and swilling beer at the end of a journey, resting aching feet, pulling on their pipes and sending the strong smell of shag to mix with the stink of livestock on their steaming clothes.

I carried the calf from the car, dumped him in a shed where other calves crowded the close-packed pens. Market men came by and slapped a lot number on him. The calf looked unhappy. They all looked unhappy, some calling constantly for their mothers, some rolling eyes and looking round, others lying down, exhausted with the bewildering rigmarole.

Prospective buyers leant over the pens, going through their time-honoured ritual of inspection, encompassing the small of each tiny back with a heavy hand and squeezing it firmly. Calves lying down were prodded and had their ears slapped to make them stand so that they could also have their backs squeezed. And as one buyer finished and the calves tried to settle again, so another would come along and repeat the whole process.

Often I longed to ask them outright why they did this, what they hoped to find out that a practised eye alone could not tell them; whether a bull calf from a dairy breed was worth twenty-five shillings or thirty, or a beefy, blood-red Sussex five pounds, six pounds or even ten. I don't suppose any of them could have told me. Calf-squeezing was the recognised thing to do. It was all part of the market mystique, the knowing look, the aimless hit with a stick, the plucking at the skin of a cow's ribs, the nod, the wink, the shifting of a greasy cap.

I walked over to the tall, tubular pens to check that Lotty had arrived. I recognised her horns along the line of quiet, cud-chewing barreners. They all seemed to be resigned to their fate and watched me go by with slow eyes. And Lotty stared at me when I reached her, her high horns seeming to raise her eye-brows into her surprised look. It was the look I had always laughed at, ever since she had stared down from the lorry on her arrival at Maywood, the first cow I had ever possessed.

She gave no other sign of recognising me. Cows don't wag a tail, come up simpering with a greeting. They just stare. But when I gripped the rail in front of her she stretched her head forward slowly. Her tongue came out and rasped my knuckles and she drew away. There were people about, hard-bitten farmers with pork-pie hats, check jackets, breeches and polished boots and gaiters. You cannot talk to a cow in the market like you can in your own cowshed. So I just mumbled: 'Cheerio, old girl,' under my breath and walked off without looking back.

'Marnin' Dave!'

I looked round quickly. There was fat, happy Ernie Carter coming towards me with his teeth-stuffed smile. He shared a farm with his brother, two miles from Maywood, and sales and markets were their life blood because they were dealers first and farmers only in the time left over.

When he reached me, I said: 'Hello, Ernie. And what's trade like today?' It was the right greeting, the one everybody asked everybody.

'Middlin', fair to middlin'. What you doing here today? Don't often see you in the market, buggered if I do.'

I smiled. 'Can't afford the time to loaf about like you wealthy dealers.'

He sucked his teeth. 'Now I'm going ter tell yer, you has ter come ter market to see what's going on. That's the trouble with biggest half the farmers, they don't get their bleedin' heads out the furrows. Cassent see beyond their own farm gates, they can't.'

I was on the point of mentioning the value of an evening or two spent with the local paper and *The Farmers' Weekly* when I remembered that he could not read or write. Instead, I said: 'Well, I only come when I have to. Can't say I enjoy it all that much.'

'What you brought today, a litter o' pigs? Good time fer pigs just now. Either muck or money they be. Coming into good money an' all this last week or two.' He spat dryly, another market mannerism heralding an important remark. 'Now I got a nice forward young gilt 'ud interest you.'

'Come now, Ernie, you know I only ever keep two sows. Sometimes I think that's two too many, with the time we spend trying to keep them and their litters in one place.'

He laughed. He knew my pigs because I hired his boar from him whenever he was needed. You could buy from Ernie, or sell to him, and you could hire from him as well, be it animal or implement. He was always ready to turn a shilling or two on anything. He looked past me to the barreners as I started to walk on. 'Ah, that's your ol' cow, ain't it? The brown and white one with the big horns?'

I paused, looking in another direction across the market as I nodded. I hoped I was not to be drawn into a long discussion about Lotty.

'Her's old but 'er's big,' he went on. 'Big frame there, and some meat on 'er an' all. Go through at eighteen or nineteen quid 'er will. That's my guess now. You'll see I ain't fer out when the cheque comes through.'

I walked on slowly. Oh well, at least Lotty would pay her damages. That should just about cover a new bike, a flannel nightie and a pair of corduroy trousers.

Ernie caught up with me, walking as though he were wading through mud, his tattered and spattered market coat just clinging to his shoulders, with little hope of meeting across his belly even if there had been any buttons left to hold it there. 'How about a drink, then? I've about done here. Time ter watch points in the pub, I reckon.'

'Just a quick one,' I replied. 'I've got the missus and kids in town and I've still got to go to the Corn Exchange and the bank.'

He laughed. 'No such thing as a quick drink on market days. My ol' woman learnt that years ago. 'Er bides home now.'

The pub was crowded and Ernie seemed to know everybody as he waded through in front of me. He bought beer and we found a calm spot towards a corner. There was a high-backed oak settle against the wall and six drovers were lined along it, with a spitoon in range on the floor between them. Pungent blue smoke from their pipes drifted about them and they sucked in hollow cheeks and spat and supped and talked in low tones with long pauses. Stubble bristled on their faces and I wondered again as I studied it. It was silly really. So many countrymen I knew had stubble on their faces and I had never seen them clean shaven, nor yet with a beard. Day after day the stubble always seemed to be the same length, like on the faces of these drovers now, so I imagined they must shave with scissors and just keep it cropped that way. How their wives must have suffered when they came to them with beer on their breath and eighth-inch, smoke-laden stubble.

Three dogs were spaced out at the drovers' feet, two sheep-dogs and a wicked looking, smooth-coated brown job that had bull terrier in him somewhere back along the line. The dogs were trying to sleep off the chase to market, but hackles were slightly raised and eyes kept opening as each suspected his neighbour of wanting to start something. Drovers' dogs led a rough, tough life, fiercely proud of their command over silly sheep or beligerent bullock and adoring the master who hit them, swore at them, kicked them and only threw them bones scraped clean by the butcher, or a stale loaf late at night as he staggered home sloshing with beer.

Ernie greeted the drovers. He knew three of them by name. As he spoke the brown dog reared up and scratched into his ear with a low growl of satisfaction. The other two dogs warned him they were watching and his master kicked him and said some-thing to him that was quite unintelligible to me. The dog gave a final, delightful hoick into his ear and subsided with a long sigh.

The drovers had been talking about warts on bullocks. 'Fair smothered wi' 'em that lot was, s'marnin',' said the one called Charlie.

'Ain't no cure neither,' said Silas, the small one on the end, with a sharp face like a ferret under a large cap.

'Now that's jest where you be wrong,' Ernie broke into the conversation. He sucked his teeth, removed his cap from his bald head and replaced it again. He liked to control the conver-sation in a pub and in the Six Bells, in our village, he usually had his own way. 'Now I'm going ter tell you about curing warts on bullocks,' he went on.

The drovers seemed prepared to listen. There could be a free round of beer here.

'You knows that Farmer Cornes over Warehorn, don't ye, Harry?'

Harry was the big man with the brown dog. He nodded thoughtfully and rubbed his mouth with the back of his hand before taking another swig of beer.

'Well,' Ernie continued, 'he had this herd of bullocks, yearlings they was and all good reds too, and 'ee . . .'

'You don't mean that Cornes what takes in all they Romney Marsh sheep to keep, do ye?' Silas wanted to know. 'Why, bugger me, I've a shifted sheep fer 'ee many a time.'

'No.' Ernie was not used to being interrupted. 'T'other one. Some relation, cousin I think. He's the one had these red bullocks and 'ee grazed 'em on . . .'

'I knows the one you means now.' This time Charlie interrupted. He removed his pipe and leant over and spat into the spitoon. 'Used ter have a big, tall stockman.'

'That's 'im,' agreed Harry. 'Tall fella, what were 'is name? Died 'ee did. Died in the shit house down the end of 'is garden. Frank! That's 'im. Nasty shock that were fer 'is daughter when 'er found 'im.'

There was silence, perhaps in reverent memory for poor Frank. Ernie shifted his cap, drank some beer, sucked his teeth in readiness to carry on.

But another drover mused: 'Buggered if I'd like ter die like that, sittin' in the shit house wi' me trousers down.' The dog at his feet rolled the whites of his eyes at him and tapped his tail in agreement.

Ernie tried again. 'Well now, this Farmer Cornes, 'ee grazed them red bullocks on some grass wot was growin' in between stubs of trees, and after a few days . . .'

'That daughter now,' Silas interrupted again, ' 'er wot found 'im in the shit house, 'er was the one wot weren't quite right in the head. Nellie, they called 'er, didn't 'em?'

Harry nodded. 'Aye, good lookin' wench fer all that. Big with it.'

A drover who had not talked before, a large man with heavy jowls, leant forward and knocked his pipe out on his boot. 'Fanny mad 'er were.' His voice was gravelly and he sounded as though he spoke from experience.

There were swigs of beer all round, a belch from Charlie and gurgles as pipes were sucked again. As nobody seemed to want to elaborate on Nellie's morals, Ernie continued: 'Well, afore long, grazin' between these tree stubs, some o' they bullocks got warts on their faces and necks. Grut big warts an' all. Proper spoiled the look of 'em, it did. Farmer Cornes told I about it here, in this very market. Asked me if I knowed a cure.' He seemed satisfied that he had their attention at last. It was time for him to swallow some more beer and suck his teeth again for necessary effect.

'That there Nellie.' Ferret-faced Silas sucked to keep his pipe going. 'That Nellie, 'er was the one wot went on the bus with the football team.'

'Fanny mad 'er were,' the drover with the heavy jowls repeated again, dolefully now.

Harry had been staring down at the brown dog. Now he looked up at me for the first time, as though to make sure I was listening. 'Aye, good lookin' wench, 'er were. Big with it,' he repeated. 'Stopped the bus by a wood they did. And Nellie took 'em all on, one after t'other.'

'Good God!' I exclaimed. 'Never!'

'So they do say.' Harry nodded solemnly. 'Alf Raddle telled I, and 'ee were there.'

'Aye, fanny mad 'er were,' Heavy Jowls explained again.

'Charged elevenpence halfpenny each, 'er did,' Silas added.

'Elevenpence halfpenny?' I laughed. 'She *must* have been simple.'

Harry looked up at me again, slowly shaking his head and with a straight face. 'Not so bloody simple. A shilling, that's what 'er charged normal. But 'er give 'em discount, see? Ha'-penny discount 'cos there was several on 'em.'

And the brown dog raised his head and yawned loudly because he had heard it all before.

Ernie was smiling and nodding slowly. By his expression I could tell that he had heard it all before as well. He realised the whole story had to unfold before he could command their undivided attention. Now he was free to continue. 'So I says to Farmer Cornes, "take a wire brush to 'em," I says, "brush at they ol' warts till they bleeds. And then cover 'em wi' Stockholm tar." '

The drovers were all listening, nodding as though they knew of this cure all along.

'Now I'm going ter tell yer, that's what 'ee did. And the tar dried up and took the warts orf with it, clean as a whistle.' He drained his glass and belched. 'Old Harris give I that wrinkle, the old vet what used ter be over Headcorn. But tar ain't a mite o' good if you don't take a wire brush to they ol' warts first, mind.'

'Aye, old Harris,' Charlie said, 'weren't 'ee the one what allus drove round with a black pony and trap?'

'Well,' I said, quickly, 'I must be off!' I suspected that the ramifications spreading from old Vet Harris could well last until closing time. I slapped Ernie on the shoulder. 'See you, Ernie. We'll have the other half in the Six Bells.' I waved at the line of drovers. They just nodded and sucked their pipes. Everybody knew that all young men were hasty fools.

After the market, going into the Corn Exchange was like entering the Holy of Holies. Lecterns were spaced across the wide floor as though a convention of preachers was expected, to intone solemn sermons up to the ringing rafters. But, instead of bibles, each lectern was dotted with little bags of seed corn, malting barley, samples of cow cake, calf meal and compund fertiliser. And behind the lecterns stood men in sober clothes, some smiling, some serious, all wearing hats and overcoats against the chill of the large hall, each presiding over his own little spot on the floor, waiting to be approached by farmers and never to be seen to go touting after trade. These gentlemen always seemed to me to be anxious to keep up appearances, as though they were determined to be a cut above the rowdy rabble in the market; even above the shouting auctioneers, and some of them could boast letters after their names. After all, they were the representatives of big and important firms, with connections in London, maybe even with buyers on the Baltic.

My particular rep was fat little Frank Weller with the thick glasses. He always like to pretend he was Managing Director. 'I'm expecting a new shipment of phosphate into the Pool of London next week.' Or, 'I've been promised the first batch of the new S.27 ryegrass seed from the bulking up plots at Rothamstead.' Anyway he, or rather his firm, had been supplying the owner of Maywood for years, probably ever since Colonel was a colt. It was he whom Checky had told me about soon after I had bought the farm from him. The very same Frank who had drawn up at the farm that wet day and disappeared into the stable, dying for a pee. And while so engaged had reached up to a shelf above him to tilt a tin to see what it contained. Only to find it brimming with creosote, which slopped down over his exposed part. So I could never see Frank Weller without remembering Checky's story about him and how he had danced up and down the lane, blowing on it to bring relief. And as he tended to be pompous, to lecture me from his lectern because I was only small fry, sometimes I was sorely tempted to enquire after his penis, to know whether it had suffered lasting damage after its baptism of fire.

I could have changed my merchant, snubbed Frank by sauntering up to another lectern for quotes. But I didn't. I listened to his tedious advice about the fertilisers I must use for the hops, the amount of sulphate of ammonia to apply to produce the 'early bite' of grass, the seed mixtures I should buy for the best three year leys, and he had better put me down for another ton of cow cake while the price was right, hadn't he? I knew his prices were as keen as I could get anywhere and the credit he gave was the longest. And when you are constantly in hock to a merchant for six months' supplies he has got you by the balls anyway.

But this day my business with Frank was brief. Time was getting short and I had to wait my turn while he held the floor with another farmer. And I kicked my heels during the cheque writing ritual. Many of the older farmers found writing tedious so they never reckoned to fill in their own cheques. They just passed the book over to the rep, or whoever, and scrawled a wavy signature when he had finished filling in the details. And as this was always another opportunity for Frank to show off, I had to wait while he changed spectacles with loud snappings of cases, polished a lens, tested his fountain pen, adjusted his cuffs and wrote slowly and with constant reference to the invoice beside him.

I approached as the old farmer walked away. 'Morning, Mr Weller.' Once I had called him Frank and the frozen stare I had received suggested that that familiarity was only permissible if you were in credit, or had known him for upwards of ten years.

He changed his glasses, snapped the cases, returned them to his pocket and then looked at me. 'Ah, good morning, Mr Creaton, sir.'

I fished a cheque from my pocket and popped it on the lectern. 'Can't stop. Just came to pay you this. Bung it in quick and it won't bounce.'

Oh hell, it never paid to be flippant with Frank. I should have posted it. Out came the reading glasses again, and the receipt book, and the sheet of twopenny stamps, and the fountain pen. Without a word he studied the cheque to make sure I had not forgotten to dot an i, wrote out the receipt and stuck on the twopenny stamp.

He handed it to me. 'Thank you, sir.' He straightened up and started on the spectacles routine. 'Now I'm glad you've come in because I want to work out your potash requirement with you. My stocks are limited and I want to be as fair as I can to all my customers.'

'Well, I really can't stop now,' I cut in. It was amazing how many salesmen still fed you the shortage line — a sure fire seller when everything was scarce. But now they seemed unable to get out of the habit even though supplies were improving all the time. And it always annoyed me, made me feel as though I was being taken for a fool. But then Frank always made me feel that way. 'Look,' I continued, 'put me down for half a ton of cow cake on your next delivery our way, and I'd better have a couple of bags of calf nuts as well.'

'Very well.' Glasses again, the invoice book, the pen. 'Perhaps I had better see if I can fit you in with a visit. I want to talk to you about your hop powders as well. I'm giving a very good price on Bordeau for early delivery, which I don't want you to miss.'

I thought: that'll be left over stock from last year. But I said: 'Fine, call in anytime. You'll find me somewhere about the farm, that's for sure.' And I escaped, waving goodbye with my receipt, before he had time to produce and peruse his diary to discuss a date for his visit. He looked a trifle upset because visits by appointment were important to him. They placed him above the typical traveller flogging round with patent medicines for livestock, or yard brooms, or a special line in wellies.

I slipped the receipt into my pocket, telling myself to remember to file it when I got back home. Blessed paperwork, it always got squeezed out by the pressure of other tasks. It had caused me some embarrassment on the last occasion Frank had visited Maywood. The feeding of my in-tray, my out-tray and my pending file was achieved by tossing everything on to my desk as it arrived. It grew into a slippery mountain, putting a terrible strain on Olive's tidy mind because it was more than she dare do even to give it the odd flick with a duster. Nothing could be disturbed because I knew where everything was. Some unconscious computer in my brain registered the exact location of bills, forms, circulars, tax matters or letters from the bank manager so that I was able to put my hand on a particular one with the minimum of shuffling.

But the higher the mountain grew, the longer it took to locate all but the most recent letters, the larger the total of unpaid bills hidden within it and the stronger my language at the sight of it. Until the task could be put off no longer and I would slide into the office after tea, with the spirit of a schoolboy facing Latin prep, and plod through the pile into the far watches of the night. And when I crept cold into bed, to cadge warmth from Olive, I would feel glad that the job was done, but despondent because the bills I had paid always totalled more than my pessimistic estimate.

Anyhow, my paper pile was approaching one of its zeniths on the occasion of Frank Weller's last visit to Maywood. As usual he had refused my invitation indoors and we were conducting our business in the yard. He sat in his car with all his papers to hand around him while I peered through the window. It would have been easier to have sat beside him, but the passenger door was always kept firmly locked against me — probably because my boots were too dirty.

During the course of his lecture he referred to a letter he had sent me two or three weeks previously, drawing my attention to pending price changes.

'Oh, I don't think I can have received that,' said I, innocently.

'You should have done.' He looked up at me over his glasses with pale-blue watery eyes. 'I've already had an excellent response from nearly all my farmers, who are wisely buying in at existing prices. It was an important letter, setting out as it did . . .'

'Just a tick. I'll go and check up.'

To my surprise he opened the car door to come with me. He had only once come into the house before and I presumed that that single sight of my desk, offering him no square inch to set out his own papers, had decided him to stay in his car in future. Now it seemed as though he did not trust me to find his important circular.

I ushered him through into the office. I approached the desk, both hands raised and fingers spread. 'Now, missives from your illustrious firm are usually to be found about here.' I knew the envelopes well. Invoices, statements, circulars, each had its own particular look and feel and I extracted all I could find and tossed them down, one by one on the corner of the desk in front of him. 'There you are, take your pick.'

He had been changing spectacles again. But the confident case snapping was missing. Gingerly he lifted the letters, turning them over slowly one by one. All the colour had drained from his cheeks. 'But Mr Creaton, sir, you, you haven't even *opened* them.'

I laughed. 'Not yet. No. I don't get much time for office work, you know.'

Reverently he replaced the letters on the desk. He changed his spectacles without a word and walked out of the house rather sadly. He seemed to have forgotten all about his important circular and it was the only time I ever saw Frank Weller deflated.

'I could only get Mildred a red flannel nightie,' Olive said, on the drive home from market.

'Oh, I'm sure she'll like it,' Mother replied, reassuringly from the back seat. 'Red's such a lovely warm colour.'

I laughed. 'I wonder what it'll do for old Jack. P'raps he'll start chasing her round the bedroom again. Bet he hasn't done that for a few years.'

There was a hiss from behind me. 'Ssh, darling, really!'

'What's wrong with old Jack chasing Mildred round the bedroom in a red flannel nightie?' I protested.

She sighed. 'You know what I mean.' She would never be

drawn into what she called smutty arguments. So she changed the subject and asked Donald: 'Is Mummy's bike still all right?'

He was standing on the seat keeping an eye on it out of the back window. Cob had a boot that was a development from the old dickie and the new bike stood upright in it, suitably lashed in position.

I growled: 'It had better be, all fifteen pounds, nineteen shillings and sixpence worth of it, saddle bag and bell extra. Well, at least we didn't have to buy them. We can salvage them off the old bike.'

Olive said, patiently: 'Never mind, Lotty's paying.'

'Lotty's going to die,' Donald reminded her, seriously.

'Poor Lotty,' Mother said. 'But still, what fun she gave us when she first arrived. D'you remember the oceans of milk she flooded us with before you started to send it away in the churn? All the masses of butter I made?' She gave a gay little laugh. 'I often think of those busy days.'

We were nearing her cottage. I could see her in the rear view mirror, straightening her hat and tucking in the unruly wisps of grey hair. 'Now, Donald, help me find all my bits and pieces, there's a dear.' She gathered two overflowing carrier bags towards her and jammed the contents into them more firmly. Then she rummaged in her pocket for a hanky and blew her nose loudly — always a sign that she was about to make a move. It was also her final act before retiring to bed at night. Back home, ever since I could remember, the sound of Mother blowing her nose on retiring had always been referred to as The Last Trump.

Now she was ready. Soon I drew up beside the path leading across the corner of the village green to her cottage. She kissed Olive and the children and I carried her bags to the gate.

She took them and kissed me too. 'You run along. I can manage now. I expect you've got masses to do.' She dumped a carrier on the ground and banged her hand against her thigh. 'Ah! Here comes my little old man to greet me. Hello, Guffy, my old faithful.'

Guffy was a Scottie, square backed and strong smelling. He advanced towards her, ears back and screwing his bum round until she bent down to pat him. And as she gathered up her bags, walked up the path and disappeared into the porch, he swaggered slowly after her.

Our dogs heard us coming and we met them bounding up the lane barking. They scrabbled round to follow us, overtook us and jostled each other to be first back into the yard to welcome us as soon as we stopped.

'Sadie! Pat! Down, down! Both of you, DOWN!' Olive was trying to get her door open. Cherry was clinging firmly to her neck and looking decidedly unhappy.

I got out, leaving my door open. 'Down you two! What's the matter with you? We've only been gone a few hours.'

They came racing round and leapt into the car, jamming themselves between the steering wheel and the seat, back legs scratching for a footing in their race to get first greeting from Olive. They were yapping and wriggling. Cherry started to cry and Donald looked uncertain at such a boisterous greeting. Already Pat was half over the seat as he tried to lick his face.

'Out, you two, *out!*' I shouted as I leant into the car and hauled them back.

Pat quietened down almost immediately at my rough handling. He sat quivering on his haunches. But Sadie kept yapping, wriggling and snapping her jaws. She looked up at me and she didn't see me. She pushed past me and blundered against the car.

'Oh God! She's going into a fit! Stay in the car.' I slammed the door.

Now she was growling, snapping, staring and froth was beginning to line her jaws. In a moment she would go down but now she looked like a mad dog. I knew I had to catch her, haul her along, get her into the dark of the woodshed. And I was scared. She was baring her teeth hideously, growling and jerking as though preparing to attack me. Yet her gaze didn't register. As I walked up to her she looked right through me and started to stagger, unable to control her movements. I grabbed her by the collar and the scruff of the neck in one handful and her teeth snapped together ferociously as I pulled her after me. She yapped without forming the sound properly and her whole body leapt about in great spasms so that several times I nearly lost my grip.

But I made it to the woodshed, pushed open the door and dragged her inside. And as soon as I let go of her she staggered for a few paces and fell heavily on her side.

'Poor old girl,' I looked down at her, now no longer my lovely Sadie but a grotesque, grovelling creature that I was powerless

114

to help. '*Why* did you get so excited? You poor old thing. I wish I could help you.' But she didn't know me. She never even knew I was there as she jerked and frothed and cried, and blood came from her tongue where she had bitten it, and mixed with the froth and the earth that stuck to it.

I went out, taking my bike, the axe and the saw with me so that only the harmless pile of logs remained. I shut the door to leave her in the dark.

It usually took about an hour, sometimes longer, for her to come out of a fit. Soon she would rear up, try to stand, fall down and stagger to stand again. And then would start the long walk, not knowing where she was going, not caring, not seeing, bumping into things, staggering, walking on again, panting, panting, while her tongue lolled from her mouth dripping with blood and saliva. Once I had tried to tie her up, to stop her hurting herself as she walked. But it had only distressed her even more as she tangled in the lead and I had to release her. It seemed as though she had to walk freely, aimlessly, to move her limbs in regular rhythm to bring herself back to sanity.

When I had unloaded Olive's new bike and wheeled it into the large pantry out of harm's way, I went back to look at Sadie. She was still lying there, still jerking and paddling with her feet, but only feebly now. This was strange. She should have been up by now and starting on her long walk. I went in to her, knelt down beside her and lifted her head on to my knees. There was no resistance, hardly a jerk and her eyes were only half open and glazed.

'What's the matter, old girl? Have you tired yourself out? Perhaps you just want to sleep it off, do you?' I stroked her head. She felt cold. It would be as well to get her a rug and wrap her in it.

As I started to get up, Olive came in. 'How is she?'

'I don't know. Can't make her out. She's never behaved like this before after a fit. But then it's so long since she's had one.' I lifted her head back on to my lap and now she was still. She seemed asleep.

Olive knelt down beside me. She put her hand on Sadie's chest. She pressed, moved her fingers, pressed again. She looked round at me, startled. 'I can't feel any heartbeat. I think, I think she's dead.'

'Dead? No! She can't be.' But her nose was against my hand and I knew I could feel no breath.

'The fit must have given her a heart attack.' She put her arm around me. She leant over my lap to stroke the still head. 'Poor, dear Sadie. Oh poor Sadie.'

Side by side we knelt over her and with arms around each other. I was numb; my mouth and my eyes were dry. Olive was silent, still. I squeezed her to me and I felt a tear splash down on to my hand.

I waited until dark to bury Sadie; until the milking was finished and the boys had gone home; until the sad tea time was over and Donald had cried himself to sleep. Then I carried her to the orchard and I hung a hurricane lamp in the branch of a tree. There was enough light. Only I couldn't see to dig properly for the tears that swamped my eyes.

9

FORTUNATELY FOR ALL of us we had Ditty. She was an almost fully-grown tabby cat, with white tips to her paws, and had been clever enough, and persistent enough, to make a home for herself with the dogs under the kitchen table on a more or less permanent basis. And when Sadie died, quite unashamedly Ditty took over her basket. Of course she could not replace her. But she did her cheeky best to fill the horrid gap, indoors at any rate.

Perhaps I should admit right away that while Olive loved dogs she could not abide cats. Dogs did as they were told; well, mostly. At least they recognised you and were pleased to see you, and stayed on the floor. But a cat about the house was not to be trusted. Turn your back and she would leap on the table, stick her head in the milk jug, her paw in the butter and leave footprints on the tablecloth. It was all most unhygienic. Cats belonged outside where they could catch rats and mice and generally make themselves useful.

And it was outside where Ditty originally came from. She was the offspring of the itinerant tom, Henry. He had arrived at Maywood, liked the look of the place and taken up residence in the oast house soon after I had bought the farm. He came and went as he pleased, often disappearing for days on end in lonely searches for sex and returning, battered about the ears and scowling as he demanded milk at the dairy door.

Sometimes Henry brought a mistress home with him and installed her in the oast house. Half wild creatures they were that he had persuaded away from some far off barn or farmyard, probably with glowing descriptions of his pad and the abundance of mice to be found among the corn sacks. He was a rotten mouser himself. He only ever caught what he needed to go with the milk. I often told Pete and Bert that I reckoned he actually encouraged the mice breeding in the oast house to build up good stocks to attract a girl friend. And when he persuaded one to come and stay we only ever caught flashing glimpses of her. But none of his mistresses ever stayed long. They were all fiendishly efficient mousers, cleared the oast of rodents in no time and moved on to better hunting grounds and a change of lover.

Until Ann Boleyn arrived. She was a tabby with a white tummy and actually allowed us to get a good look at her two or three days later. There was an outside stairway leading to a door in the first floor of the oast house and she sat on the landing, staring down at us as we went about our work. But we could not get near her, however stealthily we approached. As soon as you started up the steps she would be gone, through the cat hole in the door and across the cooling floor to the tall press at the far end of the oast house. If you climbed the steps and followed her she would be eyeing you from behind the press, half scared and half prepared to make friends, yet diving down through the hole to the floor below if you took a step forward. Once there she could lose herself among the piled-up sacks of corn, or dash into the roundel and escape through one of the air holes let into the outside wall.

Gradually she became tamer, moving openly about the farm buildings and staring at us from various vantage points. We left milk for her on the oast house steps and soon she came to drink it while we were still in sight, alternately lapping and looking round. Then she discovered that milk came from the cowshed, that Henry got his by just going there and shouting for it, and one day she braved the hissing of the milking machine and the shifting of the cows and crept in after him.

But we could never get near enough to touch her. You could stand quite close and she would purr as she drank. Yet as soon as you bent down to stroke her she was off, along behind the mangers, stopping in the dark corner and staring back with her white shirt front shining, while Daisy, at the end of the line of cows, blew down into the manger and looked through to her.

Once Pete followed her, inching along the passage towards her with his hand out. He invited her, in a high voice, to come to him, showering her with endearments: 'Come on, yer pretty little bugger, come ter ol' Pete. I won't hurt yer, yer silly little sod.'

She seemed prepared to let him touch her. His hand was almost on her when she suddenly realised she could be trapped. The only way out was over the dwarf wall into the manger, past Daisy's blowing nostrils and then a hazardous journey through cows' legs to the open door. But a cat usually looks upwards for escape if possible. Which is what Ann Boleyn did. And she scaled Daisy's surprised face and was on to her back in a flash of white, then leaping from cow to cow in her dash to the doorway. She really left the old girls guessing.

One day Pete decided: 'That lil' ol' cat's going ter have kittens. Look at 'er lil' titties showing.' She had just demolished a saucer of milk and was sitting with her hind legs spread, purring happily to herself as she licked her tummy.

'Her'll go away and have 'em, I'll lay,' Bert said, 'like all the others. This is the fourth one ol' Henry's brought here, ain't it? They all buggered orf.'

Henry strolled out of the dairy, licking his whiskers with long sweeps of his tongue. Bert swept him up into his arms. The old cat looked surprised at such affection. He had felt the toe of Bert's boot on more than one occasion when caught trying to help himself from the milk cooler. But if Bert felt like being friendly it was all right by him and he went on preening himself, purring loudly between licks.

'Ah, but you'm a randy ol' devil, ain't yer!' Bert was scratching the base of his whiskers and Henry was curling them forward with approval. 'Loves 'em all and then they leaves yer. Only I reckon you drives 'em away, yer yellow-eyed ol' sod. Henry. Henry the bloody Eighth all right you be. Cor, lumme, you don't arf stink.' He dropped him suddenly and Henry walked away, whiskers bristling and tail swishing at the insult.

The dogs were the first to let us know that Ann Boleyn had given birth. They chased her whenever they got the chance, which wasn't often because she was too wary. And they always gave a few loud snorts at the oast house door in passing, if they thought she was inside. But now they were standing outside the door, whimpering and cocking their heads from side to side at an unfamiliar sound.

Much to their disgust I left them outside and went in with Donald. And he found the kittens, mewing in a nest deep among the corn sacks.

He had to squeeze through to reach them. 'There's two, Daddy.'

'Two? Is that all? P'raps you can't see them all.'

'Yes two.' He twisted round to face me. 'Look, two!' To prove it he had one in each hand and they were both protesting feebly.

'Yes, I see. But put them back or Ann Boleyn won't find them again.'

She had returned and was pacing the sacks, not daring to go to them but calling loudly to reassure them — and probably telling us to push off and stop interfering.

As soon as we had gone she lugged them off to another hiding place. There were a hundred hideouts around the oast house for her to choose from and unless the kittens mewed it would take all day to find them.

Donald came flying to find me when he discovered they were missing from the original nest. I tried to explain that a cat wanted to be alone with her kittens when they were first born and she did not like being disturbed. Especially Ann Boleyn because she was half wild and would not even let anyone touch her. But hunt the kittens is compulsive play for a small boy and really Ann Boleyn was an utter fool. As Donald discovered each new nest, stroked the kittens, examined them closely to see if their eyes were open yet and toddled off again, so she returned to them and took them somewhere else. But Donald soon learnt that he had only to stand and listen to locate them, because even if the kittens didn't mew, she gave the game away herself by purring so proudly as she licked them.

However, in the end she became thoroughly unnerved by the whole experience. It was probably her first litter and I'm sure she did not mean to commit infanticide. But one day I happened to glance up as I passed the oast house steps. There she was, standing on the landing looking down at me and with a kitten dangling from her jaws. And the fool opened her mouth and meowed at me, sending her kitten plunging to its death. I picked it up and it twitched but there was no saving it. When I looked up to swear at her, Ann Boleyn had disappeared through the hole in the door.

So Donald was forbidden to enter the oast house until the remaining kitten had its eyes open and could get about. Then we promised him he would be allowed to see it again and take it bread and milk to lap.

Meanwhile Henry took himself off. He had shown no interest in being a father and had left the oast house severely alone since Ann Boleyn's confinement. He prowled round the yard as usual, suffered having the dogs sniff under his tail in passing and sat down among the chickens for a good scratch. For three days he used the cowshed as his bedroom, curling up to sleep on the hay in the corner. Then he was gone. I wasn't surprised. I always thought of him as a confirmed bachelor, a loner who liked his sex but wanted no complications. It was natural for him to shrug off all responsibility and take off on one of his jaunts. But he never came back. We asked around but nobody had seen him. There were vermin traps about the countryside; there were foxes. I suppose poor old Henry just ran out of lives. But he had certainly lived the nine he had been given to the full.

And as soon as she had weaned her solitary female kitten Ann Boleyn vanished too. She had become more than usually vicious with her. Cats swear at their kittens when it's time to cut the apron strings, but Ann Boleyn boxed her ears, growled, spat at her and really carried things too far. But the kitten persisted in pestering her and in the end Ann Boleyn just disappeared one night and Donald found the kitten crying in the oast house.

By then he considered she was his anyway. He had tamed her because to begin with she had showed her wild side, sitting up on the sacks and spitting at him, backing away and lashing out at him when he came close. But before long he had her in his arms and soon there were struggling introductions to the dogs, only they were not at all sure that was a good idea. Yet they accepted her, bowled her over and licked her bum. At least it was preferable to put up with a kitten than suffer more of the interminable waits outside the oast house while Donald played inside.

It was Cherry who called the kitten Ditty. Donald held her up to her and said: 'See, Cherry? Kitten, kitten, kitty, kitty.'

Ditty was the nearest to it in her vocabulary, and she bashed her on the head with a rag doll to christen her.

Well, now that Ann Boleyn had cleared off Olive was faced with a problem. Cats belonged outdoors, she had told Donald several times when he had tried to bring the kitten in.

'Ditty can't sleep on her own *now*, Mummy,' he announced, holding the kitten in his arms just inside the back door.

'We can make a little bed for her in the woodshed. She'll be all right.' Olive was ironing at the kitchen table.

'She'll be cold without her mummy.'

'We'll give her a box with a nice warm piece of blanket.'

'She *might* run away.'

'Not if we shut the door.'

'I 'spect she'll be frikened.' Donald was stroking her energetically.

Olive walked to the Rayburn. She changed the flat iron she had been using for the one that had been getting hot. I was on my way out but had stopped, pretending to read the paper while I listened to the discussion.

As Olive seemed to be stuck for an answer, Donald pressed home his advantage. 'Sadie and Pat sleep in the kit-chun. Ditty could sleep with them.'

'I said no and I mean no.'

'Why *not*? It's not *fair*. The dogs do.' Pat was sitting on his haunches beside him, trying hard to control his jealousy of Ditty. Suddenly Donald screwed up his face and kicked him. 'You can't sleep in the kit-chun either, Pat. *You've* got to sleep in the woodshed too.'

Pat yelped and walked away, his tail between his legs with the tip waving rapidly. He rolled his eyes miserably.

'No, Donald!' I shouted. 'Just you stroke Pat and tell him you're sorry. He'll think you don't love him now you've got Ditty. Kicking him's the best way to make him bite her.'

Rather grudgingly he held out his hand. 'Sorry, Pat.' And the dog bustled up to him, licking at his hand and nosing Ditty to show no hard feelings. But she spat at his blundering movement and dabbed at him with her little claws.

Donald gave up and departed. When I looked out of the window he was heading for the chickens, obviously intent on involving Ditty in his games with them. Pat plodded after him and sank to his belly to watch.

'Why can't the blessed cat come in?' I asked.

'Don't you start as well.' Olive continued ironing without looking up. 'You know what it would be. She'd be into everything, in the sink, on the table, paddling germs all over Cherry's things. It's difficult enough keeping them clean as it is.'

' "You've got to eat a peck of dirt before you die." ' I laughed, quoting my mother.

'*You* may want to. But I don't want *her* to and a cat in the kitchen . . . '

'Never mind.' I patted her on the bottom and went about my work. A stand-up argument had never yet persuaded her to change her mind.

That night Ditty was given a box in the woodshed. And she took an instant dislike to it, in spite of the warm nest of hay wrapped in a piece of old blanket. She missed the musty smell of the oast house with the lingering spoor of her mother, the purring white belly still there to snuggle against during merciful moments in the brutal weaning. Donald really tried to make her comfortable, pinning her down firmly with one hand while he wrapped her in the blanket with the other. But she always unravelled herself before he could get to the door and came chasing after him. So in the end he had to leave her crying.

His bedroom window overlooked the backyard. He leapt out of bed for one last listen as Olive carried the candle from the room. 'Ditty's still crying,' he said, accusingly.

'She'll soon settle down. I've heard you cry when you don't want to go to bed. And Cherry. She often stands up in her cot and cries at bedtime, doesn't she?' She kissed him goodnight again and pulled the covers over him. 'Ditty'll be fine in the morning, you see.'

But the pitiful mews were still coming from the woodshed when I let the dogs out for a last run. I looked across at Olive, standing with her back to me by the Rayburn and filling a hot water bottle. 'She's still crying.'

'I can hear.' She screwed the top on the bottle, put it on the table and took the kettle to refill it at the sink. 'Oh well, p'raps you'd better bring her in. But it'll only be for tonight, mind. Just until she gets used to being without her mother.'

When the dogs returned I popped Ditty in the basket with Pat. At first he was none too keen on the idea and he looked up at me with his ears back and his eyes imploring. 'Must I have her?' But Ditty was all for it. Pat didn't smell a bit like Mum but at least he was warm. Soon she was purring, pummelling Pat's tummy and teasing his coat with her claws. And Pat could not resist that. He put his chin down on the rim of the basket with a sigh and wriggled over to give her more tummy to work on.

So began the battle to house-train Ditty. As she wasn't one of those sleek suburban cats, descended from generations of nicely-mannered moggies, it raged for weeks. A cat is curious at the best of times, has a will of her own, knows just what she wants and the best way to get it. And she never admits defeat. No self-respecting cat goes slinking off with her ears back and her tail between her legs. She will sit and face you, stare you out and then start to lick herself to show you you're making a fuss about nothing. If all else fails, have a good lick while you think out another way round the problem. That's their motto.

That is what makes cats attractive — to me, at any rate. But not to Olive. And certainly not where Ditty was concerned. Being descended from a half-wild mother and a lone ranging father, she had no idea what living in a house was all about. Food did not come nicely presented on a saucer, it had to be hunted for; scratched out of the sticky bits in the sink basket, stalked after over the table and pounced on behind the cornflakes packet, leapt for up the back of the high chair with a quick dive down over Cherry's shoulder to the well-stocked tray. And when Olive gave chase she didn't cringe, nor make for the dark corner behind the old armchair — not unless she wanted to relieve herself. No, she fled upwards, a swift scrabble up the dresser to the top and from there a flying leap to the saucepan shelf, from where she could look down defiantly and spit out at attempts to retrieve her.

From across the farmyard Pete and Bert followed the running battle to house-train Ditty with great amusement. There would come the rattle of a falling saucepan, a desperate, wild scream from Olive, the shriek of the cat.

'Watch out!' One of them would exclaim.

'Cor, bugger me, 'ere 'er comes again,' the other would reply as the back door flew open and Ditty was hurled across the yard. I found myself joining in the laughter.

If the dogs were there they always sided with Olive. They would go bounding out after the cat, barking madly, only to come to a slithering, stupid halt as she turned on them and called their bluff.

But Ditty was persistent. A dust-up with Olive and a sprawling fall across the yard did not put her off and she was back indoors at the first opportunity, as cheeky as ever. If the door remained firmly shut against her, and it usually did, there was always the window sill. It gave a grandstand view of the sink. If she saw Olive working there she would prowl up and down, peering through the glass, screwing up her face and opening her pink mouth wide, sparking off a series of vituperative exchanges through the steamy glass. And she knew the precise moment, the exact movement which signified that Olive was about to relent. She would rush down and be at the back door to swagger in with a 'brrrp' and tail raised high as soon as it was open wide enough.

So in the end Olive and Ditty reached a kind of understanding. Ditty gave up mountaineering in the kitchen so long as Olive made sure she left out nothing to tempt her up from the floor. She gave up shitting behind the armchair in exchange for the pleasure of pestering Olive to let her out and in, out and in. She discovered the comfort of the beds but agreed to sleep only on Donald's and to vacate that on the dot of lights out. And with Olive determined to stamp out all begging for food by animals at meal times, Ditty agreed to abide by the rule, which didn't include hiding behind my chair and scratching my leg for a surreptitious scrap or two.

Thus neither of them relinquished any of her dogged determination and from this grew mutual respect. From which, in time, grew a love for each other that could neither be shown nor admitted.

It was a few weeks after Ditty had taken over Sadie's empty basket that I awoke at three o'clock one morning. As usual I had been sleeping soundly and now I found myself in that irritating state of semi-consciousness when you know that something is not quite right, and why it is not right, and yet you persist in dreaming that you are taking the necessary steps to put it right.

I opened my eyes again. The moon was streaming through the branches of the cherry tree straight on to the bed and the tom cat I had been chasing away in my dream was chanting lustily outside. I reared up to listen. Oh, sod him, let him yowl. I glanced down at Olive, dark hair sprawled over the pillow, face unnaturally pale in the moonlight. She was sleeping peacefully so I lay back with a sigh, vaguely wondering where the tom cat had come from. Probably one of old Jack's. His smallholding was crawling with cats.

Suddenly Olive was awake. 'That blasted cat!' She sat up with a jerk, frowning at the window. 'If it wakes up the children I'll murder it.'

Already she was sitting on the side of the bed, fishing for her slippers. And as she got them on and started to pull on her dressing gown, Ditty gave an answering wail from the kitchen.

I groaned. 'Oh God, she *is* in love. I thought p'raps she might be.' She had been showing all the signs for the last few days, giving tender little 'brrrps' and throwing herself at your feet, rolling on her back and lifting her paws behind her ears as she practised her routine for inviting a tom to a session of slap and tickle.

She called again from the kitchen and now Donald was awake. Unlike his father he experienced no state of semi-consciousness and was straightway in an informative mood. With the voice of a town crier, he called: 'Mummy! Ditty's crying in the kitchun.'

'Ssh!' hissed Olive, fumbling to light the candle, 'you'll wake Cherry.' She swept out of the room and I rolled over to her side of the bed. It was always warmer than mine, softly scented, luxurious. I had every confidence she would sort things out satisfactorily.

Drowsily I heard the amorous tom repeat his invitation to come outside, spurred to greater efforts by Ditty's evidently encouraging reply.

Then I was wide awake again. '*Mummy!* Ditty's got a little friend outsi-i-de.'

'Ssh!' came from halfway down the stairs. There was a peeved whimper from Cherry and Ditty answered again from the kitchen, just as I heard Olive fling herself at the door. By the

sound of her onslaught she seemed prepared to put the cat to
sleep with but a single blow.

Reluctantly I got out of bed to go and keep Donald quiet.
There was a sound of determined finger-sucking from Cherry's
room as she fought to keep track of a dream. With any luck she
would drop off again if I could placate Donald.

'Come here, you blasted cat!' I heard Olive hiss from the
kitchen, just as I reached Donald's door.

'Hello, Daddy. That blasted cat's on the tiles,' he informed
me, confidentially. I was trying hard to remember when we had
ever talked of a cat on the tiles when he nearly split my ear-
drums with: 'Dit, Dit, DITTY!'

'Shut up!' I hissed, 'you'll wake Cherry. Now go to sleep.'
Some hopes.

There was a squawk from the kitchen and a rattle of saucepans. Ditty was obviously back to her mountaineering tricks.
Being in love was a whole new ball game, manifestly excusing
her from all her previous ladies' agreements.

'Meow – meow – wow – wow?' came from outside.

'Ditty's little friend wants to come in, Daddy. You go and let
him in, Daddy. Mummy won't,' he added, wisely.

'Go to sleep. Ditty can go out and meet him in the morning.'
I pushed him back down in the bed and pulled the covers up
with a jerk. Toy cars cascaded to the floor and a lorry, complete
with its load of milk churns, took a header off the end of the bed.

'That was a big crash!' Donald was laughing.

Olive was cross. She came tearing up from the kitchen, two
stairs at a time, candleflame cringing. Being thwarted by the
cat had magnified the sound of crashing cars. As soon as she
came into the room she spotted me, groping frantically for
milk churns as they rolled across the floor.

'Whatever are you doing? Are you *trying* to wake Cherry?'

'I was only trying to keep Donald quiet.'

'It sounds like it.'

'Mummy,' Donald was standing up in bed now, 'look at funny
Daddy crawling on the floor. Did you hear that big, big crash?'

'I should think I did! Now, you lie down and go to sleep,
there's a good boy.' She tucked him into bed again. I stood up,
dumped a double handful of churns on the end of the bed and
made for the door.

Olive picked up the candle and frowned, with a fierce whisper: 'Don't you go sliding off to bed again just yet. Help me catch that wretched animal and we'll put her outside. Then p'raps we'll get some sleep.'

'I want Ditty in my bed. I can keep her quiet, Mummy.'

'You go to sleep. You can have Ditty in the morning.' Olive pushed past me. 'If she lives that long,' she murmured, under her breath.

We listened at Cherry's door. The finger-sucking had almost stopped. She was back in her dream again. 'That's one blessing, anyway.' I tried to strike a note of cheerfulness.

The feline duet was mounting to a crescendo as we reached the kitchen. Ditty was weaving her way in and out of the saucepans, trying out deep husky notes that we had never heard from her before. I stood still and looked up at her. 'Ooh! You do sound a right sexy little madam. No wonder the old tom's going crazy out there if you make promises like that.'

'Never mind about that! You'll have to climb up on the dresser to get her down. It's the only way.' Olive spoke from bitter experience.

As I pulled a chair out from beneath the table to use as a step up, Pat yawned loudly to remind me he was there. He strolled out with a long stretch, swished his tail and jabbed his nose against Olive's thigh. She stroked him absently as she watched me climb, and he sat back on his haunches and regarded me with a doleful expression.

I had the lovesick cat cornered. She was shaping up to me, her love song turning into hisses as she struck out at me. Then I had her, firmly by the scruff of the neck and was just preparing to lift her up between the saucepans when:

'Mummy, why is Daddy standing on the dresser?'

It was foolish of me to look round to show the reason. I should have concentrated on the job in hand because Ditty sensed the moment of advantage. She whipped up her hind legs to scratch me. I yelled, my grip on her neck slackened and she leapt over and used my body as an escape route to the floor, her claws piercing my pyjamas. I swore as a saucepan clattered after her, and Pat howled and hastened to his basket, convinced I'd thrown it at him.

Olive had been on the point of scolding Donald. Instead I

got called a clumsy clot as she dived to catch Ditty, missed, and picked up the saucepan instead.

'I'll catch her!' Donald cried, glad of a chance to redeem himself. He sped after her, throwing himself to the floor as she went to ground behind the armchair. And from there she growled and spat as she prepared to take on all comers. But he had a way with her and in a moment was hauling her out by her tail.

Olive pounced on her. 'Right, madam, now I've got you! If it's tom cat you want, then tom cat you shall have!' And she hurried towards the back door.

So far as Pat was concerned this could only mean action stations. He reached the door first and waited, prancing and whining.

Outside, judging by the mounting excitement of his demands, the tom cat had a shrewd idea that things were panning his way. He was caterwauling lustily, quite carried away by his desire, completely unprepared for Pat to come bounding out into the night.

They met in a flurry of claws and snapping teeth, from which the tom evacuated rapidly with a leap up the fence. And there he stood his ground, with arched back and tail like a flue brush, determined to get what he had come for, dog or no dog. Of course Pat jumped up to dislodge him, only to receive a deadly accurate left, right, planted smartly on his nose, which sent him backing away growling and shaking his head to take away the sting. He was trying to understand what had happened, why what had started out as just a routine dash after Ditty had turned into a sudden confrontation with a stinking tom. But it was all too much to worry about in the middle of the night, so he started back for his basket. And he couldn't have cared less when Ditty went sailing over his head on her way to her night's enjoyment.

Back in bed I settled down to sleep. Only a couple of hours and I would have to be up again, leaping across the room to silence the alarum on the dressing table. It was the only place to put it to ensure that I got out of bed at five thirty. So I snuggled up to gather warmth from Olive and tried to shut out the sounds of cats courting. I started to glow, to drop off cosily.

'D'you think she'll be all right?' Olive was still alert.

'Wh-o-o?'

129

'Ditty, of course.'

'Oh, for Chrissake. You're the one who flung her out into the night.'

'I know.' She sat up, letting in a draught of cold air. 'But she doesn't sound very happy.' Now she was thoroughly contrite.

'Go to sleep. Cats always make that bloody row when they're courting, you know that.'

'Yes. But . . . I mean, it's her first experience, isn't it? And we don't know who the tom is. I never got a chance to look at him. He might be a terrible mangey old thing. Quite unsuitable. He might even be rough with her.'

'Huh! Hark who's talking! Thought you were meant to be a cat hater. She'll be all right and a tom's a tom in her happy condition. He's probably one of Jack's ragged old lot, anyway.'

She leant back. Good, I could get some sleep.

There was a crescendo of blood curdling screams from outside. She shot up again. 'He's forcing himself on her! I'd better see she's all right.' Now she was out of bed and shuffling for her slippers again. 'After all, I did rather throw her at him, didn't I? Didn't give her a chance to get to know him gradually.'

'Oh hell. Women! ' I turned over with a sigh.

I heard her rummaging in the bedside drawer. Soon there was the flash of a torch, then the squeak as she raised the window. 'There they are. They're just sitting hunched up on the lawn staring at one another and making that horrible noise. Yes, I think you're right. It *looks* like one of Jack's cats. Yes, it's that big black one that comes round sometimes. Oh well, I suppose he's all right. At least she's not trying to run away.'

'Good. So glad you approve. Now drive them off, shut the window and come back to bed.'

She hissed at them and flashed the torch. But they just stared back and swore roundly. So she gave up and came in cold beside me. And then we heard them move away.

When I went down to the kitchen to make the early cup of tea, Ditty was waiting on the window sill. I opened the door and she ran in with her usual 'brrrp'.

'Well, madam, did you enjoy yourself?'

She ignored me. She strolled up to Pat with her tail in the air and he stirred sleepily in his basket as she rubbed her cheek against him. Then she hopped into Sadie's basket, sniffed round for a second or two and sat bolt upright with her back towards us.

'Come on, you can tell *us*. We won't let on, will we, Pat?'

But she raised a white-tipped paw, licked it for a few moments and started to wash her face.

10

UNLESS YOU WERE a specialist, or a genius, or perhaps if you had been fortunate enough to inherit your farm and stock free of mortgage or overdraft at the bank, then you were unlikely to make much money on a small mixed farm.

Of course, there seemed to be a report of a different genius every week in the farming magazines. There were articles on farmers who had started with just a few hundred pounds of their own, on farms much the same size as Maywood, and in next to no time had amassed small fortunes in pedigree livestock and all the latest machinery. There were always pictures to prove it. Sometimes one of the farmer himself, not with his livestock but stepping out of every farmer's dream, the wonderful new Land Rover that was then starting to nose its way all over the world.

The only time for reading was late in the evening. There was always some job or another that needed finishing after tea, winter or summer, so I was tired when I came to slump back in the chair. But I tried hard to keep awake as I read avidly of these paragons, wondering at their skills and trying to see the secrets of their success, puzzling as to why none of their animals ever seemed to break out, or get sick, or failed to conceive according to plan, or generally behaved in the cussed ways that mine frequently did. And then I would doze off and dream that everything I had read in the article was coming true at Maywood.

When I awoke to reality, perhaps to a kiss on my cheek and 'if you want to sleep, why don't you come to bed?' I would point to the page, explain my dream and say: 'Oh well, it's the way of life that counts really, I suppose. Count your blessings and all that,' followed by a hollow laugh.

Olive would smile. 'P'raps so. But it's a pity so much money always has to be ploughed back, just when we do make some. It would be nice to have a bit of spare cash to splash around once in a while.'

'One day there will be. There *must* be. There must be a cash return for all our hard slog, at some time or another.' It was my stock reply, the spur that drove me on on the rare occasions when the joy of the work itself failed to inspire me.

The cows were the mainstay at Maywood. The monthly milk cheque had to cover wages, bought in feeding stuffs for animals, wife and family, mortgage and overdraft interest payments and as many other running expenses as possible. The hop crop was supposed to provide the profit while the pigs and the sheep made worthy and regular contributions of dung, in addition to welcome cheques now and then from sales of piglets, lambs and wool. That was the theory anyway. The geniuses in the articles managed to make their fortunes even without the hops.

But my pigs had always paid in their small way, provided I discounted the hours spent chasing them. They were the first animals I'd had at Maywood, not counting old Colonel. I had started with the two pregnant sows, Skinny and Fatso. And I was full of ideas about piglets having free access to a field, where they could roam happily with their mothers, growing into sturdy, healthy weaners to be sold at eight weeks old for fattening.

Fattening pigs was a specialist's job. I did not have the correct, purpose-built pig fattening houses at Maywood, nor the inclination to stuff rows of squealing pigs with food, with the dedication and attention to detail necessary to achieve the right weights at the right ages, and with the minimum amount of food intake, and back fat on the carcass, to make the whole costly exercise pay. But I was prepared to breed the piglets and rear them into strong, outdoor types that would fatten readily and economically once the specialist bought them.

Skinny and Fatso thought life in the open was a good idea too. They had been reared by a specialist, and had they not come to Maywood they would have spent the rest of their days

133

punching out piglets in cramped farrowing pens. And once each litter was reared, their only relaxation would have been a stroll down the passage for a quick how d'you do with the boar to set them off again. So they appreciated the pig meadow behind the sties, the heady tang of turf and the acorns and other goodies to be found hiding in it. They liked it so much that it seemed a pity to have to stop in one meadow when the wide world with all its interesting smells was only just beyond the fence. And once they had broken through there was really no stopping them after that. Time after time we tried to keep them in and I began to work myself up into a frenzy each time they found a new way out. Until I realised they never strayed far away, did little or no damage and that the piglets thrived on scavenging in the wood, along the hedgerows and around the farmyard.

With two litters a year to cope with a sow leads a busy life. Some breeders managed to get three litters out of a sow each year, by taking advantage of the fact that she will come in season immediately after farrowing, and by weaning each litter at six weeks instead of eight. So it is no wonder a sow soon gets worn out. And by the time Skinny had produced over a hundred piglets, and Fatso seventy, it was time for them to go. So I sent them to market to be sold complete with their last litters. It was easier that way. Let somebody else less familiar with them fatten them out for their final rôles as fillings for a thousand pork pies. I knew them too well.

I had saved two of Skinny's gilts from her last litter but one, so that by the time she and Fatso departed the gilts would be ready to go to the boar.

These gilts were alike as two peas, adored one another and went everywhere together as they grew up. They grazed side by side, never lost sight of each other on expeditions into the wood to rummage through the leaves, and insisted on squashing up together in the same sty at night. That was the only time we heard them tiff — if the one jammed up against the wall decided to get up and stumble over her sister to go and spend a penny. Then there would be a spot of sleepy swearing, a grumbling change of position and a sort of 'Oh well, if you're going to have a pee I may as well join you.' And they would grunt and argue as they rooted about to settle down again. Otherwise they never had a cross word and even fed from the same trough without squabbling, changing from end to end by mutual consent to assure each other that the food was the same all the way along.

It was Mother who named them Martha and Mary, not that I could see any likeness in their characters to the holy sisters of Bethany. But on one of her visits she had come with me to look at the gilts and they had been preparing for a siesta in the sty. One was already lying down comfortably, unconcerned as her sister fussed around, worrying at bits of straw, rooting about and kicking up a dust as she prepared her side of the bed to her liking. So the one lying down became Mary and the busy one Martha. But it took a careful look to tell one from the other.

So Martha and Mary were the daughters of Bill, Ernie Carter's old boar, who had numbered Skinny and Fatso on his calling list of sows around the parish. He was a fine boar, threw large litters of long pigs and despite his advancing years was still as randy as ever. I am sure he would have been only too delighted to continue his twice yearly visits to Maywood and perfectly prepared to perform on his own daughters. But a change was called for.

It was uneconomic to buy a boar, just for two sows. So I rang up Ernie to see what he could suggest. I heard him sucking his teeth as he listened to my problem.

Then he said: 'Now I'm going ter tell yer. I've been thinking about that, I have. I knowed there was several of yer thinking about breeding from old Bill's daughters, so I says to meself: "Ernie, you better watch points". So I bin and bought another boar.'

'Good. That was clever of you.'

He chuckled at the compliment. 'Oh aye, a nice enough young boar 'e be, an' all. Hereward, they calls 'im. Full pedigree 'e be and that's why 'ees got such a posh name. Forty guineas I paid for 'un, pick of the bunch 'e were over to Harry Batt's dispersal sale. Never paid such money for a pig before, that I ain't. But same as I allus say, the best be the cheapest.'

'When can you bring him to Maywood?'

'Your gilts ready?'

'Should be next week.' I chuckled. 'They'll both be on together, I expect. They were brimming together last time round. Will that matter?'

'Two, three, six together, that don't matter. This 'ere Hereward ull make short work o' they. You'll soon see when I brings 'im.'

And the following Monday he arrived with Hereward, lurching in the trailer behind his car. We threw the pig net off him and he jumped down. Then he swaggered off, nose high and sniffing the air with all the confidence and expectancy of a sailor stepping off along the waterfront.

Pete and Bert were standing by, ready to help drive him to the sty we had prepared for him. They looked him over critically, Pete chewing a stem of grass and Bert with his hands clasped behind his back.

Pete said: ' 'E ain't so well hung as ol' Bill, that's for sure.'

Bert shook his head, slowly 'No fear, that 'e ain't. Proper whipper-snapper 'e be. Ol' Bill ud make two of 'e.' He sniffed and spat. 'No,' he decided, ' 'e ain't got knackers enough there, I'd say.'

Hereward paused, holding his head high and smacking his chops at these insults. Ernie was walking behind and he stopped removed his check cap and scratched the bald dome of his head, anaemic above his ruddy cheeks. 'Course 'e ain't so big. 'Ees only a young un still.' He prodded Hereward and the boar gave a peeved squeal of protest as he stamped forward again. Ernie smiled. 'But just you wait 'til you sees 'im go, though. 'E don't hang about. Knocks spots orf of ol' Bill for gettin' on wi' the job.' He sucked his teeth and frowned seriously. 'And the blood's there, mind, that's what counts. Good blood 'e be. The best money can buy.' Ernie seemed keen to justify the record price he had paid for the young boar.

'Oh, ah.' The boys nodded together as they raised their arms and manoeuvred to steer Hereward into the sty. But they did not look convinced as they hung over the wall looking down at him. Blood lines were abstract and the size of the animal's testicles was real. Certainly Hereward was smaller than old Bill, who had become progressively coarser and more cumbersome with each visit, and although he always sounded as keen as mustard seemed to take longer and longer working himself up to action. But this was a fine long pig, with all the characteristics demanded for throwing litters to become high-grade baconers, and I was quite hopeful that he would do just that with Martha and Mary.

The gilts seemed unaware of his arrival. They were grazing quietly across the meadow, close together as usual and interested only in each other's company. But I knew they would have got wind of him because a sow can smell a boar out a mile and more away. But only when she's ready.

'So you'll just have to wait, my lad,' I said to Hereward, as he paced the sty, grunting his disapproval at finding it empty. And he held his head high and glared at us as we walked away.

Every other Tuesday Stivvy Wild and his brother Reuben came clattering down to the farm in their mobile emporium. That's what they called it, written in large letters on either side of the box body of their pre-war Ford lorry. It was really a travelling extension of their village shop, which was situated several rattling miles away, and in it you could buy anything from a tin kettle, a broom, or any one of the pots and pans hanging in swaying clusters from the ceiling, to a can of baked beans, a pound of rice weighed out from a sack, or even a pair of army surplus man's combinations. And if you hummed and ha-ed over something, either Stivvy or Reuben, whoever happened to have his hands free in the squashed confines of the van, would thrust the article at you saying: 'That's it, you take it, try 'un out, don't matter if you ain't got the money now, pay next time, or when you can.' Or they were perfectly prepared to barter for eggs, vegetables, apples, chicken corn, even for live chickens or ducks and there was usually a crate of startled chickens lashed on the cab. On a visit to the parent shop I discovered that bartered fowls were let loose in the garden behind the shop, to scratch in the flower beds and croon in and out of the outbuildings, even into the shop itself, while they waited to fill orders from customers for oven-ready chickens. If one started to lay she was granted an instant reprieve, as were ones that went broody, and once I saw an old hen hatching out a clutch of eggs at the foot of the shop counter, flashing a beady eye at the customers from her seat behind a sack of potatoes.

The arrival of the Wild's emporium was always something of an event. It was important enough for Pete and Bert to knock off for a while, saunter down the lane and climb aboard to see if there were any bargains. Sometimes Stivvy had a message from their mother because he called at their cottage on his way down to Maywood. And perhaps Pete was instructed that it was time he bought a new beret, or Bert one of the second-hand bus drivers' jackets because they were good value, or that they should both try the new batch of grey woollen gloves for size and she would pay next time.

I never did understand the Wild's method of accounting. They never wrote anything down at the time and yet they seemed to keep track of all the transactions. Only when Bert took a fancy to a five-shilling lamb's foot pocket knife, and talked them into accepting payment at sixpence a fortnight, he was certain they let him off the last two payments. He had been marking them off on the calendar in the dairy and there were only eight grubby crosses showing when Stivvy declared he had been paid in full. So Bert did not argue.

But profit seemed to be of secondary importance to Stivvy and Reuben. I think they just liked the travelling, the two days each week spent touring the countryside, visiting the outlying farms and cottages; two days when they left their wives to look after the shop and enjoyed themselves. I felt sure they would both have sooner been farmers than shopkeepers.

They were never in a hurry to move on, often spending up to an hour or more traipsing around, or just leaning over a gate talking and looking at the cattle or the pigs. But there were certain hidden profits from their country rounds in those days of food shortage — invisible earnings, you could say.

Stivvy was the one to talk. He was a small, wizened man in his fifties, with a long nose and a walrus moustache, that gathered dew drops in winter and beads of perspiration in summer. And he had a pipe, all burnt down round the top of the bowl, which he spent more time filling and using endless matches lighting than actually smoking. Reuben was a year or two younger, quieter, and would listen to his brother's talk with a set grin, displaying a row of over-large false teeth which, I felt sure, were only worn for outings in the emporium because he took them out and popped them in his pocket when he wanted to eat. He could bite into an apple and chew it with the greatest of relish with just gums alone.

It was the pigs that Stivvy loved best of all. He always followed the progress of each litter and would stop talking, mid-sentence, if piglets happened by. Then he would discuss their condition, the length of their bodies and declare it was a 'right marvel' the way they had grown since his last visit and how much did I want for that particular one? He was always on the look out for pigs to fatten in his sties behind the shop.

At that time meat was still rationed and there was talk that joints of pork, or home-cured bacon were always available 'under the counter' to favoured customers at the Wilds' village shop. In fact Stivvy made no secret of the wealthy customers he supplied. He was always boasting and once told us a story of where his big mouth had landed him.

We were in the stack-plat, drawn there by a litter of pigs rooting around among the loose straw, and Stivvy had his eye on two of them. He was always prepared to pay a few shillings over the market price for them, and would pitch up a day or two later with a trailer behind his car to take them away and pay cash for them.

'They two'll do us fine,' he said, pointing to two piglets rooting about on their own. 'Give they another four months of my tender care and they'll kill out a treat, I'll lay.'

Reuben grinned at me and nodded. 'Will do if they be like them last ones we had orf of you.' His teeth dropped with a click as he finished speaking.

'Beats me how you get licenses for all the pigs you kill,' I said, naïvely.

Stivvy was filling his pipe. He pressed the tobacco roughly into the worn bowl and left strands of it falling down the sides like creepers. 'Ah now,' he said, striking a match and holding it over the pipe. 'Sometimes that can be a problem.' He looked at me and winked with great exaggeration, screwing up his eye and his cheek and half his walrus whiskers. The flame burnt merrily along the match towards his fingers and just before it touched them he sucked it down through the tobacco. He managed two puffs before it went out. He lit another match and while it flared and started to burn, he went on: 'Like when us killed that grut big sod last autumn. Eh, Reuben?'

'Aye. Fifteen score 'ee were, if 'ee were a pound.' Reuben continued grinning.

I was watching the match, mesmerised by the flame advancing on Stivvy's fingers. Why didn't he light the ragged ends of tobacco and have done with it? Two or three more puffs and the match went out, leaving the pipe as cold as before.

He struck another match and now he did set the tobacco glowing and the creepers curling upwards. And then he stopped puffing, started to talk again looking over the flame, leaving the pipe to go out and the match to die in a pinch of charcoal between his fingers. So he worked his way through the box of matches as he talked of his 'grut big sod of a pig' and the trouble it had caused.

Because it was such a big pig he had boasted to many people about it. And when the local pig killer had been and done his stuff, leaving the carcass with its hind trotters fixed high up on a beam and the tip of its snout nearly touching the floor, Stivvy and Reuben had felt obliged to celebrate the prospect of profits to come with a few extra beers down at the pub.

'There were only the usual crowd down there, weren't there Reuben?' The pipe was really starting to burn at last, but the box of matches was still held at the ready.

'Aye,' Reuben agreed, 'and there weren't one of 'em as ain't killed his own pig at some time or t'other.' He clicked his teeth, like a signal for Stivvy to continue.

So they could not understand it when the two strangers in suits walked into the shop the following afternoon. Was he Mr Stephen Wild? Could they have a word with him in private? They were from the CID. They understood he had killed a pig and could they see the necessary licence?

Stivvy sucked his pipe and frowned at me. 'Fair knocked I back, I can tell 'e. All me innards turned and I shit meself.'

Reuben stopped grinning. 'Aye. Never did know who telled on us. Tried to say we'd forgot clean about the licence, but that weren't no good.'

The men from the CID demanded to view the body. They looked it up and down, made notes in black notebooks fastened with elastic bands and told Stivvy he would have to accompany them to the police station. And, of course, they would need to take the pig along as well as evidence.

The plain-clothes men backed their car up the narrow lane beside the shop, to where a gate led into the garden and the shed where the pig was hanging. 'Buggered if 'er didn't want some shiftin' too.' Stivvy lit another match. 'And they chaps never give we a hand neither. They just followed

140

we about, pointin' and orderin' while us struggled with that grut sod o' a pig until us had 'er curled up in the boot of the car.'

One of the plain-clothes men shut the lid of the boot and locked it. Stivvy wiped the sweat from his brow and the other man told him to go indoors and fetch his coat. He could well be in custody for quite some time, he added, sternly.

So Stivvy and Reuben crept back into the parlour behind the shop for a hurried consultation. Suddenly their whole world had been turned upside down and they were at a loss to know what to do for the best. They talked of ringing up their solicitor, but decided against it because the woman in the telephone exchange would hear all about their trouble. They discussed how many other unlicensed pig killings Stivvy should admit to because everybody knew the police always asked what other offences should be taken into account. And who would do Stivvy's work about the shop because sure as fate he was going to be locked up. And what about the wealthy customers? Stivvy always dealt with them personally and somebody was going to have to warn them about the sudden end of all black-market transactions. And suppose they became implicated? Phew! Big names were involved and it didn't bear thinking about. Then there was the round. Reuben would never manage that on his own because he was no good at driving the lorry.

'Wretched pigs, wish you'd never had nothing to do with them,' said Myrtle, Stivvy's wife, his second wife and twenty years his junior.

Stivvy sniffed and squirted out a stream of saliva and tobacco juice. He jabbed his finger into his pipe, struck another match and looked at me through the flame. 'As if 'er cared. I'll lay 'er was thinking 'er'd be glad to see the back of I.' (Stivvy and Myrtle had fallen out of love in the war, when Myrtle had been called up to join the ATS and Stivvy was too old for the army. She had blamed him for being unable to get her with child and so give her exemption from military service. Only Stivvy always stoutly maintained that it was Myrtle who was barren.)

'Any road,' Stivvy continued, 'five minutes went by, then ten, then quarter of an hour while us argued about the best things to do what with me away locked up.'

Reuben clicked his teeth. 'And then I says: "Funny they

buggers leaving we in 'ere talkin' like this. For all they knows us could be escaping." '

Stivvy chuckled through a cloud of smoke. 'Only it were *they* what escaped. Cunning buggers. CID my arse. Spivs more like. Drove orf they did, pig an' all and us never did hear no more of 'em.'

Reuben grinned. 'Aye. Pig an' all. Couldn't very well report the theft to the police, now could us?'

11

THE DAY AFTER Hereward, the boar, arrived at Maywood, it was obvious that Martha and Mary were ready to make his acquaintance. I let them out into the meadow as usual and they toddled off, side by side, taking hurried little bites of grass and grunting seriously to one another. It was not their usual casual conversation about the smell of the grass, or where they would go today, if it should be into the wood for a carefree rummage through the leaf mould, or across to the cowshed for a quick lick along the mangers. It was important talk, accompanied by much agitated tail-swishing and jostling against one another, and they never moved far away from their sty.

They had not seen Hereward, but they knew he was there. Yesterday they had taken no notice of his arrival and had been deaf to his impatient grunts as he paced his new sty, rooting under the heavy cast-iron pig trough and chucking it about the place, behaving like a spoilt child locked in his room. Today was different. Now they made their way by degrees right up to the door of his sty, talking loudly so that he could hear and really being very blatant about their interest in him.

'What shall us do?' Pete asked, cautiously. 'Shall us let one into 'im at a time?' He was gazing down on the boar over the wall of the sty. Hereward was eyeing him coldly, his head thrust up so that he could see from behind his long ears.

Bert was beside him. 'No. Let the young bugger loose in the meadow, I say. If us puts one of 'em in with 'im, us'll have hell's own job getting her out again and t'other one in.'

That made sense. So I opened the door of the sty and Hereward marched into the meadow with a great show of rapid grunting and with his tail curled proudly. He walked straight past the gilts and stopped with his back towards them, champing his chops and looking sternly across the meadow.

Now Hereward was a proud young boar, not lacking in experience and his stance made it quite obvious that he intended to take charge of these simpering gilts. There was a proper procedure to be followed, formalities to be observed, the first and most important of which was that he should give his intended a good root up the belly with his snout.

The gilts approached warily, uttering provocative, high-pitched grunts. He rolled his eyes, turned slowly to face them and grunted quickly and deeply, marking time with his front feet to add weight to his speech of welcome.

'He don't know which one to choose first,' Bert decided.

'Ain't nothing to choose between 'em.' Pete shifted his beret to the back of his head and settled back against the wall to watch. 'Don't suppose 'ee can tell the difference between 'em. Ain't nothing *to* choose.'

'How d'you know? You ain't a boar.'

'Course I know.'

'Oh, stop arguing you two. You'll make him feel self-conscious.'

As Martha was the nearer to him, Hereward turned his attention to her. He faced her, talking to her breathlessly, chucking her under the chin with his shining snout. And she answered him with excited little squeals while she stodged up and down with her hind legs, preparing a firm foundation for him. Which encouraged him to swing round at right angles to her, bury his snout in her belly and heave her hindquarters clean off the ground. She squealed with delight at such attention and Mary was seized with a fit of jealousy.

Just then I heard the familiar rattle of the Wilds' travelling emporium, followed by the undulating note of its hooter as the lorry pulled up in the lane. There was a clear view across to the yard and in a moment Donald appeared and went racing to greet them while Pat barked from behind. They had paid us a visit in the pig meadow earlier, but had soon left in search of more amusing pursuits. Donald found adult pigs boring creatures and

Pat was half afraid of them. But Stivvy was always good for a sweet, so there was no time to be lost in climbing aboard the emporium.

Cherry shouted from her playpen. It was an early spring day, with a winter-washed sun shining warmly. Such a nice day that Olive had set up the playpen on a piece of tarpaulin, across the backyard and within sight of the kitchen window. There Cherry could practise walking and keep herself amused watching all that was going on – the chickens prating as they wandered about their business; the ducks preening beside the pond and splashing into the water with loud quacks and flicking tails, with Sinbad, the drake, in ardent pursuit; Colonel dozing in the sun with his head over the hedge and Ditty sitting staring at Cherry, wisely just out of reach of a grasping hand through the bars of the playpen.

In no time Stivvy and Reuben alighted from the lorry. While Reuben opened up the emporium and greeted Donald with a sweet, Stivvy walked purposefully across towards us. He stopped to waggle his moustache at Cherry and touched his cap to Olive as she bustled from the back door, clutching her purse on her way to the emporium.

Stivvy joined Bert and myself at the gate, while Pete paced about in the meadow keeping Mary at bay to await her turn. He wiped the surplus moisture from his moustache with the back of his hand and rummaged in his pocket for his pipe. He filled it to overflowing as he watched Hereward at work, but when he came to lighting it he had to concentrate on it behind cupped hands because a sneaky breeze kept interfering. He held the match box over the bowl to help the pipe draw and looked back across the farmyard through the smoke curling from beneath his drooping moustache. 'Don't see they weaners runnin' around anywhere. Ain't sold 'em, have yer?' He looked disappointed.

'Not yet. They're shut up with their mothers on account of the boar being in the meadow. They all go to market next week and the old sows go with them.'

'I could do with one o' they. Going ter sell us one, be yer? I'll take one orf your hands today.'

I laughed. 'In the emporium?'

'I've got a sack to put 'im in. He won't hurt on the floor.'

'You'll lose customers if you start carting a pig around with you.' I wondered how the rich aroma of a pig would mix with the strong smells of paraffin, jute sacks, oranges, onions, spices, cotton clothing and pipe smoke that wafted from the emporium as soon as the doors opened.

'Lor, bless you, my customers have seen a lil' ol' pig afore now in my lorry. Country folk they be, all of 'em. Like as not I'll have some offers to buy 'im afore I gets 'im home. What d'you say then?'

'All right, just one from old Skinny's litter as she's got the most. Can't spare any more because I want to show that the sows throw big litters when they go to market. It might tempt buyers to go on breeding from them instead of fattening them out. The old girls might get a longer lease of life that way.'

Stivvy looked up at me and he was frowning a puzzled look, which surprised me because I thought he would understand a sentimental feeling for old sows. Oh well, there was no point in trying to explain. So I said: 'You fetch your sack and you can choose which pig you want.'

With Skinny shut away inside the sty we looked down on the litter snuffling about in the open yard outside. There were thirteen altogether and apart from the usual runt there wasn't much to choose between any of them. As usual Skinny had done them proud. She was a bag of bones herself but they were long and lively, with the slightly coarse look to their coats which showed they had been reared out of doors. And Stivvy knew this meant any one of them would thrive and do well once it was confined to a fattening sty. With any luck they would fetch fifty shillings each in the market. I might even get fifty pounds for the lot, including Skinny, if a buyer thought she could produce another litter like this.

Anyway, that's what I told Skivvy when he asked about a price for the one he liked the look of.

'Fifty bob?' He sucked on his pipe and it gurgled. So he shook it and wiped the mouthpiece on his trousers as he thought. He would expect to pay more than the market price for the pick of the litter. 'Right you are then. Three quid for that 'un. Can't say fairer than that, now can I?'

'Okay by me.'

'Done!' He spat on his hand and held it out for me to shake. I gripped it, but I could never get used to sealing a bargain

146

with him without a little shudder. Fortunately deals within the emporium were exempt from spitting handshakes. Perhaps he had found they were bad for trade with housewives. But he was a stickler for keeping up old customs and once I had found myself forced into abiding by another old tradition when I happened to meet him in a pub. Saliva was involved then, too. Reuben was with him and when I noticed them I walked over with my beer to join them. Soon Stivvy slid his glass across the bar towards me. There was about an inch of beer left in the bottom. 'Drink up!' he said, seriously sucking his moustache.

I frowned. 'That's your beer.'

'Course it be. But I wants to buy you a drink. So I says "drink up" and you must finish my beer. That's the proper way. The old-fashioned way. Shows us be friends.'

Reuben nodded in agreement. I looked at the dregs of beer and remembered how they had swilled around the ragged fringe of Stivvy's walrus whiskers. But I could see he was quite serious. He would be offended if I refused. So I drained the glass and banged it down on the bar. Not so bad after all.

But we were hardly halfway through the old custom. As soon as the full, frothing glasses of beer were placed before us, Stivvy leant over and lifted my glass. 'Now I has to take the top orf your'n,' he said, with a glint of pleasure in his eyes and his moustache lengthening in anticipation.

And 'taking the top orf' involved swallowing over half the contents of my glass, all neatly strained through his moustache. Well, once you accept a drink you have to complete the round, if you know your manners. Only before I had a chance to offer my dregs, to say 'drink up' and then have a go at 'taking the top orf', Reuben got in first. He shoved his glass towards me. 'Drink up!' and I had to knock back the swillings from his false teeth.

Anyway, to pay for the pig Stivvy peeled off three pound notes from the wad in his back pocket. I slipped into the sty, grabbed the pig he had chosen by the back leg and hauled it out. It squealed as though it was trying to burst its lungs and Skinny shouted abuse from inside the sty.

The pig was heavy, firm, a good fifty pounds in weight. And by the way he struggled, evidently he could think of no good reason as to why he should be dragged away from his brothers and sisters and his calling mother.

Stivvy shut the yard door behind me. He opened the mouth of the sack and held it ready. I grasped the pig by one ear and his tail, swung him up and, while he was still wondering, popped him arse first into the sack.

All would have been well, only that pig was a pretty quick thinker. He had been caught unawares once, in the sty, and it wasn't going to happen again. Before Stivvy had time to close the neck of the sack over him he leapt out and made off as though determined never to return.

I watched him heading off in the direction of the pond. 'You clumsy old fool, Stivvy, now look what you've done!'

'You let the bugger go afore I was ready.'

'Pete! Bert! Give us a hand.'

The pig was rounding the pond, disturbing three ducks as they carefully combed their quills. They bundled into the water with loud quacks of annoyance and Sinbad bustled over in a bow wave from the other side, asking what all the trouble was about in his loudest falsetto. He was halfway across when, as usual, he decided that a spot of sex solved all problems. So he singled out one of the three, chased her in a flurry of spray, grabbed her by the back of the head with his bill and pulled himself aboard. Then he proceeded to elicit her agreement by threatening to drown her, thrusting her head deep under the water while he paddled about on her, wobbling from side to side. At last he allowed her up for air, raped and repentant. And he left her spluttering and flapping as he sailed away, singing in his silly little voice to a deep-throated chorus of approval from his dutiful wives.

Now the pig was making for the freedom of the open road. He was beating across the backyard to shouts of encouragement from Cherry, making for the gate and the gap past the back door of the drawn-up emporium.

'Stop him, Reuben!'

'Olive! Turn him back!'

Stivvy and I screamed simultaneously as we pursued the creature.

In the nick of time Reuben stumbled down the steps from the emporium, closely followed by an agile leap from Donald and an anxious look from Olive. She was peering round from the top step, her arms full of the goods thrust on her by Rueben for her approval.

Faced with this unexpected opposition the pig braked violently and stood still, snorting anxiously as he tried to decide whether to risk running the gauntlet of a dash out under the unfamiliar, creaking emporium. But Pat put paid to that. He came ambling by from the front of the lorry, delighted that Donald had alighted at last and quite unaware that a pig chase was in progress. But when the pig backed away he spotted him. He sat on his haunches, pricked his ears and growled importantly. Pat had a healthy respect for the sows, but he was very brave when it came to confronting piglets. And by the way he was quivering I knew he was fighting the temptation of a quick, snarling chase.

I threatened him with dire punishment if he moved an inch as we came up behind the pig. Now that escape into the lane had been denied him, he snorted and spun round, weighing up the chances of a rapid retreat. On his left Stivvy and I were coming forward, crouching, arms stretched like slip fielders. On his right the boys closed in, Pete making encouraging noises meant to put the pig at his ease, while Bert sniffed and repeatedly assured us that we had not got a hope in hell of catching a pig in the open.

Dead ahead Cherry watched from her playpen, suddenly silent in serious appreciation of this grown-ups' game.

And it was on the playpen that the pig seemed to be pinning his hopes. He was staring at it earnestly. Perhaps he remembered it from a few weeks previously, when he had come across it on one of his first excursions with his brothers and sisters. Olive had set it up outside the back door to give it a good clean and while she was back indoors the piglets happened by. It must have reminded them of their creep feed because they spent a few happy minutes popping in and out between the bars. And they scampered off chortling to one another when the back door flew open and Olive came out clapping her hands.

I could read the pig's thoughts as he peered at it, raising his head and huffing as he took a few paces forward. He knew Cherry was no opposition. One quick dash through the bars and he would be away. So I was ready for him when he charged.

Only he had forgotten that he had grown and put on weight and his premature snorts of triumph turned to squeals of grief as the bars gripped him firmly by the shoulders. He pushed but they would not part for him. The playpen jerked forward, Cherry lost her balance, sat firmly on her bottom and started to scream. A second or two later I had the pig by the back leg and hauled him clear.

This time we made sure of getting our pig in the poke. Stivvy chuckled as he carried the writhing bundle to Cherry, now in the comfort of her mother's arms. But she would not smile, however much he waggled his whiskers or the pig snuffled and squeaked in the sack. She just stared at him with wide, brown eyes and sucked her fingers solemnly.

So now we were free to make our purchases, squashed in the emporium and trying not to stand on the pig as he lay quietly at last in his poke.

When Stivvy and Reuben drove away, with a wave and a hoot in a cloud of exhaust, we remembered Hereward. We could just see him in the meadow, still lounging on Mary. And when we came to him again he was on the point of dropping off to sleep.

12

THERE WERE ALWAYS pleasures at Maywood which more than made up for the hard times. Little things to look forward to when a dreary day loomed from beyond the dark and shivering dawn and I thought I must be mad to be a farmer, leaping from a warm bed to silence an alarum at an ungodly hour. But outside there was the friendly warmth in the cowshed and the lazy greetings from the cows, standing up, stretching out of the long night, shitting thoughtfully and rolling eyes of recognition. Or perhaps the sight of a new litter of pigs, born only yesterday, rummaging at the sow's teats to encourage her to let her milk down. And afterwards, bellies full, all snoring in a heap of twitching limbs. But when one roused and stretched and wanted to spend a penny, who taught it that it must stagger over to the corner of the sty and do it in the proper place? I could watch them and wonder and easily forget the latest letter from the bank manager.

Of course the weather was never right for everything. It is always either the farmer's friend or his enemy. When rain is right for roots it harms the hay, or when sun shines on ripe corn at harvest it parches the pastures. The worst was rain on ready-to-carry hay. All plans had to be abandoned while the hay spoiled. It would dry again, but never be the same with the lively green turning to bedraggled brown, the gay new scent often becoming a musty reminder of dark clouds when the stack was opened in winter, instead of the welcome armful of remembered sunshine. Yet old Colonel was the one who derived pleasure from rain on hay. We laughed at his relief at being let off work, the satisfied swish of his tail when we removed his harness and his hastening, stamping steps to get back to his field in case the rain stopped and we changed our minds.

But of all the pleasures, the one that gave me the most satisfaction was 'turning out time' and the sight of winter-yarded heifers greeting new grass in spring.

The twins, Primrose and Prunella, were now eighteen months old and had been in the bullock lodge since the previous autumn with five younger females. The part they occupied was a cosy nine yards long by five yards wide, covered in on three sides and under a thick thatch roof. The fourth side was post and rails dividing the lodge from the hard yard beyond, which led past the pond and down to the back of the house.

The bullock lodge had an earth floor and before the heifers had come in for the winter we had covered it with bundles of green faggots and a thick layer of straw so that they could lie dry. And through the winter we had added more straw every other day or so, with the result that the thatched roof became lower and lower as the floor-covering thickened.

Cherry was also eighteen months old now. She watched from behind the rails of the yard as I opened the gate and Donald followed me in, proudly brandishing a stick like a fully fledged stockman. We stodged over the piled up, hoof-packed dung to drive them out. Suspicious creatures, they could see the gate was open, they could smell the new grass on the hurrying breeze, the winter sentence was over and yet they hesitated, afraid of freedom. The twins stood side by side, stretching their heads forward and blowing anxiously at the open gate and the drop down into the yard. They were the leaders; it was up to them to make the first move and the others would follow.

'Go on, you fools!' I urged them forward and they dug their front feet deeper into the dung as I smacked them smartly on their rumps.

Cherry shouted something in her own language.

Donald said: 'She wants to know why you smacked her two beauties.' Ever since she had started to talk gibberish he had assumed the rôle of her interpreter, rendering a free translation of her remarks whenever he thought it appropriate.

'Because your beauties are being silly,' I called across to her. The twins were always referred to as Cherry's because they had all been born on the same day. Sometimes I had carried her to the yard and she would hold out her hand to them over the rails, shouting boldly until they came close and started to stretch out long, exploring tongues. Then she would draw back and cling to me, whimpering if I started to hold her closer to them. But the yard was visible from the kitchen window, and she could sit in her high chair and point across to the heifers if there was nothing more interesting to occupy her. Or perhaps she wanted to distract her mother's attention, to stop her forcing food into her mouth that she was none too keen on eating. Then there were shouted orders for us all to look out of the window and gaze upon her two beautiful twin heifers.

Prunella was the first to take the plunge out of the dark winter prison into the spring sunshine. She blew boldly, flashed her tail and half jumped, half slithered out on to the hard yard. There she stood still, straddle-legged, blinking in the bright sunlight and wondering what to do next.

Primrose joined her and they stood side by side while memories of a wall-free world came back to them; of a wide, warm sky instead of the night-black thatch; of hardness under their hooves. The sun felt good on their backs as it scratched with hot fingers through their ragged brown winter coats. Their thighs tingled where the dung had caked on them in hard little lumps and they stamped their feet to relieve the itchy feeling.

They looked at each other, ran a few steps, kicked out with their hind legs and stopped dead. Primrose stretched her head forward and blew at the ground. Prunella copied her and they rolled their eyes at each other. They agreed they felt fine, strangely elated. Why not take off? What's to stop them? Yes, let's! And away they went and it was wonderful. They had quite forgotten what a grand, free place the bright world was.

In a moment the sun and the sudden scope had gone to their heads like wine. There was no movement too crazy to try out in their excited dance. Soon their mates joined in, leaping out of the shed in an abandoned frenzy of delight, surprising themselves at their own capers. Sudden bursts of speed ended in frantic leaps, landings on all fours, straddled, wobbling uncertainly and with looks of bewilderment followed by snorts of impatient breath as they took off again.

Donald was laughing beside me. I looked across at Cherry and she was bubbling with fat chuckles as she watched the scatty heifers, prancing, snorting, speeding, swirling. I ran over, swept her up into my arms and danced round with her. 'Just look at your two beauties! Aren't they silly. They're all silly with spring fever.' And I ran with her, skirting the pond while she bounced up and down, through scattering chickens in long-legged escape, and disturbed ducks, launching themselves on the pond with cries of astonishment. From the safety of my arms she pointed and laughed and told me so much that I wished I could understand.

I dumped her on the doorstep, out of the way of charging heifers, and I joined Donald in his efforts to take command and drive them to where Pete and Bert were waiting in the lane.

When, at last, we drove them into the meadow, and shut the gate behind the last high kicker, we leant against it and watched them as they raced round in jagged circles. Soon Primrose and Prunella stopped together, snatched at the grass eagerly, snorted and settled down to some serious grazing, remembering and relishing the delectable taste after the dry winter tack.

Pete said: 'Buggered if they ain't grown. Now they'm in the open they look a right pretty pair, don't 'em? Couple of doers there, right enough.'

Bert spat. 'Won't be long afore they'm ready for the bull. Give they a couple or three months at grass and they'll be fit for it, I'll lay.'

Pete scratched his head through his beret. 'Yeah, as soon as they gets rid of them winter coats and into their summer best they'll look ready for it. Three months and we won't know 'em and then they'll be ready for to be introduced to the gent with the rubber apron and the glass rod.' He chuckled and turned to me. 'What d'you reckon? Give 'em another year and they'll be ready to calve down, I say.'

I nodded. 'Looks like it. We'll see how they do, but I expect they'll be ready for AI come September.'

Bert was counting on his fingers. 'That'll bring 'em to calve June.'

'Clever boy!'

Pete said: 'Oh, 'ee's good at workin' out pregnancy dates, that 'ee is. Randy young bugger.'

But Bert ignored the jibe. 'June,' he mused, 'that ain't much of a month to have two heifers calving, what with the haying an' all.'

'June's all right,' I said, 'the milk price starts to rise in July and they'll be able to settle in nicely before the autumn calvers start.'

We hung on the gate, watching as the heifers grazed in a close bunch. They had scattered in the first delirium of freedom in sunshine coupled with the intoxicating smell on new grass. But now they had come together again, wanting each other's company as they missed the confines of the winter quarters. They needed time to get used to how wide the world was and how far away the sky.

'Wonder if they'll milk like ol' Daisy.' Pete broke the silence.

'Hope they don't kick like 'er did!' Bert laughed. 'Wham! Bang! Remember how 'er used to let fly?'

We smiled at the memory of their kicking mother. It was easy to look back and smile, but at the time it had brought frustration and anger as the gallons of milk disappeared in sorry trickles down the drain. It was easy to smile at anything, leaning over a gate in spring sunshine, watching heifers enjoy themselves at turning out time.

Work was waiting everywhere, but let it wait. The thrusting hop shoots needed untangling and training up the strings. The alleys between the rows wanted cultivating yet again. Hops, springing corn and pastures alike were waiting for top dressings of fertiliser, and the stodged-up, chewed-up kale field had still to be ploughed. The ewes needed 'dagging' where the spring grass had loosened their dung and it was time for the lambs to be tailed and castrated. And now we had turned the heifers out there was the back breaking, sweating job of heaving out their dung and carting it away to steam and rot in the midden behind the oast house. So what? Of course we had to hang about and keep a sharp eye on heifers turned out to new grass, in case they blew with the unaccustomed richness.

We watched them for a while longer. Donald got fed up with playing at being a grown-up, copying us as we leant against the gate, one foot nonchalantly on the bottom bar. He wandered off to release Pat, whining from the woodshed, where he had been incarcerated in case he was tempted to chase the jubilant heifers.

When he returned, with Pat prancing beside him and licking at his face with grateful thanks, I straightened up and took a step backwards. 'Oh well, this won't do.'

'No,' Pete agreed. 'Suppose us better make a start.'

Bert sighed. 'Aye, bloody work. Wish I were a heifer. Nowt to do all day 'cept eat and sleep in the sun.'

There was a weak place in the hedge at the far end of the meadow where we had turned the heifers. If I did not mend it now they would be sure to find it as soon as they got fed up with grazing, and started to inspect their new domain. And once young heifers tasted the fun of breaking out it was a job to keep them in anywhere.

So I gathered up an axe, pliers, a length of barbed wire and some stakes and bundled them all together. As I prepared to lift them on to my shoulder, Donald called from outside the back door. 'Wait for me! Wait till I've finished feeding Corky and Choppy.'

He was holding a bottle of milk in each hand and two month-old sop lambs were tugging at the teats, sucking back the contents with the unsteady intensity of a couple of wineoes.

It had been Olive's idea that Donald should rear a sop lamb. She could remember when she was a child and the pleasure she had found in having a lamb of her own to look after. So when one of the ewes gave birth to triplets, and only looked like producing enough milk for two lambs, I tucked the weakest one under my coat and carried it down to the house on a wet March day.

'Who wants a surprise?' I asked, as I walked into the kitchen.

'I do.' Donald answered automatically. He was under the table, trying to interest Pat in lending his body as a race track for dinky cars. 'Brrm! Brrm!' as he manoeuvred a car along the dog's nose, between his ears, fast into the straight down his back and squealing for the bend round his waving tail.

'Then you'd better see what it is.' I held the lamb firmly out of sight.

He walked over, still full of boredom at being cooped up

indoors on a wet day. Cherry shouted something over her shoulder from where she was standing against the armchair, busy throttling a doll as she tugged to remove its skin-tight knickers.

Olive looked at me suspiciously from the sink. 'What are you up to now?'

'Nothing. Come on, Donald, bet you can't guess.'

He frowned, still uncertain whether it was worth joining in my game. Then the lamb struggled and gave a muffled bleat. 'You've got a lamb!' Immediately his face was alight and he pulled at my coat. 'Let me see, let me see. Can I have it?'

I stood the lamb on the floor. It wobbled and bleated loudly, opening its tiny pointed mouth wide and quivering its pink tongue. Its black eyes glistened in their sockets of wool and it tried a few unsteady steps.

Pat growled from under the table and Ditty was suddenly awake, springing from Sadie's basket to the seat of a chair and hissing enthusiastically as she eyed the lamb through the bars.

'You can have it if you look after it,' I promised. 'But that means stopping whatever you're doing and feeding it at the right times. And you'll have to wash up the bottle and teat afterwards and be sure they're nice and clean.'

'I will! I will!' He knelt on the floor and looked into the lamb's face. 'Hello, Corky, I'll look after you.' The name just came to him without a thought.

'But he'll have to live outside,' Olive warned. 'It'll be too hot for him in here and he can't take off his woolley coat to come indoors like you can.'

'He can sleep in the woodshed until he's old enough to live in the orchard,' I added.

But Donald was too busy talking to the lamb to listen to us. Then Pat yawned loudly because it was time somebody told him just what was going on. He strolled over, sniffed at the lamb, licked him under the tail and sat on his haunches as close to Donald as possible.

And Cherry came over, leading her now naked doll by the hand. She squatted down in front of the lamb and lectured him on the doll's sleeping habits, demonstrating how she closed her eyes each time she laid her on the floor. The lamb bleated in disbelief and staggered forward because milk was really what he had in mind.

157

A sop lamb can be a pest. It will follow you about, get under your feet just when you're busiest and loudly accuse you of deliberately trying to starve it — just like a hungry cat. But we knew it would be good experience for Donald to have one to look after. And as well as giving him joy, I wanted to make him realise that once the lamb was weaned it would join the rest of the crop and one day go off to market in the usual way. That was what livestock farming was all about.

Only we did not bargain on landing him with two lambs to care for. Yet the next day I hurried into the kitchen again and this time the lamb under my coat was half dead, abandoned at birth in the rain while its mother turned all her attention to her other two lambs. I revived it in front of the Rayburn and Donald helped to massage it and get it to suck some warm milk laced with a drop or two of whisky. After a whole day of looking after Corky he was already full of confidence, sure of knowing all there was to know about lambs. And as soon as the new lamb was on his feet and taking notice, he called him Choppy and prevailed on me not to return him to his mother. Of course Corky wanted a friend to keep him company at night in the lonely woodshed, he argued.

So he took charge of Corky and Choppy. But there were times when they got the better of him. They were not submissive like the chickens. Or like Pat. Even Ditty could be made to cringe and stay in one place if he was firm enough with her. But the lambs were something else. After a week there was no ordering them about and they had absolutely no manners when it was feed time. They bunted and bleated and wriggled to get at the teats on the bottles of milk. When he did manage to get them with a teat each and sucking properly, either one or the other would suddenly jerk upwards and send the bottle flying from his grasp. And that meant the other one had to stop drinking while he tried to retrieve the bottle and wipe the teat as both lambs furiously charged at him because he was their dam.

More than once he came dragging back to the kitchen with tears in his eyes, clutching both bottles and choking with threats to the lambs as they frisked after him, demanding to be allowed to finish their feed. Then Olive had to down tools and take charge of one while he fed the other, and it was easy now he had two hands to grip one bottle.

A week later still and he had control of them at feed time, grasping the bottles with white knuckles as he fought against their exuberance. And once their thirst was assuaged for a while they were docile, quite happy to walk about beside him without worrying, or to sit down suddenly with their ungainly legs tucked under them and doze off. They were too sleepy to bother when Cherry rolled up and perched dolls on their backs, could not care less when chickens stalked by and swore at them for lying in the middle of their parade ground and were quite happy to have their backsides licked by Pat before he settled down beside them, because by now he felt responsible for them as well.

But once the drowsy effect of the milk had worn off, once its energy had started coursing into their blood streams, they took on new rôles. Now they were athletes, adventurers and intrepid explorers all rolled into one. They staged elaborate races across the yard, races that sometimes involved a complete circuit of the pond and set the ducks swearing, races that always had to end in quick-fire hopscotch, played travelling sideways and jumping with all fours clear of the ground. Or there was a rise in the ground to be conquered, or the old tree trunk outside the wood-shed to be climbed and held against invaders. 'I'm the king of the castle, get down you dirty rascal.' And from there they charged off into the unknown behind the privy, fetching up in a rattle of dead leaves under the sprawling quince tree, panting and eyeing each other as they wondered whether they dared move, then wriggling their tails and wandering off side by side because they had suddenly lost interest in that game.

Now they were a month old as I waited for Donald to finish feeding them, before coming with me across the meadow to mend the gap in the hedge. As soon as the last of the milk drained into the last teat he tore the bottles away, raced indoors to put them in the sink for his mother to deal with while the lambs looked after him, stupidly flopping their ears. When he appeared again they trotted behind him and followed us into the lane, now lagging behind, now catching us up and racing ahead with sudden bursts of speed. And for a start Ditty came too, bounding with her tail in the air, joining us as we went through the gate into the meadow, leaping up the gatepost and hanging on just below the top, looking round at us with her ears back to make sure we were watching, swanking at how sharp her claws were before she heaved herself on to the top. And that was as far as she intended to go. She sat upright and watched us pass through the gate. And she scowled down at the lambs as they skipped over the ruts and snuffled at the new grass.

Donald called her: 'Come on, Ditty, you can come too.'

But she ignored him. Silly boy, didn't he realise that she had only jumped on the gatepost because it was the very best place for her to wash her whiskers? And she only paused in her licking long enough to look down as Pat squeezed under the gate and came plodding after us.

We walked across the meadow in sunshine and it was the sort of day that made up, in one fell swoop, for the worst that winter could throw at you. A day when clods and cold conglomerates had changed into living things, shooting with shy stems, a million and more arteries to lift the sap from the sleeping soil and spawn a coverlet of green flecked with all the colours of the rainbow, draped over the farm from the tallest tree and flowing over the fields and hedgerows into the darkest corner of the deepest ditch.

Primrose and Prunella had stopped eating. They walked cautiously towards us and when they were close Primrose belched. She was full. She really could not face another bite. It had been a meal worth waiting a whole winter for.

Donald held out his hand and walked slowly towards her. She backed away.

'Silly Primrose, it's only me.'

In the yard she would have stood still, lowered her head for him to scratch the really itchy patch just behind the base of her curving horns. She would have rasped his sleeve with her tongue. But already the free field whispered wild words to her and told her not to tarry with humans now, tempted her to independence with the feel of firm turf under her hooves, while a soft breeze played round her ears with tales of the far fields it had come from and where it would take her if she followed. So she shook her head, flashed her tail and kicked her heels and led a stampede after the breeze. But it was only a short run, which petered out in just a few moments because they were all much too full and sadly out of training for any more capers.

Corky and Choppy were alarmed at the sudden flurry of hooves. They had been following us at a distance, already overawed by the wide meadow and constantly considering turning back. But they felt they had passed the point of no return and it was safer to keep Pat's reassuring figure in view. But when the heifers charged, and Pat yelped and scurried because they had taken him by surprise, the lambs scattered helter-skelter to the nearest hedgerow and stood quivering, bleating and blaming each other for the foolhardy idea of leaving the security of the farmyard.

Donald raced to their rescue. Pat gave a sidelong glance at the now stationary, blowing heifers and hurried after him. I kept going with my load of stakes and axe over my shoulder and the coil of barbed wire hanging from them. When I reached the weak place in the hedge I threw them to the ground with relief. As I took off my jacket and prepared to work, Donald walked slowly along the hedge towards me, coaxing the lambs to follow while Pat strolled along behind.

Over the hedge at this spot there was a small shaw, spreading along from a pond to the right and filling a dell between the meadows. The hedge was weak because the sweet green gloom from the hazel, the chestnut and the birch leaves robbed it of all but the slanting rays of the morning sun. The hawthorn had to struggle upwards in paltry competition, weak at the knees and unfit to fend off an attack from a determined cow. Certainly not from Colonel. Over the years it had been one of his favourite escape routes, before the electric fence put paid to much of his wanderings.

As I drove in the first stake with the heel of the axe there was a horrified shriek as a magpie flopped down from the shaw and landed in the meadow. He eyed me, dipping and raising his tail like the end of a see-saw.

I stared at him and spat.

'Oh good morning, Mister Magpie,
Now, say I, here's spit in your eye.'

Donald arrived and the magpie fluttered off and landed again at a safer distance. 'Why d'you say that? Why spit Mister Magpie?'

'One magpie's bad luck. We say, "One for sorrow, two for joy". So if you see one magpie on his own then you have to spit and say that rhyme and then it's all right.'

'Do I have to say it now?'

'Of course. You can see Mister Magpie and you don't want bad luck, do you?'

He spat enthusiastically and repeated the words after me. The magpie saw no good reason why he should be insulted a second time, turned his back on us and hopped off towards the pond. And as he did so his mate hurtled over the hedge and landed nearby, just as if someone had lobbed her over.

Donald spat and started again. 'Good morning, Mister Magpie...'

'No. You don't have to say it again. Now there's two. Two for joy, remember?'

Obviously I was talking gibberish. He turned to Pat and spoke to him instead.

I returned to my task. The lambs were nuzzling at the hedge. They had found a trail of ivy and were picking off the leaves, devouring them with sharp bites and rapid movements of their little jaws. They were enjoying it immensely. Judging by their expressions its discovery had made their walk well worthwhile. It was good for them too. Ivy holds magic properties for lambs and more than once I had turned a sickly lamb into a thriving one by feeding it on a diet of ivy.

There was a rustle in the shaw and I caught the quick movement of a grey squirrel. He had leapt from the slender trunk of a silver birch and hurried through the leaves. Now he was staring at me, standing up to get a better view over clumps of primroses. His tail was flared and arched, ready for instant take-off.

I beckoned to Donald. He hurried up beside me and peered through the hedge. Pat joined him and blundered through barking because he was sure I had spotted a rabbit. The squirrel hurled himself at the nearest tree, spiralled round it so that he could climb unseen and then peered down at us from a high branch, chattering and scolding Pat for giving him such a fright.

Shaking my fist at him, I called: 'Stop swearing, you cocky little devil. If I had a gun I'd shoot you.'

Donald looked worried. 'Why d'you want to shoot him?'

'Because he's a thief. We used to have little red squirrels all over England until somebody brought over some of these grey squirrels from America. They let a few loose in Bedfordshire, the other side of London, and put a few more in the London Zoo. That was only about fifty years ago. And now they've killed all the red squirrels because they're bigger and bolder. They raid the nests of baby red squirrels and they raid birds' nests too. And the little grey squirrel pinches fruit from the orchards and he'll even steal peas from the garden if he thinks you're not looking. Sometimes he doesn't even care if you *are* looking. He'll steal them just the same if he thinks he can get away up a tree before you can catch him. He's what we call vermin and . . .'

I looked down at Donald. He was not listening but staring up at the squirrel, pointing with a finger just in front of his nose, glancing down at Pat and whispering to him to make sure he had spotted it.

Pat could see it all right. He was whining and shifting his feet as he sat on his haunches.

'Go on! See him off!' I urged him.

He flew at the tree, barking and jumping up at the trunk. The squirrel scampered up into the swaying heights, flung himself into the air towards a branch of the next tree, landed on its thin tip and clung tightly as the bough bent down and down. Then he clambered up the branch to the stem, rushed along another branch and in a few seconds he had travelled the length of the shaw, leaving the flustered tree tops swinging and swaying.

While I finished mending the hedge Donald wandered off to play round the pond. Corky and Choppy settled down to regurgitate milk curds mixed with ivy leaves and then to snooze. Pat came slinking back from his fruitless squirrel chase, his tongue out, his tail down and bending bursting bluebell shoots under his paws. He squeezed through the hedge, sniffed at me in passing and ambled over and licked the lambs. They ignored him so he moved on. Then he caught sight of Donald, fanned his tail gently and sank down on the cool turf with a sigh, where he could keep his eye on everybody.

It was a morning for exploring. It was too good a day to spend the rest of it doubled up training hop shoots. That work could go on waiting for me for another hour without spoiling while I walked through the meadows. I salved my conscience by assuring myself that I should see how the grass in the hayfields was growing, that the rabbits were not cropping the young corn and that, anyway, it was rude not to spend time admiring Nature when she had gone to so much trouble with her spring outfit.

I joined Donald by the pond. He was clutching a handful

of king-cups and the mud oozed on his boots from where he had stodged to reach them. When he saw me he held out his fistful of fat yellow faces. 'I've picked them for Mummy.'

'She'll love them.' The marshy smell was strong where he had disturbed the mud. 'Good job you didn't get stuck.'

'Course I didn't!' Why were grown-ups so stupid sometimes? Then he was pointing across the pond. 'Look at that funny bird! It's having a wash.'

A sedge warbler had flashed at the water, beating brown wings at the edge of the pond and dipping her tiny, badger-striped head. She was only there for a few moments and then she was off with an excited 'tek-tek', like a dart aimed at the low bushes growing at that end of the shaw. When she disappeared there was a reproving 'churr-rr-rr' from her mate, followed by some pretty harsh chatters and squeaks for having left him in charge of the nest. But really he was glad to see her safely back because soon he started to serenade her with a throatful of bubbling warbles.

'I expect she's sitting on eggs,' I said. 'Birds get hot when they're broody. And thirsty. She felt like a dip to cool her down. Now she'll be back on the nest with her wet feathers and that all helps to hatch the eggs out.'

He looked at me quickly: 'Let's look for the nest.'

'No. We might make her desert it.'

'Hum.' He had forgotten that possibility. We had talked about it before. 'I hope the squirrel doesn't find it though.'

'No, he won't find it. He won't go looking in bushes by the pond.'

We left the lambs to sleep. I hung up my jacket on a stake in the hedge and shoved the bunch of king-cups in the top pocket. They looked like a giant button-hole. And we went through to a meadow where we were saving the grass for hay. I had harrowed it and rolled it early in the spring, as soon as it was dry enough, and had dressed it with one of Frank Weller's special fertiliser mixtures for pastures. As I did not possess a machine for the purpose I had broadcast the fertiliser by hand, clasping a basin in the crook of one arm and pacing the field in two yard strips like the sower that went forth to sow. Now I could see the results of my labours and here and there a thin, yellowish hoop in the darker green showed where I had failed to achieve a completely even spread. But these streaks of yellow were few and far between and mostly the grass grew strongly, thick in the bottom with the indigenous Kent wild white clover, spiked in places with the pointed leaves of vetch and sometimes woven with delicate threads of trefoil. I shuffled my feet through it and it looked like growing into a heavy crop. Given some good spring rains it would do. 'A shower of rain in May, is worth a load of hay.' I muttered the old saw to myself as I plodded along.

I was lost in my study of the grass. A good crop was so important. Get it safely into the rick and it saved the nasty, nagging worry of not having enough fodder to see the animals through a late spring. For the moment I had forgotten Donald. And then I felt a hot hand come into mine. I gripped it and smiled down at him with a feeling of huge pleasure.

In front of us a lark startled into the sky. It rose higher and higher, fluttering striped wings, singing, trilling, filling the high sky with non stop praise. We stopped and watched it until it was just a speck in the blue and listened as its song fell all around us.

I sang up to it, lustily:

> 'Hark! Hark! the lark at heaven's gate sings
> And Phoebus 'gins arise,
> His steeds to water at those springs
> On chaliced flowers that lies
> On cha—ha—liced flowers that lies;'

I paused and looked down at my son. He was studying me as though I was mad. So I pumped his arm up and down. 'Come on! Hark! Hark! the lark at heaven's gate sings . . .'

'Hark, hark, lark, lark. Daddy, what's heaven's gate?'

'There! Up there! All that blue. That's heaven's gate. Right up there where the lark's singing.' And I pulled him by the hand and started to run, jumping up and down through the grass until he was laughing helplessly and Pat was barking and bounding beside us.

The meadow sloped down to a stream. We reached the trees that lined the bank and I threw myself against one and slithered down the trunk until I was sitting on the ground. Donald flung himself down beside me, laughing and wrestling with Pat when he came nosing into him. Soon he lay still, pretending exhaustion, and the dog gave a last snort and buried his nose in his side.

The stream was still full, slowly swirling, eddying, emptying the heavy harvest of February and March rains. I looked down into the water from where I sat. Below me it was quarrelling with the root of a tree that curved from the bank, spitting at it and clawing to dislodge the twigs that had caught there. I threw a stick and as it floated away I glanced over to the opposite bank.

'We're being watched,' I said, quietly.

Smart in his copper, bronze and purple suit, a cock pheasant paused as he strolled out of a copse. He tilted his glossy green head as he flashed an eye at us and his scarlet wattles seemed on fire. And the pointing tufts above his ears lent him arrogance as he continued on his morning constitutional, over his private moss-pile carpet, woven with primroses, bluebells and cringing anemonies.

I watched him disappear into a thicket, slowly drawing his long tail after him. And a moment later he uttered his raucous, abrupt crow. Perhaps one of his harem was nesting just there and he was giving her a few well chosen words of encouragement as he passed by on his rounds.

The sun was warm on my face as it struck through the dappled shade. It would have been easy to have lounged there all morning; easy to forget about the work crying out to be done while I sat and watched the comings and goings. Birds, besotted with love, were careless of our intrusion as they called from every vantage point; while those already saddled with heavy responsibilities whizzed about on terribly important errands. Thirty yards upstream, on the other bank, a rabbit loped across the far end of the pheasant's pile carpet. He stopped where the sun shone on a patch of grass. The coast was clear, the sun was warm, so it seemed just the place to have a wash and brush up. But no sooner had he started than he bolted in a flash of white tail.

Donald had jumped up, fidgeting to be on the move again. Pat agreed that it was a good idea. 'Let's have a race, Dad. Race you to the white tree.' He kept moving away, now crouching under starter's orders, now stealing another step or two towards a may tree, pale green and whitening into bloom further along the bank. 'Race you! Are you ready? I'll have this much start. No, *this* much. Ready, steady, go!'

I jumped to my feet and chased after him. Pat won easily. But I managed to achieve a dead heat with Donald for second place. And I said we should award ourselves prizes. I reached up and picked three sprays of may blossom. Then I stuck one into his jersey, one into my shirt button-hole and one into the buckle of Pat's collar. So we continued on our walk sporting our sweet-smelling badges of spring.

Corky and Choppy were wandering across the meadow when we returned. They were looking lost, ambling to no purpose as they looked around them, trying to see something they recognised to latch on to. When Donald called they stood and stared. But when he called again and ran towards them, they rushed at him, bleating and blaming him for deserting them.

So they followed us home, staging a race or two and several scurries of hop-scotch. And the heifers watched us pass. They were lying in a tight bunch, chewing their cud, eyes half closed as they delighted in this second helping of new spring grass.

13

THE TELEPHONE RANG and it was Mother.

'Hello, is that you, David? Now listen, darling . . .' No how
are you; how's Olive and the children? Pleasantries were for
letter writing and the phone had to be used as rapidly as possible and only for imparting absolutely essential information.
'Ruth and Co have asked me to go on holiday to Switzerland
with them.'

'That'll be nice for you. You'll have to start getting in training for your mountaineering again.' (Ruth and Co were my elder
sister and her family, and the thought flashed through my mind
how noble of them to ask Mother to accompany them again.
The last time they had taken her to Switzerland they had spent
the whole holiday panting after her up goat tracks leading to
the elusive summits of mountains, gathering up bits and pieces
that fell from her bouncing rucksack — ballast they had loaded
on her at the start of each day in a vain effort to slow her down.)

'Yes, I will.' She allowed herself time for a little laugh. 'But
I'm wondering what to do about dear old Guffy. *Do you* think
you could look after him for me? Last time Mrs Gilbert had
him and that was splendid because of course he's great friends
with little Susie. You remember her little Yorkshire terrier?
They play so nicely together. But she's going to be away at the
same time and I don't really want to put my little old man in
kennels. He'd be simply miserable.'

'Of course we'll have him.' She always referred to her dour,
ten-year-old Scottie as 'my little old man'. Actually he had been

Ruth's dog in the first place, but soon after she moved from Maywood to Jessamine Cottage, Mother had Guffy to stay with her while Ruth moved house. And, like the man who came to dinner, Guffy made himself at home and had remained ever since. Mother was glad to have him and Ruth did not press for his return because the more he advanced in years, the smellier he became. Quite sensibly she argued that as Mother's sense of smell was so bad it did not really matter and anyway the old dog was company for her.

'We can easily look after him,' I went on, 'and he and Pat get along okay. At least they don't fight.'

'Oh good. Hurrah! I'm so glad that's settled. I'll write back to Ruth tonight and tell her it'll be all right. Now I must rummage around and try and find my passport. And I'll have to get some Swiss francs from the bank. What fun! Goodbye, darling.'

The phone clicked and burred in my ear before I had time to answer. I smiled to myself as I thought of the number of times I'd told her that a local call only cost a penny for umpteen minutes. But for all the years she had been a subscriber she'd had it firmly fixed in her mind that a telephone was an expensive luxury and not to be used for idle chatter. This was in the days of toll calls and trunk calls and the pips that went every three minutes. And if she made one of these calls, or even if she received one, the first sound of the pips was the signal for her to say: 'Well, there go the pips so I'll ring off now.' Which she did, even if the conversation happened to be in mid sentence.

Although Guffy could put on all the swagger and pride of a fearless Scottie, at heart he was a very sensitive creature. I was always convinced that he was self-conscious about his b.o. as well. On a visit to Mother I had only to mention that he was smelling a wee bit strong, and was she giving him too much meat again, and his ears would lie flat while he looked away sadly. Then, when we had resumed our conversation, he would sit up, cock a leg and begin a loud, slow licking of his private parts. And this led to a violent scratching session, all the way up his broad back, across his ribs, lifting his head in ecstasy as he worked up to his neck and rattled away at his collar, until Mother prodded him with her toe and shouted at him to be

169

quiet. Which made him sink to the floor again with a sigh and a sorry look, as though he realised all he had succeeded in doing was to stir up an even stronger smell.

At Jessamine Cottage Guffy had his basket in what Mother called her 'glory hole'. It was a small room leading off the kitchen, where she bunged everything that had no fixed abode about the cottage. The room was already overloaded with heavy bookcases, bulging with Bibles and black-bound religious books, tedious tomes written by verbose Victorian vicars, a few privately published and many of them inscribed and given as birthday or Christmas presents to long-dead members of the family. (My sister Ruth had a theory that the givers got sanctimonious kicks, but that nobody ever read the books, only it was the done thing to display them. Certainly many of them had uncut pages.) Although they overflowed the bookcases, spilled over other discarded furniture and helped to prop up a broken-legged table, Mother always insisted that none could be disposed of to make more room in her small cottage. But she was never averse to grabbing a hefty one for a door-stop, or several of them at once when she had a craze for pressing wild flowers. Anyway, the glory hole was Guffy's sanctuary and he threaded his way slowly through brooms, garden tools, old seed boxes and discarded, mud-caked boots to reach the comfort of his basket. Once there he guarded the room with his life.

Mother never locked a door, front or back, and would cheerfully leave the cottage for hours on end without worry. From the road it was only a few steps round a curving path to the front door, which was screened by a thick laurel hedge. And once I popped in to see her in passing and found the door wide open and the cottage empty — except for Guffy, and he growled at me as I popped my head round the door of the glory hole.

'All on your own?' I asked. But he kept growling and refused to budge or even recognise me. If Mother left the cottage open to the four winds that was her affair, but he was determined to hold his glory hole against all comers.

I shut the front door, locked it with the huge, rusty key, left a note and went out by the back door. At least that would deter any odd bod just wandering in from the road and helping himself, I thought.

But when I next met Mother, she frowned. 'I'm very cross

with you.' She had a way of throwing back her shoulders and staring you in the eye when annoyed.

'Why? What have I done now?'

'You have no business locking my front door.'

'Hell! You left it wide open for anybody to march in.'

'It is my front door. I'll lock it or leave it open as I choose.' She screwed up her nose and blew down it and thumped her tummy in an anxious mannerism.

'Well *you've* no business leaving it open when you're out,' I shouted back. 'You're placing temptation in people's way and that's wicked. Everyone says you ought to lock up when you go out.'

She calmed down and gave a short sigh. 'Oh well, we'll see.' Which always meant that she intended to carry on exactly as before. She had some nice things about the cottage, antiques handed down. But they meant very little to her. So often, as children quarrelling over possessions, she had lectured us: 'Store not up for yourselves treasures upon earth, where moth and rust doth corrupt and where thieves break through and steal.' Except they never did break into Jessamine Cottage, or any house where she had ever lived for that matter. We always said she kept her guardian angel working overtime.

Certainly Guffy never cared a hoot who wandered in and out, so long as they kept out of the glory hole. But in it, behind the door, there was a low cupboard leading under the stairs. It was dark and musty inside, you had to bend double to enter and it housed the electricity meter. So it was bad luck on the meter reader when Guffy strolled in one day and captured him in the cupboard. And there he held him until Mother just happened to hear his shouts from the bottom of the garden and came to his rescue.

'Poor man, he was really quite white with fright,' she told us. 'I had to sit him down at the kitchen table and make him a nice cup of tea to cheer him up. And, of course, Guffy made great friends with him then, once he was out of the glory hole.'

So Guffy came to us for his summer holidays. I fetched him in Cob, complete with his basket, blanket and all the windows open. He sat solidly on his square, black bum on the seat beside me, not altogether sure that being taken on holiday was a good idea. As Mother had settled him in the car he had listened patiently to her glowing promises of what fun he was going to have with fields to run in, rabbits to chase and all the other animals to make friends with. It reminded me of her encouragement to me years before, when trying to cheer me up at the start of another dreary journey to boarding school. And when she kissed him goodbye on his high-smelling forehead, he looked up at her with the same misery.

On the short journey to Maywood I glanced down and spoke to him reassuringly from time to time. And each time he rolled the whites of his eyes up at me from under his bushy, black eyebrows: 'Och, mon, yer ken I'm no looking forward tae a holiday wi' you.'

And he was not immediately happy at the welcome he received on our arrival at the farm. Donald came running across to greet us as I drove into the yard. He pulled open the passenger door, embraced Guffy as he sat on the seat and straightaway staggered back, exclaiming: 'Pouf, Guffy, you *do* stink!'

The old dog had been quite impressed at the warmth of the embrace, wagging his six-inch tail and giving a wriggle of delight because he was fairly fond of Donald. As small boys went he was quite kind, more considerate than some of the little wretches at home, who barred his way and taunted him if he made the mistake of taking a stroll across the village green just as the school turned out. But now, at being told he stank, his ears went back and he lowered himself to the ground with as much hurt pride as his stumpy legs and barrel body would allow.

But Olive was laughing and calling to him as she came out of the back door. The day was hot and she wore a sun top and grey shorts as she came towards him, bending forward and clapping her hands. She seemed particularly jubilant. She liked hot weather and I thought this accounted for her extra high spirits.

Guffy was really a ladies' man. This was the sort of greeting he understood and knew just how to deal with. He walked forward, screwing his arse round, baring his white teeth and pretending to be taken with a fit of sneezing — an approach which he had perfected over the years and always proved to be most fetching.

'Guffy stinks, Mummy,' Donald warned her, loudly.

'Hello, Guffy! Dear old Guffy. You can't help it, can you, old boy?'

He rolled on his back, still grinning and sneezing, revealing his rather matted chest where Mother could never bring herself to brush and comb out all the tangles because it made him squeal — and sometimes snap in a most ungentlemanly manner.

Olive patted his chest. She straightened up and continued rubbing him with the toe of her sandal. She seemed to be having a little trouble keeping her balance on one foot. 'Whew! You *are* a bit high, aren't you, old fellow? It must be the hot weather. Never mind, I'll soon give you a good brushing. You'll like that.'

'We could always give him a bath in the pond,' I suggested.

'Yes, yes,' Donald agreed.

'No. Poor Guffy! Let him settle in first.' She stopped rubbing his tummy and he rolled upright. 'Come on, let's get your luggage.' She walked to the car with a carefree shrug. Guffy shook himself and strutted after her.

She reached inside the car and picked up the basket with its tattered blanket. As she drew it out and walked towards the house, she held it at arm's length while she turned her head away and pinched her nostrils. With a little snatch of song: 'Ho! Ho! Ho! I smell a smell, said the Wobbly Man,' she executed a rather unsteady pirouette and the blanket lifted and threatened to fly from the basket.

I tried to make up my mind whether she was trying to emulate the Wobbly Man, or if the lurch was unintentional.

Donald shrieked with laughter. 'Pouff! Pouff! Guffy's stinky basket.'

'Pouff! Pouff!' Cherry echoed from where she was squatting near the back door, naked except for knickers. She thought she ought to add her voice because we were all laughing. But she was too busy shaping mud puddings and wiping her hands on her tummy to pay any serious attention to us.

As for Guffy, he immediately realised he was being ridiculed. His ears went back, his tail down and he slouched apologetically after Olive.

Until Pat bounded into the yard. Straightaway Guffy was the sturdy Scottie, tail upright and twitching, lifting his nose to sniff Pat's balls as they circled suspiciously after each other. They had not seen one another for several weeks and so all the formalities had to be observed. I always felt that it only needed a wrong word or action from either of them to start a scrap.

'Now, now, Pat, talk nicely to Guffy. He's your guest.' Olive had paused to watch them, still clutching the basket at arm's length. The dogs pranced playfully at one another, ears askew, tails wild. 'That's good boys,' she continued to gaze at them. I thought it strange. I had presumed there was some urgency to give the basket and blanket a good wash and get them dry before bedtime.

By now I was standing beside her. She looked at me and smiled and her face was flushed. She thrust out her lower lip and blew up over her face so that her hair fluttered. 'Phew! It's hot, isn't it?'

I sniffed, loudly. 'God, woman, you smell like a brewery!' I was puzzled. My wife was no drinker. One well-watered gin and orange was her limit. Two and she considered she had been quite reckless. But now the booze on her breath explained her light-hearted behaviour.

'Oh, the wine! I'd forgotten all about it! Must get it finished.' She sped indoors, flinging Guffy's basket down outside the door. Pat raced after her and Guffy followed as fast as he could.

Inside the kitchen it smelt like the heaven of a drunkard. It was racking-off time for the spring-fermented wines and the table was glowing with jars of liquid, yellow and transparent as a watery dawn. Some jars were raised on upturned basins and from these rubber tubes sprouted, syphoning the wine from the lees into lower jars, sending it bubbling up in strings of tiny sequins. Primrose, dandelion and cowslip, each a different shade of yellow, gurgled innocently onwards towards staggering maturity. Surely, I thought, the odd mouthful swallowed inadvertently in starting the syphoning had not caused Olive's joviality. There was no strength to these brews yet, and anyway I knew how careful she was to spit out mouthfuls into the sink like a wine taster. She always behaved as though immature wine was poisonous.

Then I spotted the culprits. On the draining board stood two jars of blood-red elderberry wine, heavy with the heady heat of last September. And below them in the sink a row of bottles stood on parade, some already filled, others waiting expectantly with the syphon pipe draped over them, empty and awaiting the next good suck to start it flowing again. Evidently the wine tasted good and it must have seemed refreshing on a hot day.

Olive gave me a sly smile. She lifted the pipe to her mouth to start filling the next bottle. 'This elderberry tastes as though it'll be good when it matures.' She sucked, jammed the flowing end of the pipe in the next bottle and swallowed. 'Mmm! Too good to spit out. Try some.'

She reached across the draining board for a glass. She's even provided herself with a sampling glass, I thought. She removed the pipe, splashed some wine into the glass and passed it to me with one hand while she returned the pipe with the other.

I held it to my nose, pretending to test the bouquet. 'Ah, a fruity and naughty little number.' I wrapped my arm around her and pulled her against me.

'Don't play the fool. Drink it!' Her eyes were shining.

I drank and it was sweet and strong.

'Good, isn't it? You can feel it tingling all the way down. I'm sure it's the best I've ever made. Much better than the last lot. That tasted like red vinegar. Phew!'

She blew out another blast of wine-laced breath, raised her eyebrows and blinked quickly. 'Strong, too. I really feel quite swimmy and I've only had a few sips. D'you realise I've made five gallons of elderberry altogether. If it's all like this . . .'

'You'll get as tight as a tick just bottling it.' The bare thigh below her shorts was inviting and I slapped her playfully.

'Nonsense. I just feel nice and happy. But if you don't let me go that bottle will overflow.' She twisted away from me, removed the pipe and started filling the next bottle. 'Let's see, I shall get twelve bottles from these two jars so that'll be thirty altogether of elderberry. Every year you say you'd like to have an oast house party so why don't we this year? Now we've got all this booze? After hop picking. Baked spuds in the ashes under the fires, bread, cheese and elderberry wine. That should go down fine. It'll make a change from cider, won't it? Everybody has cider.'

'You'll have them all drunk. Look what it's done to you.' I pinned her in my arms from behind.

Donald marched into the kitchen, calling Pat and Guffy out to play. 'Why are you holding Mummy like that?'

'Because she'd fall down if I let go of her. Or else she'd roll across the floor like the Wobbly Man.'

He laughed. 'Let go of her. Let me see! Let me see!'

She dug me in the ribs with her elbow. 'Come on, let me go! I'll never get this wine finished before tea time.'

I released her quickly, holding my arms wide. Donald was leaning forward, watching intently. He started to chuckle as she swayed from side to side. Suddenly she pounced towards him and he shrieked with laughter, darting out of the back door with the dogs barking in pursuit.

It was surprising what a change of routine and some fairly violent exercise did for Guffy's b.o. Or perhaps it was the change of diet, less of the lashings of lights and the blue-stained, reject meat that Mother bought weekly from the stall in Ashford market, or commissioned other friends in the village to buy for her if she wasn't going herself. And this meat she then boiled and boiled in a large saucepan until the windows in her cottage wept copiously and every room stank of simmering lights. (The ubiquitous tins of dog meat had yet to find their way on to the shelves in the shops. And if you kept a dog, and were an ordinary mortal, you relied on condemned meat from the knacker men's stalls. But, if you had a pretty face, you could charm lumps of lights from the local butcher.)

Whatever it was, whether less meat, more exercise or even the compulsory dip in the pond next morning, Guffy soon smelt less vile. From the first day, as soon as he came splashing out of the pond, shaking himself and rolling on the hard yard to relieve the tingles, he forgot his first doubts and set out to pack the maximum amount of activity into his holiday. He treated Maywood like a health farm. He followed Pat on great excursions across the fields, but where Pat loped along with his comfortable stride, Guffy had to run full tilt to keep up. With the result that when the rabbiting was over, when the last hedgerow had been explored, the last ditch scrambled through and the final patch of brambles had clawed at his tough coat until there were just no more rabbits, or squirrels, or rats or birds or stoats left to put up and chase, it was all Guffy could do just to get himself home, dragging, panting, a meadow and a half behind Pat and not a single burst of speed left in him to avoid the cows if they came charging and blowing up to him. Which they often did because they never got used to seeing this strange little black creature crossing their meadow.

And they found him all the more interesting just because he did not run away. When they came at him, all legs and udders, horns low and menacing and with the most fearful threats on their breath, he just stopped and squared up to them, snarling as best he could through his exhaustion. Horrified at having their bluff called, the skittish cows skidded to ungainly halts and circled him with heads thrust forward, great cowards not daring to touch him and only too willing to give ground if he snapped. So Guffy usually arrived home long minutes after Pat, slowly crossing the meadow and occasionally glancing behind him to the following cows, who seemed to be the only creatures on the farm to find a fatal attraction in his spoor.

But one day Guffy went exploring on his own, which ended up with us all in a dither. He was in disgrace for chasing Corky and Choppy and I had hurt his Scottish pride by giving him a good hiding. So he took himself off, giving a backward glance that conveyed his opinion of me most forcibly.

The sop lambs lived in the orchard, which was next to the farmyard. Now they were weaned they had lost most of their frisky ways and were fast becoming staid sheep. Really they should have joined the other sheep weeks ago. But it was one of those jobs that had never got done. Not that it was my fault. Several times I had said I was going to move them and each time I was met with glum looks and tearful protests from Donald.

'You know they've got to join the other sheep sometime,' I argued, on the last occasion.

'But they won't have any friends,' he sniffed.

'Oh, they'll soon make friends. Besides, they're almost grownups now and they can look after themselves. And grown-up sheep should all be together.'

Olive put her arm round him and said: 'We'll leave them a little longer. But soon they'll have to go because they need a change of pasture. Sheep don't like eating the same old grass all the time. Anyway, you'll still be able to see them after we move them.' And when he had run off, tears drying in the glow of victory, she said: 'He'll soon forget them. Now they're weaned he visits them less and less and they've given up running to the fence when they see him. Another week or two and he won't mind at all when they join the other sheep.'

But whether they were weaned or not, Pat still regarded

Corky and Choppy as part of his responsibilities. And when he had not got anything better to do he squeezed under the gate into the orchard and ambled over to have a word with them. If they were grazing they paused and stared at him for a moment, then took no more notice of him as he came up and sniffed them and flopped down nearby. And it was this friendship with the lambs that made Guffy so jealous because he was not allowed anywhere near them.

Pat guarded them as though they were bones between his paws. He was pleased to have Guffy follow him anywhere, except into the orchard with the lambs. The first time Pat visited them after Guffy's arrival they were only some twenty yards inside the gate. As usual he eased himself under the gate and shook himself when he stood up on the other side. But when Guffy came scurrying towards the gate, ears forward, tail straight, anxious to keep up on another new adventure, Pat sprang round and faced him through the gate, hackles up, ears half back, tail arched and growling menacingly.

It was quite obvious that Guffy realised Pat meant every word he said. His ears went flat, he sank to his solid stern and turned his head away as though he could not bear to hear another word.

Pat continued on his way, walking slowly, still grumbling warnings for the first few yards, then waving his tail gently as he came up to the lambs and passed the time of day with them. He lowered himself to his belly to watch them graze as he always did.

Guffy's ears shot forward as he watched. He whined a little and he quivered. It wasn't fair. Why couldn't he go close to the lambs as well? But it was more than he dared do to try so he turned away, swaggered off to the backyard and sank down to sulk in the shade.

So it was no wonder he took the first opportunity that presented itself a few days later. The coast was clear and he set off to introduce himself to the lambs. I happened to be crossing the yard just as he went haring across the orchard.

I yelled at him: 'Guffy! Come back here, sir! *Here*, you little sod!'

He kept going. He knew I was too far away to catch him. It was now or never if he was ever going to meet the lambs.

178

Corky and Choppy looked up startled. They came together and faced this strange black creature bearing down on them. They stamped their feet but he kept coming. They ran in a quick circle and stamped again. Still he came and now the only thing to do was run, run like the wind with the bleats beating out of them in staccato cries for help.

I yelled and yelled as I ran into the orchard. But Guffy could not hear. He was barking with excitement. This was better than a rabbit chase, much more fun because the lambs kept going in circles and didn't disappear down holes. He had never run so fast, never swerved with the same speed and once he cornered so abruptly that he tripped and rolled over twice before regaining his scrabbling feet.

And I chased him, screaming at him and threatening him with instant death. There is no surer way of losing your temper with a dog than to see him sheep worrying. The thrill hits them like a drug. Soon they become incapable of kicking the habit.

So when I caught him I thrashed the living daylights out of him. And he skedaddled when I let him go, ears back but thoroughly unrepentant in the glance that he gave me, just determined to push off somewhere, anywhere where he would never have the misfortune of setting eyes on me again.

'Good riddance, you black bag of haggis,' I fumed after him. 'Don't you dare chase sheep again or you'll get shot on sight.' And I went about my business deciding I would make friends with him again after the lesson had had time to sink well in.

He disappeared for the rest of the day. When we called the cows in for the evening milking I asked the boys if they had seen him anywhere. No. So I left them milking and started to search. Donald came with me. So did Pat, but he did not seem to have missed Guffy at all and he tagged along after us with his tongue hanging out and a resigned expression on his face. As we kept whistling and calling he presumed his presence was required wherever we went.

We searched the oast house, the stack-plat, the bullock lodge, the calf pens, the cart shed and even the pigsties. Our calls echoed through the wood and vied with the bird song. But there was no sign of him. I began to think that he must have decided to shake the dust of Maywood from his paws for ever and push off the three miles home. There was nothing for it but to start up Cob and drive slowly to Mother's cottage in the hope of finding him.

I went to the cowshed to tell the boys. The milking machine was hissing and pulsating and the engine throbbed monotonously from its cubby hole in the corner of the food store. As I turned to go I noticed that Bluebell, Popsi and Little Lotty all had their heads forward and were staring keenly beyond the manger at the wooden wall of the food store.

'I suppose that bloody hound's not in there?' I asked.

'Ain't seen 'im.' Bert bent to massage the last of the milk into the cluster on Daisy's udder.

I went to the food store and opened the door. No Guffy, just the increased noise of the engine. I shut the door again and walked the narrow passage beyond the mangers past the staring cows. It led nowhere, but then I heard the sound that had attracted their attention. Guffy was whining and his faint cries seemed to be coming from under the wooden floor of the food store. There was a gap between it and the earth. It was blocked off with a board jammed across the small entrance. Evidently he had knocked it down and crawled in and could not get back.

We located him from inside the food store, pulled up one of the century-old floor boards and yanked him out. He crouched down and looked up at me apologetically, just daring to quiver his tail. His coat was draped in cobwebs and suddenly my stomach turned over as I noticed white dust clinging to his eyebrows, his whiskers and his beard.

Immediately Pete voiced my fear: 'He ain't been eating that rat poison, has 'e?'

There were holes in the old floor and sometimes we trickled poison down through them if we suspected that rats were casing the joint. It was mixed with some flour and sugar, appetising enough for Guffy to want to sample now that he was on his hardy, health farm diet. Why else would he have knocked the board down that guarded the only entrance under the floor? He must have smelt the sugary mixture and decided to squeeze in for a taste. The worst thoughts raced through my head as I bundled him under my arm and made for the kitchen.

'Quick!' I shouted, 'what's the antidote for rat poison?'

'Why, what's the matter?' Olive looked up from laying the tea table. 'Oh, you've found him!'

'Yes, little sod. Under the food store floor. Stuffing back rat poison.'

'No! Are you sure?'

'Course I'm sure! Look at his beard and face, will you? It's white with the stuff. He looks like a canine Father Christmas.' Guffy was struggling to get down and be allowed to greet Olive. Certainly he was very lively and showed no ill effects as yet. 'Hold still!' I commanded him. 'Just let me wash this muck off your face for a start.' I hauled him over the sink, turned on the cold tap and doused the flour from his face.

He struggled so strongly that I had to put him down. He hurried over to Olive and shook himself, spattering her bare legs with the drips from his now bedraggled face.

'Oh, Guffy!' She hopped up and down and he sidled close to her, going into his sneezing routine.

She bent down and held his head in her hands. 'You really ought to have your stomach pumped out.' The nursing training came flooding to the fore. She looked up at me: 'We'll have to make him sick. That's all we *can* do.'

'What? Shove a feather down his throat?'

'No, silly. Salt and water. Get him to swallow some salt and water.'

She hurried to the sink to prepare the purgative. Donald was kneeling up on a chair and he looked down over the back, anxiously sucking his fingers and asking if it was going to hurt Guffy. Cherry was on the other side of the table, energetically banging it with a spoon. She didn't know about anybody else, but she was hungry and what about some tea? Ditty walked in smoothly through the open door. She froze when she saw me holding Guffy. She turned and walked out again with an angry swish of her tail. She had made no attempt to disguise her dislike of this smelly stranger and had sworn at him roundly whenever he came near her. She hadn't seen him for the last few hours and as far as she was concerned that was good riddance to bad rubbish. Now she was furious to find him back in her kitchen again.

Olive hurried over with a jug of salt and water and a tablespoon. I sat Guffy up on his haunches, knelt behind him and pinned him between my knees. Then I gripped his snout and tried to prize open his jaws.

181

Now Guffy had really had enough of it for one day. He held his strong teeth tight shut, rolled his eyes up at me and growled threateningly. I was no friend of his.

'Come now, my little old man,' I coaxed. I nipped his lips against his teeth and his mouth opened. 'Quick! Bung some in!'

Olive slopped a brimming spoonful on to his tongue. 'Hold his mouth shut!'

'You rub his throat.'

'Mind he doesn't *choke*.'

'Stop snarling and swallow, you sod!'

Some went down and the rest dribbled down his chest. He spluttered and hoicked and I felt hopeful.

Donald said: 'He doesn't like that.'

'Course he doesn't. It's meant to make him sick. Come on, let's get some more down him.'

Which was easier said than done now he'd had a taste of it. I was surprised at how strong he was as I wrestled with him and tried to avoid his determined snaps.

So we had to bind his jaws together, pull out his cheek and dribble the saline into him, rubbing his clammy throat, coaxing him and pleading with him to swallow for his own good. He stared back at us defiantly as the liquid oozed out through his teeth.

But he did swallow some and Olive sat back on her heels. 'He doesn't seem to want to be sick. Are you *sure* he ate some poison?'

'Well, I *think* so. I mean, you saw it all over his face.'

'It must be white with flour everywhere under that floor just from the milled corn you mix there. Doesn't mean to say he ate the poison. P'raps we're putting him all through this for nothing. He may have just been chasing a mouse under there and got stuck. That's more likely. He could only have knocked that board down if he was really excited to get after something. You know how frantic he gets.'

'Mmm. P'raps you're right. But I felt sure . . .'

'Anyway, I thought you said dogs and cats can sick up this new poison if they happen to eat it.' Already she was untying the gag.

'Oh yes. It did say that on the packet, now I come to think about it. I'd forgotten in the excitement. I was only thinking

182

how dreadful to have to greet Mother with news of a dead Guffy when she comes back.' I patted him on the tummy and released him. 'Never mind, old fellow, if you're going to be sick I'm sure the salt will do you good in the long run.'

He bundled up to Olive, forgiving her instantly for the part she had played in his ordeal.

An hour later he still showed no signs of illness. All he could think about was his evening meal that Olive was preparing. When she put it down he wolfed every scrap, belched, scratched and settled down in his basket for a sleep.

The next morning he stretched to greet me when I went into the kitchen. Obviously he felt thoroughly fit and it seemed we could be friends again. I knelt down and made a fuss of him. And when I opened the back door to go out he scurried ahead of me. Halfway across the yard he stopped and looked back. 'Och, mon, 'tis a grand day.'

Then Pat trotted out and he hurried up to him, anxious to discuss how to spend the next day of his holiday.

14

TOM HARRIS LIVED from catching rabbits. And when we had
carted the last of the hay from the fields to the bulging rick, and
the close-shaven brown stubbles were starting to spike again
with new, pale green, he came swinging down the lane on his
bike. He found it hard to steer because three brace of rabbits
hung from each handlebar and their dead heads swung and col-
lided with each swerve of the bike, while he pedalled with his
knees sticking out sideways because the rabbits hung in the way
of normal riding. Two more brace were draped over the crossbar,
a narrow-bladed draining spade protruded over the rear wheel
and a bulging sack was strapped to his back with binder twine
across his chest.

Tom wobbled to a halt when he saw me coming from the cowshed. He was about thirty, with lank fair hair, sky-blue eyes and
shining red cheeks. Two brawny arms led to the handlebars and
the inside of each forearm sported a tattoo of a near-naked girl
with an hour-glass figure. They stood on arrow-pierced hearts
and the one on his right arm was inscribed AMY — TOM, and
the one on his left IVY — TOM. I don't know who Amy was
because he never said. Only I did know he had served in the
navy during the war. But Ivy was his girl friend, except he called
her his Missus, and they lived together in an old cottage, half
buried in a wood down the cart track past Pete and Bert's cottage. I just presumed that Amy was the reason why they never
married. And whenever I saw Tom's arms I always thought how

rotten for Ivy, with half of every embrace an indelible reminder of the wretched Amy.

'Hello, Tom,' I greeted him, 'you're well loaded. No need to ask if you've had a good day.'

He smiled. 'Aye. Not bad. I bin working them fields of Milton's t'other side of the May Wood. That's why I come to see you. Bloody rabbits ain't arf given that corn o' your'n a caning aside the wood.'

'You're telling me!' This was before the days of myxomatosis, and rabbits bred and thrived no matter how hard you tried to exterminate them. Only a year previously Tom had waged war on the rabbits at Maywood. For several months afterwards I hardly saw one and the yellow urine-poisoned grass that bordered the woods and the warrens began to recover. But gradually the numbers had increased again and a stealthy walk on a summer's evening could produce a hundred bobbing white tails as surprised rabbits hurried for cover.

'About time I had another go at 'em for you. I likes to work in rotation if I can and now I done Milton's I can sweep right on through with your'n.' He eased his thumb under the binder twine where it was biting into his shoulder with the weight of the sack. A corner of the sack bulged and wriggled as his ferrets changed position in their bed among the snares and pegs and paraphernalia of a rabbit catcher's sack.

'Start whenever you like,' I said. 'The sooner you clear them the better.'

'Then I'll be along later. Make a start with me snares about dusk. Pay you a bob a head same as last time. All right by you?'

'Okay, fine.' He would make three shillings and sixpence each for them — half a crown for the carcass and a shilling a skin. So the sixteen rabbits hanging from his bike right now were worth fifty-six shillings, or £2 net after he had paid Milton his shilling a head. Not bad for less than a day's work, when the farm worker's wage at that time was under £4 a week. But still, no point in arguing for more than a shilling a head. He had to take the good with the bad and every man to his own trade. It would not have suited me to spend my days snaring and ferreting and netting rabbits for a living, even if I had the skills required. Besides, Tom was nobody's fool. I could hang out for another threepence a rabbit and after some haggling he would agree. But there were a hundred and one places to hide dead rabbits, and as many routes through the woods to go and retrieve them, after I'd agreed with him his bag for the day. So he could easily get his rabbits for a shilling each in the end.

He smiled broadly as he prepared to mount his laden bike: 'Right then, I'll get rid of they ol' rabbits for you.' He wiped the beads of sweat from his forehead with his arm and Amy's red tits wriggled on the muscles.

'None of your gin traps now, Tom,' I said, in parting. 'I don't want to be prizing them off sheep's feet, or cows, or the old dog, come to that.'

He paused and looked at me innocently. 'Oh no. They be illegal now, you know.'

'As if that would worry you, way out here,' I scoffed.

'No. Just snares, Dave. Honest. That's all I uses now. Just snares and ferrets and maybe Ivy'll come out and help I with the long net if the place is right.' I must have looked at him quizzically because he started to ease the sack from his shoulder. 'Here you are, look in me sack. You won't find no ol' gin traps in me tackle.'

'Go on,' I slapped him on the shoulder. 'I believe you.'

He readjusted the sack. 'Tell you what, though. You come along o' I tonight, why don't yer? Help I set a few snares. Happen as us could have a sweep with the ol' long net too. After it gets dark. Acrost the bottom o' that banky meadow of your'n. Wind's just right for there, I'll lay.'

'Okay. You're on. About nine?'

'Aye, 'bout nine. I'll give you a shout.' He pressed on the pedal, heaving to steady the heavily-laden handlebars. And Amy and Ivy rolled blue hips at him as he rode away.

Ivy was with him when he came that evening. She did not look a bit like the tattooer's impression of her on Tom's arm. She was fair-skinned and dumpy in dungarees, with a homely smile and a headscarf that said PARIS under a picture of the Eiffel Tower. But it was not a souvenir of a wild weekend there because she was not that type. I don't *think* she had been any further afield than London and she was certainly no gad-about. When she was not helping Tom with his rabbits (and I'd seen her rip the skin off one quicker than a mother in a hurry peeling a vest from a child), or caring for him in their cottage, she was

186

out hoeing or hop-tying in the spring, strawberry-picking or climbing the tall ladders up the cherry trees in summer, apple-picking or potato-lifting in autumn and sometimes cycling long miles in winter to join a shivering gang of sprout-pickers. And every year she had her own bin for the hop-picking at May-wood. She could pick hops quicker than anyone and sometimes Tom joined her of an afternoon and then the big bin would fill to overflowing, long before it was time for the busheller to come round.

Country folk tend to hide their emotions in public. But it only ever took half a look at just their glances to see that Tom and Ivy were always in love. It did seem a pity that Amy had to come between them in their cottage every time Tom reached for his cup of tea or another slice of bread and jam, or sprawled his right arm sleepily across the pillow.

We walked through the cows on our way to set the snares. The sun had already set and was turning distant cumulus clouds into a range of red mountains. And as we walked with the long red light behind us, the cows eyed us suspiciously. They stared and circled and the ones lying down heaved themselves to their feet, coughed and blew through their nostrils with alarm because they did not recognise us. Tom carried his bag of tricks over his shoulder, Ivy had the extra lump of the long net in its valise while I humped a bundle of slender stakes for fixing the net. As far as the cows were concerned we were three shady characters walking through the twilight. They were making it their business to see what we were up to. I had to call them by names several times before they recognised me. And then they turned away lashing their tails — of course we knew it was you all the time.

Through the gate, we went in single file down the hedge in the cornfield. It was 'dredge' corn, oats, barley and peas growing together to be harvested, threshed and then milled together to provide a roughly-balanced milk production ration for the cows. It was turning gold already and as we walked down the sloping field the crop was thick and promising. But from the bottom edge of the corn, before the ground suddenly plunged down to the wood in a bank of short grass too steep to plough, the corn had been cropped in a ten yard wide swathe, ragged with stumpy heads and bent-back stems where the rabbits had fed while the corn fought to outgrow them and survive.

Tom dumped his sack on the ground and looked down the slope to the wood. The spikey, rabbit-cropped grass was criss-crossed with runs. 'Right. Action stations. Us'll soon lay a few surprises to put a stop to their little games.' He started to rummage in his sack.

Ivy dumped the long net and went to help him. He gave her the snares and pegs to hold and his thick fingers lingered for a second on the back of her hand. She followed him across the slope, the wire loops of the snares ranged along her hand like bangles and the brown strings draping from them. A handful of tethering pegs sprouted from one pocket of her dungarees and a bunch of slender setting pins from another. Pegs and pins had been cut and whittled from hazel, but the whiteness had gone and they were carefully weathered and soil-stained so that, to the hurrying rabbit, they looked no different from fallen twigs.

I followed them. 'Anything I can do to help?' I asked, stupidly. It was so obvious they worked as a team and I could only be a spectator.

'Presently,' Tom answered, softly and without looking up. 'When we comes to try the long net. It's better with three.'

Ivy smiled at me: 'Yes, we can do with you then all right, if we has a good run.'

Tom was squatting, studying a rabbit run. 'But first things first,' he mused. His voice was little more than a whisper and he held up his hand to Ivy without looking up. She handed him a peg and he knocked it into the turf beside the run.

I was bending over his shoulder. 'Why just there, Tom? Why not further up, or even further down the run?'

' 'Cos that's just past where 'e jumps, see? See the grass? You can tell. Some bent, some upright, where 'e lollops along.

'Oh, ah,' I said, wisely. But it all looked the same to me.

Ivy handed him the snare. He fastened the string to the peg, formed the pear-shaped noose, fixed the base into the slit at the top of a pin and poised it over the run, squatting one side of it to work so that his scent was not in the rabbit's path.

He stood up. 'There! That's a nice necklace for old coney. Strong enough to hold a bouncing buck, I'll lay. Snares grab bucks best 'cos they plunge into 'em and they're dead in a minute. Not like a doe. Her's more dainty like. Sometimes the wire

188

don't catch 'er just right. Then 'er squeals afore 'er dies and that can be a pity 'cos the ol' stoat can hear her, see?'

'So you find one half eaten rabbit in the morning,' I said.

He was moving on down the run, looking for another likely spot. 'Oh no, rabbit'll be whole orlright — 'cept 'er won't have no blood. That's what ol' stoaty likes, see, drop of warm blood. He'll never attack a dead rabbit, only a live one and, 'course, time you comes to skin it 'ees had all the blood out of it and the flesh is white as a chicken. All right for we to eat, mind. Nothing wrong with it. Only it ain't no good for I to sell. My dealers won't touch no stoat-drained rabbits. It's people, see. Funny buggers they be, people. Just 'cos that meat's a bit white they reckon there's summat the matter with it.'

By the time he had set fifty or more snares it was almost dark and, towards the end, Tom had been using a torch to study the runs. We made our way back along the edge of the corn and I looked down the slope where we had been working, down to the black mass of the wood. It was too dark to see any of the snares but I felt the place was now like a minefield, waiting silently for advancing, unsuspecting rabbits.

We walked through to Banky Meadow. It sloped more gently to the wood. What breeze there was was blowing down the slope into the wood, carrying our scent away from the rabbits we suspected were grazing above us in the dark. Here was the place for the long net, a few yards into the meadow and stretched along the line of the wood. Simple, I thought, roll the net out, prop it up and drive the rabbits into it. Why hadn't I thought of getting hold of a long net and catching the rabbits myself?

But I soon found that the setting of a net that would actually catch and hold a frightened rabbit took as much skill and experience as the ploughing of a field or the building of a well-shaped hay rick. Particularly as the work had to be done in just the starlight of a summer's night and in complete silence.

Tom's net was some one hundred yards long by three feet wide and the mesh was about two inches square. Two cords were threaded through the net top and bottom and these were tied to slender steel pins driven into the ground at each end. And all I was allowed to do was hold the bulky valise to my chest and walk backwards in fits and starts while Ivy eased out the carefully folded hanks of net with delicate fingers. It was easy to see that one false pull, or if the net had been wrongly folded into the valise in last night's darkness, and you would spend frustrating hours unravelling tangles instead of catching rabbits.

Tom came behind, pegging the bottom cord, propping up the net with sticks every three yards, adjusting, tightening, fussing until we reached the far end and he drove in the final steel pin. Even then he was not content and he walked back along the line, a shadowy figure creeping and stopping to fiddle with the net, which was now billowing gently in the breeze slipping down the hill.

Ivy was close to me. She looked up and whispered. 'Got to be just right for 'im, you know. Proper careful, my Tom. If there's twelve rabbits up there in the dark then 'tis all twelve 'e wants in the ol' net. If there's fifty then 'e wants fifty and none of 'em getting by 'cos the ol' net ain't set just right for to catch 'em.'

I peered along the net. 'Looks okay to me. Can't see how they can get through that.'

She whispered: 'Ah, but the slack's got to be just right all the way along to bag the rabbits proper when they hits the net. Don't catch 'em all else. But my Tom knows and he'll have to have it so-so.' I could just make out her smile as she searched for his returning figure.

When he came back we set off to round up the rabbits. I walked up beside one hedge from the wood, they up the other, and we spread ourselves along the top of the meadow and started back down towards the net.

I zig-zagged down the meadow and I only seemed to be driving silence before me. I searched the gloom but could see no glimmer of a retreating white tail. It seemed we had drawn a blank, gone to all the trouble of setting up the net for nothing.

Three parts of the way down the meadow I called across to where I believed I could see Tom: 'Sod all, here, mate. I reckon they must have run off before we got here.'

I heard him chuckle. 'You wants to eat more carrots, me ol' Dave. Carrots to help you see in the dark.'

A moment later the beam of his torch stabbed the darkness. He chuckled again as he played it along the net, lighting up the rabbits struggling in their bundles of mesh. 'Not so bad, not so bad,' he said, 'couple o' dozen there, I'll lay. Maybe thirty and I'll bet a bob there ain't none got away.'

Ivy joined us and he handed her the torch. 'Well done, gal.' He threw one arm carelessly over her shoulder as we walked to the struggling bundle nearest one end of the net. And while she blinded it with the torch and it stopped still, Tom pulled it from the net, broke its neck with a quick stretch and threw it kicking to the ground.

There were thirty-two altogether and I piled them into a sack and carried the warm and heavy load up and through the gate to the lane, while Tom and Ivy carefully folded and packed the net.

When they joined me, Ivy asked: 'Going to paunch 'em then, Tom?'

He grabbed the sack and tipped the rabbits out on to the grass. 'Aye, sooner it's out of 'em the better.' He laughed at the brown heap, slithering in the torchlight. 'Reckon we got enough to carry home there without taking the guts as well.'

With a quick slit from his sharp knife, a deft flick of his wrists and a hoick with his finger, he deposited the innards of the first rabbit beside the hedge. And he did five before I managed to get the warm, squirming guts out of one, while Ivy laughed at my efforts and shared the torchlight between us.

When he had finished them all, Tom said: 'Better take a brace of 'em home with you, me ol' Dave.' And he slit behind the tendon of a hind leg and threaded the back leg of another rabbit through it so that it locked on the knee joint. He lifted them, one on each hand, and plonked them astride my shoulder. 'There you are, help you make the peace with the Missus for stayin' out late. See you in the marnin'. I'll be round they snares soon after dawn and we'll have a count up when you done milking.'

He heaved the sack over his shoulder while Ivy humped the long net. We said goodnight and they melted into the darkness, two lumps exchanging soft talk as I turned to go my way home.

I hung the rabbits from a hook in the pantry ceiling. Then I blew out the lamp that Olive had left turned low on the kitchen table and crept upstairs to bed. I dreamt of rabbits running, stopping, sitting up and waving paws and daring me to catch them. And I couldn't run after them because something stopped my legs from running.

191

Suddenly I was awake. Olive had reared up in bed. 'What was that?'

I listened. Outside the first streaks of dawn fingered through the leaves of the cherry tree. Two or three birds were tentatively practicing their scales. Then the sleepy morning was ripped with the screams of a rabbit, going on and on, echoing and violently stopping.

Olive turned on me: 'God! Did you use traps last night?'

'No, snares.'

'It sounds like a rabbit in a trap. Like Tom used last time.'

'No, only snares. It'll be a doe. He warned me that sometimes a doe screams if the wire doesn't kill her straight away.'

She threw herself back on the pillow. 'It's fiendish! Why can't he just shoot them?'

'Because cartridges cost money. Anyway, he'd never cope with the numbers with just a gun. D'you realise we had thirty-two in just one sweep into the long net last night? They've just got to be killed in the greatest numbers, before they eat us out of house and home.'

But she did not answer. And she did not go to sleep again. Another rabbit screamed, then another and another. She lay there tense. I knew she was wishing there was some way she could stop their pain.

In a week Tom had covered the whole farm and paid me £9 for one hundred and eighty rabbits. At £22 for himself he had every reason to be well pleased with his week's work. I was quite happy just to be rid of the rabbits, free of their incessant chewing at the pastures and the corn, and of the poisonous little patches where they peed. Certainly I did not begrudge Tom his share. He had worked hard for it, up at dawn each day and out late at night. But he must have thought he had had a good deal because a day or two later he rode into the yard, beaming all over his ruddy face. He rummaged in an old carrier bag and from it he produced a box of chocolates for Olive, a Dinky car for Donald and a doll in a red frock for Cherry. I got a slap on the shoulder and a promise that drinks would be on him the next time we met in the Six Bells. Perhaps he had been expecting me to hold out for one and threepence a head after all.

* * *

Primrose and Prunella grew like prize cattle. In three months at grass their coats took on the sheen of brown silk, their bodies filled with puberty and there was a solemnity in their stares as they adopted the cares of adulthood. Of course they were as inquisitive as ever and nobody was allowed to walk through their meadow without being inspected. Yet they no longer rushed up but walked solidly, swishing their tails and rolling their backsides, staring and occasionally shoving a tongue up a broad nostril. Except when thunder clouds rolled and the gad-fly buzzed. Then they forgot they were adults. Their tails shot straight up and they led the field in a crazy race, full tilt, not caring, not stopping as they fled to escape the sound. And if they happened to be with Colonel in his meadow, he joined in too, laying back his ears, swivelling his stumpy tail and breaking into a gallop that left his whole gaunt body heaving. He was no lover of the gad-fly either.

By now Primrose and Prunella were bulling regularly. From their early, shy attempts, games almost of jump and chase that had gone on from time to time in the winter yard, had come the serious, compelling experience of orgasm. They paired with each other, riding and thrusting, working themselves up into sticky heats that sometimes involved one or two of the other, younger heifers in the meadow.

And early one morning, so warm that I only walked out in shirtsleeves to call the cows in for milking, I noticed that Primrose and Prunella were riding again. I decided that this time they were ready for mating.

We drove them into the loose box to await the artificial inseminator. And that was easier said than done because they enjoyed their freedom in the meadow and saw no reason why we were picking on them, trying to separate them from their mates and drive them away. Pete and Bert and I spread ourselves out and advanced on them, arms spread wide as we tried to cut them out. Several times we succeeded, while they were both so busy leaping on one another that they did not realise what we were up to. Several times we got them almost to the gate and each time, at the last moment, they came to their senses and charged past us to rejoin their mates.

In the end we had to drive the whole lot into the yard and part the twins into the loose box from there. And while the boys drove the others back, I joined the twins, coaxing them with corn to separate corners until I managed to slip the chains around their necks. When they finished the corn, went to move away and found they were tied, they eyed each other anxiously, fidgeting as they tried to understand why they couldn't stand close together because they had never been parted before. Especially they wanted to make contact today, now they were experiencing this exciting feeling again.

We never knew what time the inseminator would come. It depended on his round and the number of calls that day. But somebody had to be on hand to greet his arrival with a bucket of hot water, some soap and a towel. Inseminators expected to be waited upon. So I found myself a job to do nearby.

Soon Cherry came to find me. She was nearly two now and talkative, and I could usually understand her so had no need of Donald to be on hand as interpreter. They had been playing together, but just now he had pushed off with Pat on what was evidently a boys-only game. I could just see them advancing across the orchard to surprise a crowd of piglets, who were busily enjoying themselves while Martha and Mary slumbered in mud wallows beyond the pond.

Cherry wanted to know why her two beauties were still shut up in the loose box. There was a crack between the boards in the half-heck door and she had made several excursions to peer through this throughout the morning. She was convinced I was punishing the twins for some reason and was not inclined to believe my story that I was waiting for a man to come and see them. And as the hours dragged by, and still no man came, she got fed up with asking for the twins to be released. Instead she stood and stared at me with large brown eyes, sucking her thumb and caressing her nose thoughtfully with her forefinger. I had the feeling that not only did she consider her father to be cruel, but a downright liar into the bargain.

It was hot. There was no water in the loose box so I thought the twins would probably appreciate a drink. I told Cherry what I was going to do, held out my hand for her to accompany me and she took it without a word.

In the dairy I filled a bucket with water, carried it across to the loose box and she came in after me as I plonked it down in front of Primrose. 'There you are, my beauty, have a nice drink to pass the time.'

Primrose blew at it suspiciously, tested it gingerly and in a moment was sucking it back with gusto.

'Oh, she *is* thirsty,' I said, turning to hold out my hand for Cherry to come closer. But she had gone. Only a shaft of sunlight reflected on the straw just inside the open door. Oh dear, I *was* in her bad books. Evidently I was not going to redeem myself just by giving her two beauties a drink.

Primrose finished off the three gallons and looked up for more. Prunella stretched her head over to the extent of the chain and hopefully stuck her tongue up one nostril. I returned to the dairy, filled two buckets this time and took them back to the heifers. I put one in front of each and stood back to watch the pleasure with which they drank.

There was a rustle on the straw behind me. I turned to see Cherry coming back into the loose box. She was carefully carrying her seaside bucket, brimming with water. Without a word to me she took it slowly to Prunella and placed it beside the bucket she was drinking from. The heifer's eyes rolled and she lifted her head, water dripping from her mouth back into the bucket. Then she spotted the gaily-coloured little bucket, lowered her mouth to it and drained it with a single suck. And Cherry retrieved it and dashed off for a refill.

The inseminator arrived soon afterwards. I left him struggling into his rubber gown and wellies while I went to fetch hot water, soap and towel. And now that the promised man had actually materialised, Cherry stuck to me like a leech. She wasn't too sure about this stranger. Her natural inclination was to retreat and seek out her mother in the kitchen. But she stayed with me, her anxiety to know what this man was up to with her two beauties outweighing her fear of him.

In the orchard the piglets had been duly scattered, had raced to rouse their mothers for protection and Donald and Pat came bounding back. Donald had spotted the inseminator's arrival and watching him was better fun than chasing piglets.

There were three inseminators who covered calls in our area and we never seemed to get the same one twice running. None of them ever had much to say. It seemed to be a job that attracted morose men, particularly the one that came to do the twins. He was tall, thin, lantern-jawed and with deep-set dark eyes. Months before I had nicknamed him Sullen Sid, after he had paid us a visit and failed to utter a single word before, during or after carrying out his task. And when he had gone I had remarked to Pete what a dull old lot inseminators seemed to be. He had smiled and said: 'Yeah, I suppose they be. Still, you would be too, wouldn't yer? Suppose you had to spend your whole time going round shoving your arm up cows' arses?' It was certainly a point to be considered.

So Sullen Sid worked speechlessly while I held the twins' tails out of the way. Donald and Cherry watched silently from the doorway. They never missed a movement as Sid removed the test tube of semen mixed with egg yolk from the dry ice steaming in the flask, sucked some up into the long pipette, stuck the plunger on the end and then held the primed pipette crosswise between his teeth as he advanced on Primrose.

An arm up her backside and Primrose flicked her ears back and rolled her eyes in astonishment. She strained and Sid eased his arm backwards with a grunt, scooping out shit and dumping it at his feet. Then the reach inside again to grip the cervix, the removal of the pipette from his teeth, the introduction into the vagina and the careful threading through the cervix. Now a squirt from the plunger to send half of the semen on to one horn of the uterus. Now a change of direction to squirt the remainder on to the other horn. All done and his arm came out with a slosh and he sluiced it off in the bucket of water before preparing to deal with Prunella.

The children looked on seriously, taking in every last detail as Sullen Sid finally cleaned himself up, silently studied his cuticles and dabbed at them with the towel as he tried to remove the dark shadow of cow shit that persisted in clinging there.

And when he drove away Donald called Pat and ran off across the yard. The dog heaved himself to his feet to plod after him, while Cherry shouted, 'Wait for me' and followed as fast as she could.

I drove the twins back to the meadow. 'Sorry girls, that's all there is to it.' But they seemed satisfied. They swung their tails and walked sedately, now and then blowing at the ground because a nice bite of grass was what they were really interested in after so long.

For the rest of the day I went about my work. There were pigsties to muck out, repairs to be done to the floor of a waggon, a general clean-up needed in the stack-plat before we harvested the corn. There was never any shortage of work to find around the farmyard itself, and as I had been forced to start on it while waiting for Sullen Sid, I thought I may as well devote the day to it after he had gone.

As usual Donald and Cherry were busy with their games. Sometimes there was a chorus of protest from the ducks if they were persuaded off course, a squawk from a hen if she was squabbled over, shouts, laughter, playful growls from Pat, soft talk to dolls, screaming cornering of Dinky cars on the cowshed floor. When you are busy and children are happy you only half hear. It's the long silence, or the sudden tears that make you take notice.

In the afternoon Olive found me. She was bubbling with contained laughter and beckoning me to come. 'Have you seen what your children are up to?'

My children. It would be something bad. I looked across the yard. It was a normal enough scene. Cherry was kneeling over her dolls and chatting to them. Pat was a yard or two away, upright and watching, and Donald stood nearby. And then I saw that he held a small medicine bottle in one hand and a length of straw in the other. Even as I watched he dipped the straw in the bottle, sucked the end, withdrew it, held it crosswise in his teeth while he lifted Cherry's skirt and then prodded it against her bottom.

Olive spluttered. 'Oh no! Not her as well! He's already inseminated Pat and two chickens, as well as all the dolls.'

15

WE TOOK IT in turns to take Colonel to Boney Jackson, the blacksmith. Now that his life was leisurely, the old horse only needed shoeing about every two months. Sometimes the shoes lasted even longer, with only soft meadows to pull the cart through, or loose earth in the hop garden when he plodded up and down the alleys pulling the harrow.

But with corn harvest coming, and then the hop-picking, there was serious work for him to do and I wanted him properly shod. Besides, there was the hop-powdering to be done. He hated that. And if he could find the slightest excuse for getting out of it, like a loose shoe and pretending lameness, he would.

Hop-powdering was the only time when Colonel really worked hard. He had to, to get out of the way of the suffocating powder billowing up into the green bines from the whirring machine he pulled. I always powdered the hops late at night, or very early in the morning, whenever the air was still, allowing the powder to linger and settle into every crevice of the broad leaves. Even so, Colonel knew very well that if he slackened his speed it only needed the whisper of a following breeze for the drifting powder to catch up with him and make him splutter. But, conversely, if he happened to sense the merest zephyr fanning into his face, he slowed right down, knowing full well that the powder was disappearing harmlessly behind him.

Anyway, it was my turn to take him down to Boney Jackson. This job was a rest cure, an idle jaunt, sitting on a sack on the old horse's back, gazing over the hedgerows at the passing scene on the two-mile journey to the village. Careful note was always kept of whose turn next. Except in winter, when you had to walk to keep warm. Or if it was raining and you had to make a hood of a corn sack, draping it down over your shoulders to keep out the worst of the wet. Then each of us was quite prepared to forego his turn. If somebody else would sooner go?

The smithy was right in the village. It overlooked the large green that was cricket field in summer and football pitch in winter, standing back from the road along with other old houses, each with a long front garden leading down to the green. Only Boney Jackson's front garden was mostly a cart track leading up to the smithy attached to one end of the house. A few flowers grew; some hollyhocks struggled hopefully up through the curved tines of a long-left hay rake; two-faced pansies tried to line the track, only there were sad gaps where horses had shied on approaching the smithy. Haphazard rows of potatoes, luxuriant from all the horse dung that had been chucked on them, thrust up wherever there was space among the clutter of junk iron, cart wheels and long-dead farm implements that thronged the approaches. And to the left a path led off to the front door of the house, curling through a little lawn and past a well with a dwarf wall around it, a canopy above and a bucket hanging from the chain coiled around the wooden roller.

Colonel knew the way. He had been up that track a hundred times before and he walked willingly with his ears pricked forward. Halfway up to the smithy his chest vibrated beneath my legs as he blew out a wheezy neigh of welcome. He and Boney were old friends. I think the handful of rolled oats that was all part of the service had something to do with it.

I slid to the ground at the entrance to the smithy. A voice hailed from the darkness within: 'Cor, bugger me, ol' Colonel! Ain't seen you all summer. Thought you must be dead.'

Boney walked out, screwing up his eyes in the sunlight. He really was thin, a tall scrag of a man with a gaunt face, a jet black five o'clock shadow and tufts of black hairs sprouting from his prominent cheekbones and out of his ears. The only meaty parts of him were his arms. They were thick, bulging with muscle down to the huge hands and it seemed as though all the food he ate must go to nourish these limbs of his trade. Not that he ate very much. It was beer that Boney relied upon to keep him going, and he was usually too full of that to have much room left for food by the time he staggered back home from the pub.

Any dinner time you could find him in the Six Bells, just across the green from the smithy. Any evening, too. And if he wasn't 'laying the dust', then he was 'putting back the sweat'. He was there on Sundays as well, scrubbed and sitting prim and proper in his blue serge suit and stiff collar, drowning the memory of the chapel service he had just been forced to attend with his wife. He was a sore trial to her. She was called Chapel and I never knew whether that was actually her Christian name, or just a nickname because of her devout ways. Anyway, she did her best to rule Boney and I presumed she was only prepared to tolerate his drinking provided he attended chapel every Sunday.

And she always expected him home from the pub sober, and within a few minutes of closing time as well. If, as sometimes happened, he staggered up the track drunk and disorderly, then he found himself locked out and had to spend the night in the smithy. Local people said they could always tell when Boney had been locked out. They would see a glow from the smithy as Boney kindled his fire and bellowed it into violent life. Soon they would hear his voice, lifted in song while he bashed out the beat with his heaviest hammer on the anvil. Sometimes, they said, his repertoire lasted far into the night as he put every effort into ensuring that Chapel did not sleep either.

He came out of the smithy with one hand behind his back. Casually he scratched Colonel's forelock and the old horse blew and made his lips quiver — not so much a greeting as, 'Come on, I know you've got some oats there.' When Boney offered them to him he snuffled them up and went on fidgeting at his bit with his tongue long after they were gone.

Colonel's shoes were bespoke. There was always a set ready and waiting, hanging over a nail on the black wall behind the furnace. Boney had made them so often that he could knock them up from memory, and when he came to fit them they never needed more than the slightest adjustment. Now we were in the smithy and I was working the bellows while Boney heated the shoes. Colonel stood outside under the lean-to, old shoes removed, hooves now neatly pared and ready for the new shoes to be burnt into them.

My back was to the door. I was looking into the glowing coals as Boney shuffled a shoe with his tongs. And I was listening to the long sigh the bellows made as I slowly pulled the handle downwards — the long handle with the curved white cow horn jammed on the end, polished by years of steady movement from Boney's hand and shining red each time it reflected the firelight.

So I was startled to hear Chapel's soft voice behind me: 'Good afternoon to you, David. I see you've brought Colonel again.'

I turned quickly. 'Hello, Mrs Jackson.' This was the first time I had ever seen her in the smithy. And actually smiling. Usually all I got was a curt nod from the front of the house if she happened to be outside or checking on coming customers from a window. She was tall, wore severe, old-fashioned clothes and if we happened to pass in the village there was the same formal nod — except there would be a faint smile for the children if we happened to be there as a family. Now, more surprisingly still, she carried a tray on which were two cups of tea and a plate of home-made scones.

She hovered uncertainly. Boney went on prodding at the horseshoe in the fire and took no notice. I was just thinking I ought to take it from her and find somewhere to put it down among the clutter when Boney grunted, turned, shuffled some tools to one side of a work bench and banged the vacant space with his tongs. He returned to his work, without a word or a glance at his wife, and when she had put the tray down she drifted out of the smithy as silently as she had entered.

The firelight played on Boney's cadaverous face.

I thought I saw the trace of a smile. 'What's all this then, Boney? Afternoon tea in the smithy, whatever next?'

He pulled the horseshoe from the fire and held it glowing over the anvil. With his other hand he grasped a hammer and beat a timid tattoo on the anvil, now and then tapping the horseshoe until he was satisfied he had curved it to the right shape. Without a word he carried it outside, lifted Colonel's foot and held it between his knees. Then he fitted the shoe to the hoof, blowing away the smoke that rose into his face while the shoe burnt a bed for itself. When he was satisfied he stood up, Colonel dropped his foot and Boney plunged the shoe hissing into a nearby trough of water.

On the way back to the furnace he started to sing a hymn softly to himself and in a deep baritone: 'Dear Lord and Father of mankind, Forgive our foolish ways.' He fiddled with the fire and I worked the bellows, wondering whether I was going to be treated to the whole verse. But no, because he suddenly said: 'Her and her bloody forgiveness. The ol' hypocrite. Why, put a saddle on 'er and the devil would ride 'er.'

Evidently there had been above average strife in the Jackson household. Perhaps I ought to keep quiet. But it was so obvious that Boney's star was in the ascendency I was curious to know how he had managed to dominate his stern wife at last.

'What's up then, Boney? You seem to have got it in for her today. She been shutting you out drunk and disorderly again?'

He laughed, deeply and confidently. 'Her won't do that again, be Christ!'

'Oh?' I tried to sound casual.

And then I had the whole story, told in fits and starts as he gazed into the fire, hammered on the anvil, moved to and from burning the shoes to fit, and finally hammering in the nails that held the shoes to Colonel's hooves, and twisting off the ends that spiked out through the sides.

There had been a cricket match the day before, a Wednesday afternoon game that went on until eight o'clock and it was too dark to see to play, and anyway to go on any longer would have meant a serious loss of drinking time. Now Boney was a keen cricketer and still liked a game of a Saturday. Once he had been a demon bowler, striking terror into opposing village teams as he hurled the ball down from his great height on to the bumpy pitch. But nowadays he reckoned he 'ain't got the breath for it', and had taken to spin bowling and aiming for uneven spots where the ball would fly off at unpredictable tangents that often surprised him, let alone the batsman. Only he never played in the occasional Wednesday game. He had to work. Wednesday games were 'fer them shopkeepers and suchlike what had to work Saturdays'. But as he had a grandstand view of the village green from his smithy, he never did a great deal of work if there was a Wednesday game in progress. Once I had unwittingly arrived on a Wednesday to get Colonel shod. And we had spent most of the afternoon sitting on the edge of the water trough outside the smithy, waiting 'jest to see one more over and then us'll make a start'.

So the beer in the Six Bells tasted extra good on a Wednesday evening after a cricket match. And, of course, the game had to be analysed. Boney's criticisms as to field placings and bowling changes were listened to with respect, and with so many rounds of drink to be consumed until everybody had bought for everybody else, naturally 'drinking up time' had tended to stretch out somewhat.

Boney looked up at me, Colonel's hoof firmly between his knees and his mouth bristling with shoeing nails. ' 'Course, mind you, I weren't drunk.' The words were muffled by the mouthful of nails. 'Why, us'd only been drinking since stumps at eight. Christ! T'wud take longer than that to get I pissed.'

He positioned the shoe, drove each nail home deftly, twisted off the ends and rasped around the hoof until Colonel's feet looked far and away the newest thing about him. He slapped the old horse on the rump and Colonel nodded, rattling his bit as a reminder that now was usually the time for the second handful of oats.

Boney shuffled off into the smithy, holding a huge hand to his back and grunting. He returned with the oats and fed Colonel. He bent down to gather up his tools and groaned again as he straightened his back. I must have smiled because he said: ' 'Tis all right for you. But you wait till you gets to my age, mate. You'll get stiff everywhere 'cept where you want to be.'

He was wandering from the point. So I prompted him: 'So you weren't drunk last night?'

'Drunk? Cor, bless you, no. But 'er thought I were, old Righteous in there.' He waved a handful of tools in the direction of the house. 'Jest 'cos it were gorne eleven and I weren't home. Locked the door on me, 'er did, locked the door and me not drunk and disorderly. So I thought to meself, right, I'll see about that. T'wadden no good to bang the door to get 'er to open it. Not once 'er'd bolted it on me. So I crept to the well, see? There, right outside the door. And I lifted the catch on the chain, give the 'ol bucket a tug and sent it clatterin' down. And as it went I leans over the wall and hollars down into the well, all blood-curdlin' like. As though I'd felled in. Then I gives just one more gurglin' groan echoing down and nips over aside the door.' He chuckled deeply at the memory, and gave me an exaggerated wink. 'That did it. The light come on and I heard 'er coming. Fair frantic 'er were to draw the bolts. And as soon as the door opened I pulled 'er out, jest in 'er nightdress, nipped inside meself and bolted the door on 'er. "There," I says, "*you* bide out there, you bugger, for a change." '

'And you left her out there all night?'

' 'Course I bloody did. 'Er won't lock I out in a hurry again, I'll bet a bob.' He chuckled away to himself as he nodded goodbye and disappeared into the smithy.

I eased Colonel close to the water trough, climbed on the edge and jumped to his back.

As I rode away I heard the fire roaring. Halfway down the track his rich baritone came flooding from the darkness: 'Dear Lord and Father of mankind . . .' and then, loudly to the sound of iron on anvil: 'For — give our fool-ish ways.'

There had been a sale of furniture and effects in the village that day and as I rode Colonel up past the church, to take the narrow lane off to the left that led to Maywood, cars were revving up and moving away. Now Colonel was used to one car at a time, even the tractor spluttering by, but with so many cars starting off home and heading in both directions, he clattered his new shoes on the road and shuffled round in a bit of a state. So I slid off his back, led him into the side of the road and he nudged his nose into my armpit as I patted his neck to soothe him. Evidently he wasn't so startled as he had led me to believe. I think it was just that he was so used to having the right of way, and a few clumsy gyrations that had the cars hastily pulling into the side of the road and stopping, was his way of asserting his authority.

I was searching for a suitable launching pad to mount his high back again when I heard: 'Hello, squire of Maywood, how's the world treating you?'

Tony Gamble was on the point of getting into his car. He was a local estate agent, tubby and dark, with smarmed down black hair and heavy glasses. It was through him that I had bought Maywood from old Bill Checksfield, trying to stick to the price I had offered while Tony pretended not to be interested, sitting behind his big desk examining his nails, while the text on the wall above his head read: 'Come on Business, do your Business, go about your Business.' I was green, and he knew it, and in the end he had extracted another three hundred and fifty pounds out of me.

'Not so bad,' I smiled as he walked across to me. I saw him from time to time at sales. But it was never more than just a nodding acquaintance and now I was surprised that he seemed to want to speak to me.

He slapped Colonel on the neck. We exchanged a few pleasantries. Then he said: 'You did all right buying Maywood when you did.'

'Huh, you ought to see the size of my mortgage! Right time or not, I'll be an old man by the time I pay that off.'

'Still,' he persisted, 'you didn't pay any too much for your farm.'

'Seemed like it at the time, after you'd finished bidding me up in that charming way of yours.'

He disregarded my jibe. 'Not when you see what farms are selling for today.'

'So they tell me.' I had heard of quite ordinary small farms going for a hundred pounds an acre and more. And that was almost double what I had paid for Maywood a few years earlier. Only the other day Tony's firm had hit the headlines in the local papers when they sold a farm by auction at three hundred pounds an acre. But that was down on Romney Marsh, on the fat lands.

He patted Colonel again. 'Yes, and we're getting a heap of enquiries for farms in the Weald. No trouble to sell. It's just we can't get enough of them, that's all. So, if you ever think of selling, just let me know. I dare say we could get you double what you paid for the place. Easily clear your mortgage and give you a few thousand pounds in hand.'

'Oh, really?' I said, lamely. Colonel was getting impatient. He kicked a hind leg on the road and struck sparks from his new shoe. 'Woe, hold up, itchy feet!' I grumbled, 'just you wait till I'm ready.' I jerked his bridle and his head shot up and his ears went back. But he was thinking of the long walk home and the hours he had been without a bite to eat, except for the taste of oats at Boney's. His belly rumbled and he farted. He swished his tail and stamped again.

'Just thought I'd mention it, anyway,' Tony concluded, turning back to his car. 'Give it a thought. I'll be pleased to come over and value the farm anytime.'

I laughed and waved as I moved off. 'I'll think about it.' But what I did think about just then was what a nice business estate agents enjoyed. They could sell the same houses and farms over and over and draw their fat commission each time.

When I had mounted again in the side lane, Colonel set off for home as though there was not a moment to lose. I swayed to the rhythmic clop of his shoes on the road and mused on what Tony had said. What money I did make on the farm seemed to get swallowed up in mortgage repayments. Or just when I thought I had got the bank overdraft down to a respectable limit, suddenly a six monthly interest charge became due and shoved it back up where it was before. True, we had a simple living from the place, for which we worked long and hard hours, and that was about all. There was never anything left over for extras, neither was there an over-all improvement in my precarious financial position.

And as Colonel plodded on, down into the valley and up again, crossed the boundary of Maywood and I looked down over the farm, the thought of selling it and getting shot of all my debts was very tempting.

I told Olive what Tony had said. It could make life easier for her, I added.

'And then what would you do?' she asked. The beginnings of a smile were tickling the corners of her mouth. 'I can't imagine you being happy doing anything else but farming.' She slipped her arm through mine. 'And when you're happy, then I'm happy. When did you hear me complain that life's hard?'

I squeezed her. 'No. But I often wonder why you don't sometimes.' She glanced up at me and so I kissed her. A man was lucky to be blessed with an uncomplaining wife. 'Anyway,' I went on, 'I don't mean give up farming. Hell no! I couldn't do that. I just thought we might buy another farm where land's a bit cheaper. Make something on the deal. Exchange the millstone round my neck for a smaller one.'

'Oh well, no harm in thinking about it, I suppose.' She turned away from me, abruptly. 'Now stop it you two! *Donald*! You know she doesn't like you running your tractor over her dolls. *Cherry*! Stop pulling his hair!'

16

OUR HONEYMOON WAS the one and only holiday we'd had since we were married. Of course, in those days the annual holiday away from home was the exception rather than the rule — certainly among farmers. We stole the odd day off, packed a picnic basket, pushed Pat and the kids into Cob and drove down to Hastings or Winchelsea for a day by the seaside. And that was about as adventurous as we had time to be. There was always so much work to be done throughout the summer that we never thought to try and make time to go away for a week or longer. Anyway, neither of us was used to it. As far as Olive was concerned, regular holidays for nurses throughout the war were uncommon, and if she did get more than a few days off in a row there was nowhere to go except home. And the same applied to me on the farms I had worked on. As a matter of fact the holiday entitlement for a farm worker was one week a year. Not many even bothered to take that. They received an extra week's money in lieu — if they remembered to jog the farmer's memory. Pete and Bert never took more than their regular day and a half off each week and certainly had no wish to stay away from work for a whole week. They never remembered to jog my memory either and when, each year after hop-picking, I paid them each an extra week's money they looked at the notes and then at me as though I had gone off my rocker. Somehow they did not feel entitled to it. It seems strange, against the enlightened attitudes of today.

Anyway, if you were lucky with the weather and got your hay

safely in by early July, then there was a week, or two, or three, to spare before the corn was ready for harvesting. So that was the time to push off on holiday — provided there was no sign of copper spider or mildew on the hops so that they needed powdering. And as it happened, all these things were in our favour when Mother cycled over with the news that she had been offered the use of a large bungalow in Downderry, Cornwall, for a month while the owner was away. 'You remember Miss Hill's bungalow, don't you, darling?' she enthused. 'There's simply masses of room and it's almost on the beach. We're planning a lovely family get-together and it'd be splendid if you could come too. I'm sure the farm can manage without you for just this once.'

It was too tempting an offer to refuse. We had lived in Downderry for three years when I was a boy and I had not been back there since. Memories of those carefree days, roaming the towering cliffs and the wild seashore, came flooding back. Provided Cob could get us there and back, there was nothing to stop us. I said yes without a further thought. And long before Mother cycled home I was remembering all our old haunts; the special rock pools where we caught the most prawns when the tide went out in summer; the eerie caves echoing the surging sea on the long winter walks over rocks and grey sand to reach the forbidding Shag Rock; the twisting, tortuous cliff paths, with hanging, hair-raising bends around which we raced, sure-footed as goats as we chased elusive butterflies in summer, or followed the trail in a day-long paper chase in winter. And by the time I finished reminiscing Donald was staring at me, silent and with his mouth open. That there was another world away from Maywood and the animals such as I described was almost beyond belief. But he nodded enthusiastically when I suggested we went — so long as Pat and Ditty could come too.

Of course we took Pat. But Ditty was no traveller and the only time Donald had tried taking her in the car for a short journey, just to see if she liked it, she had fought to free herself from his embrace and leapt to the rear window swearing terribly. When we released her back at the farm she took off as though a fox was after her and we never saw her for the rest of the day. So we left her behind to prowl her own stamping ground and with Pete and Bert to feed her.

The boys were delighted to see the back of me for a fortnight because they were obviously anxious to take charge of the farm themselves. Pete was already acting like a bailiff a week before we left. Somehow I could not see Bert agreeing to the schedule of work his brother was planning once he was boss. So I had no worries that the farm and the animals would not have their best attention during our absence. And I thought the hops would probably get a good powdering, irrespective of any signs of copper spider or mildew, but just to be on the safe side. Colonel wouldn't be too pleased about that.

We slept the night in a field near Exeter on the way down to Downderry. It was asking too much of Cob to expect him to manage the journey in one bite. And of the children. So Cherry slept with six dolls crowding her off the back seat, Donald curled up in the front and Olive and I had sleeping bags under the stars. Pat sank warily to his belly beside us on the grass, only half daring to nod off, continually waking us up with his growls as he prepared for an attack from any direction. Each time I swore sleepily, fumbled for the torch and shone it on him. And he looked back at me, apologetically and surely I realised he could not be too careful with the great responsibility I had thrust on him for looking after us all in this strange, dark field?

In the early dawn Donald was out of the car and waking us up. Look at the sky! It looked as though somebody had been drawing across it with his new crayons! Olive coaxed him into the warm sleeping bag beside her. It was easier than having to rouse out at such an ungodly hour. But there was to be no more sleep. Not with the excitement of cooking breakfast in the open to come, and the long mysterious day ahead; the ferry that clanked on chains rising out of the sea and which would bear Cob bodily across to Cornwall; the crystal clear sea with deep rock pools; the dark, dripping caves — all the stories I had regaled him with yesterday, in an effort to keep him sweet-tempered when the journey had started to become unending for him and frequent fights had broken out with Cherry. She was quite content to let the miles slip by while she drilled her dolls on the back seat. But her games excluded Donald.

So we were on the road early. The children bounced in the back, vying with each other as to who would be first to see the sea. Pat had curled up on the seat beside them and was making up for all his lost sleep during the prowling night. Olive slumped down in the front seat beside me, complaining that she had been done out of her beauty sleep and intending to catch up on it. She was play-acting, never for an instant thinking that by reclining she would actually save her beauty.

The motor bike came roaring out of nowhere. Suddenly it was there, zig-zagging down the road towards us. There was no missing it. It hit us head on. The windscreen shattered and flew, peppering the side of my face and slicing my hand that gripped the top of the steering wheel. The glass missed Olive, except for filling her lap, and the children were thrown forward and down, screaming but safe with Pat on the floor behind the front seats. So Olive told me afterwards, because I bashed my chin on the steering wheel and was out for the count.

And when she turned from checking on the children, gasped at the blood smearing my face and flowing from my hand, she glanced through the open space where the windscreen had been. A scalp stuck by its blood to the edge of the roof.

On the road behind the car the rider of the bike lay dead. People had already arrived. He was only sixteen. Later we learnt that he had borrowed the big bike and was out for an unlicensed ride in the quiet of the early morning roads. He must have swept out from between the high banks of the lane and come roaring down the main road before he realised it, quite unprepared to see Cob advancing towards him.

So while I was whisked off for a sojourn in Exeter hospital, and Cob was towed away to have his bashed face straightened, Olive was left stranded with children, dog, luggage and all the bits and pieces one throws into a car at the last minute when departing on holiday. And with forty miles still to go, and no telephone at our destination to tell of her plight, the taxi she had to hire to get her to Downderry just about used up the spending money we had taken with us.

I have often pondered on why certain things happen just when they do; whether there is some giant plan mapped out for our lives, with uphills, downhills, hairpin bends and cross roads, all unexpected, unavoidable and yet negotiable provided you are prepared to rethink and re-adjust. Mother always accepted every swerve and turning in life as the Will of God. She accepted them without question — a gay little laugh and a silent prayer of thanks for things favourable, a sigh and a shift of her Cross while she waited to understand how one of God's Wonders would emerge from some sudden setback. And she often said that for every door that shuts in your face another one opens.

Which is what she said to me when I finally arrived in Downderry a week later, bandaged and bedraggled and thoroughly miserable. I was upset about the ruined holiday and my sore face, but mainly I could not get it out of my mind that I had been instrumental in killing that young lad. The inquest had been short and to the point. There were witnesses and without question it was accidental death. And yet I kept blaming myself for not swerving out of his way in the seconds when he was coming at me, even though I knew he was drawn to me like a magnet.

'Come along now, pull yourself together!' Mother never considered sympathy helped anyone get better. Determination to disregard pain was the ticket to fitness. 'Just wandering around feeling sorry for yourself won't do. Such nonsense! Life goes on and it won't stop for you.' She hurried around the bungalow as though to prove the point. And with two sisters and brothers-in-law, nephews and nieces, wife and children all milling around there was no chance of a spare spot to sulk in self-pity.

Doors banged and Mother shouted: 'Has anyone seen my towel? I know it's here somewhere.'

'Everybody! Search for Granny's towel.' Ruth appeared, dressed to face the ocean, her own towel slung over her shoulder.

Children flocked after her, impatient with buckets and beach impedimenta. 'Not *again*. We're always looking for Granny's towel.'

'Or her specs.'

'Or her handbag.'

'I'll bet she's left her towel on the beach and it's been washed away with the tide.'

'Did you, Granny? Did you leave it on the beach?'

'Of course I didn't.' Mother was indignant. 'I'm not an *utter* fool.'

'*Here* it is.' My younger sister, Mary, always found everything. 'Under your bed, as usual. I can't think why you never look there first.'

We thronged out of the bungalow for the short walk down

the lane past other bungalows, over the village street and across the rough ground to the grey sand shore. Children rushed ahead, Pat prancing between them, Guffy hurrying to keep up and Cherry shouting: 'Wait for me. Do wait for me!'

The tide was in, long slow waves were sighing at the sand and the sun silvered the edge of a dark cloud and set out across a wide stretch of uninterrupted blue.

Mother loved to bathe. But she had learnt to swim in the days of the Victorian bathing machine, and we could only suppose it was because of this that she always insisted on changing as close to the water's edge as possible. Not for her the dash from bungalow to beach in bathing costume — not even swathed in a wrap. Certainly she considered it most unseemly when Ruth, Mary and Olive went prancing ahead in skimpy swimsuits and she sighed while her son and sons-in-law followed, grunting with approval. She could come to terms with most of the modern trends, but she became excessively puritanical at the slightest suggestion of nudity. Olive always said that the greatest impetus to immerse herself in a cold sea was the thought of Mother's disapproving stare on her backside.

So Mother's changing for a swim was achieved by wriggling about under towels while the waves roared with open laughter at her feet and the children sniggered as they pretended not to look. Inevitably towels slipped exposing one mysterious part after another, and once a rogue wind snatched satin bloomers and sent them skimming across the sand, with children chasing and dogs barking in a race to be first to reach them. And when Pat pounced on them and made off, holding them high so as not to trip over, he made a fine chase of it before he could be persuaded to hand them over.

Coming in from the sea to change back again was even more of a performance. Shivering uncontrollably, because she always stayed in too long, she would try to dry herself and hold towels in position with one hand while discreetly dragging at the antiquated black bathing costume with the other. And, once it was wet, that garment seemed to defy each lurching attempt at removal so that Mother was usually quite exhausted by the time she considered she was respectable again.

For this holiday in Downderry, Christopher, Ruth's eldest boy, had come equipped with a wigwam. When assembled it was free-standing, gaily yellow, realistically painted with Red Indian insignia and just the right size for an eight-year-old to entertain an exceedingly slim squaw.

Christopher was always bursting with ideas. So after watching a particularly perilous changing session, he declared: 'I know, Granny! You can borrow my wigwam as a changing tent. We can easily set it up just where you want it.'

No sooner said than done, and the next bathing session saw Mother crawling into the wigwam clutching a new green bathing cap and dragging towels and costume after her. Pat and Guffy abandoned a search for crabs to come and watch, sitting bolt upright and whining with curiosity. When she had finally disappeared inside, and squeezed the flaps together after her with a great deal of tugging, that threatened to tear the flimsy material, the dogs remained watching, dipping their heads in attempts to peep, and when they couldn't see anything, listening first with one ear and then the other.

'Is it all right, Granny?' Christopher wanted to know.

'Fine,' came the muffled reply, 'just right.'

Sharp elbows and knees thrust at the sides and the whole wigwam heaved and threatened to take off with each change of position. The movements continued for a long time, sometimes a bare leg or an arm was thrust inadvertently through the flaps so that spellbound children laughed and the dogs became more and more interested.

But Pat and Guffy had seen Mother disappear fully clothed and they had not yet been introduced to the new, scalp-tight green bathing cap. So that when she started to emerge on hands and knees, green skin-head glistening and the folds of the old costume hanging, they backed away growling ferociously, quite unnerved by the sudden appearance of this Cornish monster of the deep. And when she stood up and started for the sea, they circled her, barking, and were not satisfied until they had seen her off into the water and the green head was bobbing safely out to sea. Even when she came in again, calling to them and pulling off the strange cap, they were still not absolutely sure and followed her, sniffing suspiciously, until she disappeared into the wigwam again.

Cornwall seemed like another world. Unable to swim with the others I prowled the seashore, walking the edge of the waves, calling the dogs after me, throwing them driftwood and watching them fling themselves into the water, uttering spluttering yaps as they raced to reach it. Soon I felt better, soon unwound, soon relaxed. And I seemed to be a thousand miles away from Maywood.

On the last evening there, with the news that Cob was mended and awaiting our collection to drive back to Kent, Olive and I walked high up into the cliffs and back into the farmlands that gaze out into the approaches of the Atlantic. We leant over a gate that was let into the grass-clad wall surrounding a field. Sheep grazed towards us, busy with anxious bites, now and then stamping a foot when they looked up and saw Pat peering through the gate. And in the next field a tractor droned, ploughing up a pasture for the short summer fallow before autumn sowing.

'Back to farming again,' I remarked. 'Nice light soil here. Easy to work by the looks of it. Not like our tough old Kent clay.'

'Mmm.' But she did not seem to have taken in what I said. She was holding her face up towards the lowering sun with her eyes half closed. 'Isn't the air soft? Soft, washed air.'

'You wouldn't say that if you were standing here in a winter gale.' I chuckled and she smiled faintly. 'But still, the winters are milder here, hardly any snow, not so much frost. And the spring comes earlier, too.'

'But I like my Kent.' She smiled. 'And I expect our old clay soil is richer really, even though it's tough to work.'

'But don't you like Cornwall too? It's sixteen years since I lived here, but all the old feeling's come back in just a week.'

'Of course I like it. And I know just the feeling you mean. Almost like another country.'

I climbed three bars of the gate and stood upright to look back over the landscape of small fields, cosy within their walls, and the few grey houses and buildings hunched under shallow roofs in folds of the ground.

'Farms are cheaper down here,' I said. 'I dare say you could get a farm the size of Maywood for half the price.'

'But it's such a long way away.'

I jumped down and Pat stood up expecting to be on the move again. We started to walk back and he followed close behind us,

214

not daring to go on ahead exploring now that he had seen the sheep.

Presently, I said: 'But home is where you make it. And with no mortgage and a low overdraft we could live better. With this soft air, easy working land, and the sea, perhaps a boat and . . .'

She laughed and started to run, pulling me after her. 'Oh well, no harm in thinking about it, I suppose. But I wonder why I picked a dreamer for a husband. You're still struck with holiday magic. It's back to reality tomorrow.'

17

HOP-PICKING TIME had the atmosphere of a huge holiday at Maywood. They say a change is as good as a rest and for the two to three weeks that it took to pick the crop the whole farm changed. It seemed a different place. From the quiet, steady rhythm of the days, from the calling of the cows for morning milking and their unhurried plod to their places, to the last bucketful of meal given to vociferous pigs at night, routines became rushed. The cows found themselves being bundled down the lane and into the shed. They looked bewildered and flashed their tails and flicked their ears as we hustled them through milking to be done before the pickers arrived. And the pigs roused themselves sleepily and gave astonished looks at the early arrival of breakfast. And when the evening feed was as late as the morning one was early, they got in everyone's way, barging up to the hop garden among departing pickers, loudly enquiring of all and sundry as to what had become of their tea and scaring the more timid folk into the bargain.

With only five acres of hops I was able to rely on local pickers. Larger hop-growers had to import pickers by the train-load from London, with all the attendant bother of providing them with huts to sleep in, ablutions, bogs and all the rest of it. To say nothing of the odd weekends when those husbands who had been left in London at work and who could afford the fare arrived in the camp, brimming with beer and starved of sex, to sing and fight and stumble over sleeping children to lay their loud-mouthed wives, who were now blossoming with country air and heavy with the heady smell of hops. And to say nothing of those hordes of children, used only to hard pavements for playgrounds and high walls for horizons, who soon tired of helping their mothers pick hops into baskets and bins and found adventure in open fields and tumbling haystacks, who chased chickens and ran scared from inquisitive cows, who left gates open and cheeked the irate farmer and who, for all their bravado, were only really prepared to approach the harnessed carthorses because they were like the coalman's horse that plodded their street, or the proud shires that pulled the brewer's dray.

But to my little band of locals, hop-picking at Maywood was their annual holiday with pay. So it was essentially a jolly time, provided it did not rain. Then they were forced to sit miserably under sacks and brollies while they heaved wet 'bines over their laps and hurried to pick off enough hops for an oasting, before they could drag off home. But in September the sun usually shines and the farm took on the air of a holiday camp. News went out by word of mouth that the hops would be ready for picking on the following Monday, Pete and Bert cycling out to inform those in outlying cottages, Mildred, their mother, telling all her cronies, who, in turn, passed it on until everybody knew and got prepared.

And we had preparations to make as well. For most of the year the oast house was used as a store for corn and sacks and junk and anything that had no fixed abode. But when it came into its own for the three weeks of hop drying each year, then it had to be cleaned out from top to bottom. And old Bill Checksfield made sure that it was done to his liking.

Checky had always dried the hops at Maywood. It was a skilled job. It still is. But more so in the old days of open anthracite fires, relying on the draught created by the cowl above, revolving to the vagaries of the wind, and with no electrically-operated extraction fans to assist on those misty autumn nights, when the dull air clung around the cowl like a grey blanket. Then the layer of hops high above the fires would scorch on the bottom while it still sweated green on the top, if the dryer didn't know what he was about, or maybe the glass of cider and the sleepy atmosphere prolonged his forty winks. And a spoiled oasting of hops could mean a big loss in the much lower price paid for a bad sample.

217

As soon as Checky heard that the hops were ready he insisted on inspecting the oast house. I went to fetch him in Cob. The car was resplendent now in repaired features, respray and sparkling new glass, while I still sported a network of scars beneath my left eye. My solicitor was claiming damages for them on my behalf. He had hovered in the background of his office, murmuring 'pain and suffering' from time to time as doctors for each side prodded my face and argued about the likely permanence of the scarring, until the doctor acting for the insurance company told me, in a final effort to minimise the claim: 'Of course, even if this scarring *is* permanent, you must realise that scars on a man's face are by no means unattractive to women.' Olive had laughed merrily at that when I told her. I had the feeling that she considered it would take more than a few sexy scars to improve my appearance.

Checky sat on the edge of his seat on the way up from the village. I should never have given him such a graphic description of the accident. I think he was expecting a motor bike to come roaring around every corner on the wrong side and was wishing he had come on his old bike after all. As far as he was concerned that was the only really safe method of transport, unless it was a cart behind old Colonel.

In the oast house he took charge. He mounted the outside steps that clung to the wall and led up to the drying floor and the cooling room. He paused on the balcony, fished for his spherical silver tobacco case, flipped open the inlaid lid with his thumb nail and broke off a lump of shag. I opened the door into the cooling room and waited while he rubbed the tobacco in his palm and gazed out across the farm from this vantage point. It was no good trying to hurry him. Fag rolling was a ritual with Checky. A hundred times I had waited and watched his thick fingers teasing the roughly-rubbed tobacco into the flimsy paper, rolling it carefully and drawing the gummed edge along the pink tongue that peeped out from under his large, white moustache. Only now his fingers had become leaner, the skin soft with retirement and the finger nails still curved but less ridged, less yellow and with even some of the white moons showing.

He pinched off stray ends of tobacco, popped the fag under his moustache and lit it with a huge flame that leapt from his battered lighter. He nodded down towards the outside of the roundel. 'Got your anthracite then. Looks about enough.'

I peered down over his shoulder at the heap of shining coals, shot near the entrance to the roundel fires. 'Same as last year.'

'Welsh, ain't it?' He looked round at me sharply, blue eyes under bushy white brows.

'Of course.' I never knew why it had to be Welsh. Anthracite was anthracite, whether it came from Wales or wherever. And Checky only muttered darkly whenever I asked him to explain. Evidently it was one of those secrets known only to hop-dryers, or else the original reason was long lost in the mists of time.

'Got enough charcoal?' He eyed the bags stacked up below the steps.

'Twenty bags. That should be more than enough.'

'How much did you pay for them?' He always made me feel I was extravagant and lacked the patience to bargain for the best price.

'One and six a bag.'

'Cor, bugger me!' He raised his cap and scratched his thick white hair. Sparks flew from his fag as he blew out in disgust. 'Who charged you that? Ol' Charlie Miller over Cat's Weasel, I'll bet a bob. Shilling, that's what you ought to have paid. Shilling a bag and not a penny more.'

I never replied. It did not seem worth trying to explain that prices had gone up since he stopped farming. Every year he told me I had paid too much for charcoal and yet it represented just about the smallest of all the hop-growing expenses.

He seemed to have a thing about charcoal because presently he said: 'One year I thought I'd got me charcoal for nothing.' He chuckled to himself, ending in a series of little coughs as the strong smoke went down the wrong way. 'Had all these ol' hop poles stacked up and no good 'cept for burnin'. Just right for charcoal, I thought. Bugger Charlie Miller. I'll burn me own. I'd seen how he done it up Cat's Weasel wood many a time. Stack the wood just right, cover it with turf and soil, set it smoulderin' in the air hole and Bob's your uncle. So that's what I done with me ol' hop poles. Right down there I done it, right where you've got your old poles stacked.'

I glanced to where the poles reared up like a wigwam. Then I moved through the door into the oast, hoping to draw him after me. There was much work still to be done and he looked set to reminisce all day.

He followed me just inside the oast and stopped again. 'Jest got it all piled up right and covered with dirt when Charlie hisself rode down the lane. Wanted to know how much charcoal I wanted for hop drying, 'e did.' He chuckled. 'He knowed, see. Somebody must have told 'im. So I showed 'im me heap. I was fair proud of it. Spent a main bit o' time on it, I can tell you. And I told Charlie I wouldn't be needin' no charcoal from him that year, nor the next p'raps, nor the one after. Not now I'd thought of using me ol' hop poles for charcoal. And all 'e did was laugh, laugh as 'e rode away, calling back that his charcoal got dearer and dearer the nearer it come to hop-picking.'

I mounted the five steps that led up on to the circular drying floor and he came after me. We stood looking down through the coarse mesh of the hop 'hair' that covered the slats, down per-haps fifteen feet to where faint light filtered in from the openings to the three fireplaces spaced round the roundel. Absently he pointed to a small tear in the hair and reminded me to get the sacking needle and mend it.

He chuckled again, removed his fag and carefully tore off a spear of paper where it had failed to burn down along the line of spittle. 'Course my hop poles was dry, weren't 'em? Brittle dry and parts of 'em pickled in creosote. Charlie knowed that. That's why he laughed. He knowed they'd want some holdin', not like green wood what smoulders steady into charcoal. Get the draught jest wrong wi' dry wood and whoosh, up 'er goes.' He laughed and blew more sparks from his fag. 'And they did, my ol' poles. Right in the middle of the night. Wind shifted, see. Whipped in me air hole and set me dry poles blazin'. The earth fell in and up she went like a Guy Fawkes bonfire. The Missus see'd it first. Jumped out of bed 'er did, screamin' that the oast house was afire. And next mornin' all I had left was a load of ashes instead o' charcoal.'

He shook his head sadly as he walked the length of the cooling floor to the tall hop press. He removed the board blocking the circular hole in the floor, lifted the heavy iron ring and dropped it back into its groove again. It was there to grip the necks of the hop pockets as they dangled down through the hole and were pressed tight full of hops. He tested the press, turning the huge wheel so that the ratchet clicked on the cogs and the plunger slowly descended through the hole in the floor. He wound it back, fixed it, removed his cap and scratched the back of his head. Not that it itched, but because he had to admit: 'Aye, dear charcoal that turned out to be that year. Extrey tanner a bag ol' Charlie made I pay 'cos I were late orderin'.'

As he walked back, to climb down and finish his inspection downstairs, he said: 'Every man to his own trade, and that's right, ain't it? Bloody sure ol' Charlie Miller wouldn't be no cop at hop drying.'

We mended the hop bins. They were simple frames of wood, draped and stitched with sacking as a receptacle for the hops, and hinged with a bolt through the crossed legs at each end so that they squashed flat for stacking, and for easier moving when negotiating the alleys in the hop garden. The bins were fairly robust and designed for rough handling. But fat women sometimes tired of their stools and tended to squat on the side of the bin for a change when picking and gossiping across to a neighbour. So frames cracked and had to be renewed. Sometimes they snapped altogether, depositing the sitter smartly into the bin backwards, cackling, kicking, skirts in the air, a sight to draw gales of laughter from all the alleys round about. Ganging up on someone and tipping him or her into a bin was one of the sports of hop-picking. So when a heavyweight toppled into a bin of her own accord, well, it was worth extra laughter.

We loaded the bins on to the waggon and Colonel pulled them up to the hop garden. And while he stopped and started along the headland we heaved them off and set them up, each at the end of an alley and advancing into the green darkness.

Colonel was sprightly. He enjoyed hop-picking as much as anybody. Although it meant that he was on the go all day and every day, harnessed into the waggon to cart the pokes of green hops down to the oast, most of his time was spent just standing about. But he knew hop-pickers brought picnics, and years of practice had taught him all the right sounds and movements to make to ensure a constant supply of titbits and plenty of fussing. He showed me up mercilessly, always pretending that he was starving, accepting anything from a crust of bread to an over-ripe tomato, relishing everything and frothing as he rattled them about over his bit to position them between his worn teeth.

In Kent a misty autumn morning is still called a 'hop-pickers' morning' by country folk, although hand-picking is a thing of the past and nowadays impersonal machines hum and flail and blow to separate the hops from the leaves and the bines. But mists hung in the valley over Maywood so that some mornings were cloaked in grey stillness, when the only movement seemed to be the occasional drip from summer-hardened leaves and when sounds were stark as they came out of the mist. The voices of the pickers chattered through the mist, the creak of a bin, the squeak of a pram, the sudden shriek as a bine was lopped down, showering a picker with cold drops and clothing her in wet leaves. Then fingers were numb with cold, hop pokes were pinched for over-skirts, babies cried and were silenced with a dummy or a bulging breast, young boys were sent searching the hedgerows for twigs and soon little fires crackled in the alleys and tin kettles blackened and started to sing.

But nobody stopped picking because it was cold, unless it was for a scalding mouthful of smoky tea. Everybody knew a hop-pickers' morning and by eight o'clock or nine, ten at the very latest, the sun would burn away the mist. Soon sacks and shawls and coats were discarded, snivel-nosed kids were hoicked out of prams and left to crawl or toddle through picked bines and drying dirt, and Mrs Buggins would take herself off for her morning pee. She was a large woman with arms like a prize fighter, her wide waist clasped in a vast black apron and one of her husband's caps firmly planted back to front on her head. Everybody knew when she went for a pee, or rather when she came back, because she would announce, with a loud cackle: 'Stung me bum on a stinging nettle again, I did!' She probably had at one time. It was doubtful whether she actually repeated the painful experience every morning. But the remark always caused a good laugh and so she always made it. Only one morning, a minute or so after she had returned, a bevy of small boys sneaked back, giggling and whispering that they had 'seen ol' Ma Buggins' full moon through the hedge'.

Pete and Bert acted as general handymen, cutting down bines with bagging hooks lashed to long poles to keep the pickers

222

supplied, moving bins down the alleys, holding out the wide-mouthed pokes as Alf Mytton, the busheller, measured out the hops from each bin, then loading the full pokes on to the waggon for the journey to the oast house. And while they worked so they kept up a constant flow of back-chat.

Because of the holiday atmosphere, as well as being in the public eye, the boys considered that their normal farm clothes were unsuitable. So, instead of their collarless, striped flannel shirts, they appeared in sports shirts, with neckerchiefs tied casually, and grey flannel trousers with turn ups and wide leather belts in place of their usual dung-spattered, blue serge trousers held up with heavy braces. And Pete discarded his beret, slicking his black hair down with brilliantine so that I hardly recognised him. But obviously Rose thought he looked marvellous. She had taken her annual holiday from the laundry to coincide with hop-picking and shared a bin with her mother. So for a whole fort-night she was able to gaze on Pete as he went about his work, offering him a cup of tea or a drink of fizzy lemonade whenever he came her way to cut down bines or move a bin. But he never stayed to chat. Courting and work could not mix. She had to wait until the evening, until the shadows lengthened and the day's oasting had started to dry above the bright fires, sending scented steam curling from the cowl.

One bin in the hop garden was reserved as the farmhouse bin. Olive and I picked into it whenever we could and it was a place for Donald and Cherry to home in on from time to time. Some-times Mother cycled over for an afternoon's picking, ostensibly to pick into our bin, only she had so many friends among the pickers that she usually ended up going from bin to bin, picking and chatting her way around. She never could stop long in one place anyway. 'There's Mrs Ongley, I must just go and have a word with her,' and a couple of hours later she would be back to help Olive again.

The fact that Olive was a State Registered Nurse seemed to impress some of the women pickers no end. From time to time one would sidle up, pick a few hops into the bin and talk of this and that. And soon she would be steering the conversation around to a discussion of some ailment that was troubling her. Once the huge Mrs Buggins shuffled over through the tangle of picked bines. She was an imposing figure in her back-to-front cap and bulging arms and silently she beckoned Olive to follow her for a consultation, deep into the green jungle of unpicked hops. There she unbuttoned her blouse, removed a colossal breast and demanded Olive's opinion of a fiery, festering boil.

Poor Mrs Junip's trouble was that she couldn't conceive. She was a slight little woman, forever popping over when Olive was on her own for 'just a little word in your ear, dear'. She was convinced a nurse could offer some magic elixir that would do the trick. Oh yes, she had consulted her doctor. All he could suggest was buying some extra flimsy underwear and, thus clad, having a hot drink with hubby before they went to bed. But nothing had come of that, in spite of being careful to observe all the recommended dates. Each day produced a new confidence about Mrs Junip's sex life, until Olive felt like a consultant stationed in her bedroom and with complete control over suggested changes from the knicker drawer.

But these visits and whispered consultations did not go unnoticed by Mrs Mabbs. She had the bin in the alley next to Olive and her trouble was the opposite of Mrs Junip's. Only she never considered it any trouble, just quite natural that she should arrive for each hop picking heavily pregnant and for the last seven years she had dropped a baby regularly every October. 'Now 'tis jest like havin' a good pee,' she told anybody who was interested.

Mrs Mabbs was always among the first to arrive in the hop garden each morning. She came looming down the lane, like a corn sack on legs, pushing her battered and squeaky pram with last year's baby peering from under the hood, the year before's sitting at the other end with his feet down between the handles, while the previous years' models straggled after her lugging stools, baskets of food and the inevitable umbrella, saucepan and kettle. (She would never risk leaving anything behind overnight, in spite of our offers to look after things for her. Perhaps she thought she might give birth ahead of time and be unable ever to retrieve her possessions.)

Her children were all lusty, grimy and clothed in penny and twopenny purchases from jumble sales. Yet they never seemed to feel the cold of a hop pickers' morning in spite of their flimsy hand-me-downs. The eldest child was a girl, Ethel. So far she was the only girl. She ruled her younger brothers with shouts and well-directed smacks, and each year she took more and more charge of them as her mother's pregnancies advanced until, last year, she had assumed total control during the annual confinement. The father, Tom, worked on the roads and left her to it, devouring his evening meal and disappearing down the pub as usual, unconcerned at the imminent arrival of yet another addition to his family. At seven he reckoned Ethel was old enough to manage the family now. And she could run for the midwife when her mother said it was time. As for the cooking, well, Mrs Mabbs always managed to be out of bed and back at the stove again the next day.

But she had to leave the long walks to the shops to Ethel for a couple of weeks. And last year, three weeks after hop picking had finished, Olive met Ethel bustling along the top road towards the village, pushing the big pram with two aboard, the others dragging behind and her own head hardly as high as the handle.

Olive greeted her brightly: 'Hello, Ethel! So Mummy's had her baby, has she?'

Ethel slackened her pace slightly. 'Yeah. Another ruddy boy.' And she hurried on, screaming at Archie not to lag behind, carrying all the cares of the large family on her determined little body.

So Mrs Mabbs sat on her stool beside her bin in the alley next to Olive. She draped a bine over her bulging belly and rapidly ripped off the hops into her upturned umbrella, spiked into the ground beside her. Her fingers were caked with the black stain from the hops and the passage of the bines across her belly left a yellowy-green streak on her apron. Ethel sat nearby, copying her mother and diligently picking into an apple box, keeping her eye on her next two brothers, who were now considered old enough to do their share of the picking. They each had baskets to pick into and were expected to fill these before being allowed off to play. Experienced pickers seldom picked directly into the bin until an hour or so before the busheller was due to come around. After several hours, hops, and particularly mist-laden hops, sunk heavily when in a large mass in the bin. And they went just as heavily into the busheller's basket when he came to measure so that the tally of the day's picking was disappointing. So they picked into boxes, baskets, sacks and upturned umbrellas, and at the last moment these were tipped into the bin so that they were light and fluffy and it took less to fill the bushel.

From where she sat Mrs Mabbs observed Mrs Junip's daily visits to Olive. And although the consultations on sexual matters were always conducted in discreet whispers or low tones, and even though Mrs Mabbs seemed fully occupied picking hops, admonishing her offspring and landing occasional, resounding smacks on wrong doers who were foolish enough to come within range, nevertheless she must have guessed the burden of these daily discussions.

Because one day she called out, loud enough for all to hear: 'Tell yer what, dearie. I'll lend yer me ol' Tom for a night. Never been known ter fail. 'E only has ter throw 'is trousers on the bed and I falls for another one.'

Poor Mrs Junip, she coloured up and crept away and never dared to approach Olive again for further consultations.

Nearly every afternoon the ice-cream man arrived. Nobody seemed to know where he came from, nor yet where he went. But as soon as hop-picking started he just arrived, doing the rounds of all the hop gardens, pedalling his tricycle with the heavy ice-cream box fixed over the front wheel and the ornate board that read: 'Alfonso. Diploma Ices.'

Sharp-eared children always heard him first: 'Ice-a-creal! Ice-a-creal!' and the bell would jangle as he slaved to shove his heavy bike up the rough track past the oast house. 'Ice-a-creal, Ice-a-creal! I scream, you scream, we all-a scream for ice cream!'

Sweating, beaming, giant black moustache sagging, he dished out halfpenny water ices, penny cornets or twopenny wafers, ladled from the ice-steaming depths of his box with a wooden spoon. Diving for the little cardboard-clad blocks of water ice was soon done. But the making of a cornet, for a grubby-faced child with her clutched penny to spend, was a labour of love. A broad smile, the delicate extraction of a cornet from the pile with outspread fingers, the spoonful of ice cream with a tail that squirmed deep into the cornet and the careful moulding of the yellowy-white dome. And he passed it to his little customer with a bow and another smile and the penny chinked into his coat pocket as he stood upright. It was less often that a child could extract twopence from a mother to spend on ice cream. But if he did, then the wafer-making machine came into action.

It swam in a jar of cloudy water, clamped to the inside of the ornate board that decorated the front of the box. It sparkled silver as Alfonso shook it free of drips, it clicked as he worked the platform up and down, brandishing it with a smile like a party conjurer about to perform a trick. The wafer went in and there was silence. Then the ice cream. But instead of levelling it off smooth, he always built it up slightly so that when the second wafer went on top, and he released the catch, the sandwich came out over-full and bulging.

'Goo on, Charlie, give us a lick,' as the lucky recipient hurriedly handed over his twopence and was pursued by less fortunate brethren.

Because the majority of their customers were busy hop-picking, Stivvy and Reuben Wild increased the number of their visits with the emporium. Instead of once a fortnight they came every week, sometimes twice a week. And the arrival of the emporium in the lane, with the blare of its hooter, was the signal for a break and a wander down to take turns climbing aboard.

All purchases were made against pay day at the end of hop-picking. Goods were put by to be collected then. And it was fun being able to consider all those extras that were normally out of reach of the weekly budget. It gave a sort of zip to the picking when it started again later.

And when everybody who wanted to had had a poke round the emporium, Stivvy and Reuben would come up and pick a few hops themselves, or idle into the oast house for a chat with Checky before moving on to visit the next hop garden on their round.

Twice during each day the busheller came round to measure out the hops. It was always wise to employ a man from outside as a busheller. The pickers felt happy that he would be impartial and measure the hops fairly. Everybody knew that a busheller could be heavy handed or light handed. And a heavy-handed one was reckoned to be a boss's man, jamming the hops into the basket so that it took more to fill a bushel. That made pickers disgruntled with a feeling of being cheated. But a light-handed busheller favoured the pickers too much and so a boss never employed one if he could help it.

But for years Alf Mytton had been coming to Maywood and was experienced enough to strike a happy medium. He was a failed farmer himself who now worked in a factory and was happy to spend his annual holiday in the hop garden. And he did the job, and went his own sweet way about it irrespective of the banter a busheller always received.

'Bushel up! Bushel up!' Alf would cry, and this was the signal for all the baskets and boxes and bags and upturned umbrellas full of hops to be emptied into the bins. And off we would start on the round, Alf leading with his basket, Pete and Bert with bundles of empty pokes to be filled, while I acted as clerk, armed with my own record book and a pen to fill in the number of bushels picked on each picker's card.

'Shove the first handful of hops into the basket real hard, that's the secret,' Alf often whispered to me as we went round, just to assure me that he was really on my side. 'Shove it in hard and they don't notice so long as you fluff the hops up nice on top and don't fill the basket quite full. That keeps 'em all happy.'

As he bushelled out the hops so he shouted out the tally. 'One!'

'One!' echoed Pete and Bert from wherever they happened to be.

'Two!' called Alf.

'Two!' came the confirmation.

And so it went on until the last of the hops was scraped from the bin. Now came the time for argument because it seldom worked out to an exact bushel. If the basket was more than half full, the picker would exclaim: 'Go on, Alf, tally up. You can call that a bushel.'

Alf would hold the basket out for a moment of weighty decision. Sometimes he would toss it into the poke and call out the next number, sometimes empty it back into the bin and push his pork-pie hat to the back of his head before moving on. He never gave any reason for his decision, or entered into an argument. But I often wondered whether favourable decisions had something to do with cups of tea offered, the odd fag that happened to be passed to him, or certainly the smile from a pretty face because often a plump bottom was patted in passing. And who would dare to accuse the busheller of being fresh?

After a couple of days of picking the question of the price per bushel arose. Usually Mrs Buggins was the first to broach the subject. She always stood sternly over her bin as her hops were measured, arms like cabers crossing her huge bosom, her fingers black with hop stain, back-to-front cap skinning all the hair from her brow.

'What's the price this year?' she would ask.

I would pretend to be totting up figures so as not to have to encounter her piercing stare. 'Sixpence a bushel, I reckon.'

'Sixpence! Can't work for sixpence!'

Already other pickers would have closed in. There would be hoots of laughter and shouts of, 'Sixpence! Can't work for sixpence!'

'Come all the way down here for sixpence a bushel!'

'You can keep your ol' hops at sixpence a bushel!'

But it was all good-humoured banter. My price would have attracted the same reaction whatever it was.

So I'd say: 'Milton's paying sixpence. So's Tiffenden, so's Cornes, so's ...'

'Down Frog's Hole they'm paying eightpence.'

'Ah, but they've only got tiny hops. Sixpence is a good price for these.'

In the end everyone knew we would settle for sevenpence a bushel and picking would resume with renewed gusto.

After the second bushelling of the day the pickers would pack up and start off home to cook the husbands' teas. Older children would crowd round the waggon, helping to load up the pokes of green hops, shouting conflicting orders to Colonel to 'gee up' and 'no whoa! whoa!' He ignored them and moved slowly along the headland, stopping by each pile of pokes, just as he had done for umpteen years before any of them were born.

But the willing help with loading the pokes was only pre-payment for a ride on the load down to the oast house.

'Give us a ride! Give us a ride!' and one by one we flung the children up on the soft, sleepy bed of hops. And from there their laughter shrilled through the lolling poles and picked bines as Colonel slowly pulled the waggon down to the oast house. The heavy wheels clonked and the woodwork creaked as the waggon rode the ruts, shivering the load each time it lurched and adding extra bursts of enjoyment.

The smell of hops makes you sleepy. Sometimes the pickers took small bagfuls home to make up hop pillows if they, or perhaps a friend, suffered from insomnia. So after a full day in the hop garden, and then a ride nestled among soft and quivering pokes of hops, it was no wonder that some children were distinctly drowsy by the time we lifted them down from the load and set them unsteadily on their feet, to stagger off and catch up home-going mothers. Certainly Donald and Cherry never needed any rocking and often it was as much as Olive could do to get their tea down them before they nodded off over the table.

So now the pokes of green hops were heaved from the waggon up to the balcony of the oast house, and from there were carried up the five steps and shot out on the hop hair over the drying floor. Already Checky had set the charcoal glowing on the fires below and large lumps of anthracite were beginning to catch. The suffocating heat rose upwards through the bare floor and we smothered it with cold hops, while Checky was there in his shirtsleeves, cap on the back of his head and resting on a froth of white hair, red face glowing and sparks from his fag flying as he brandished a hay rake and waded among the hops, raking them until they were as level as duck weed on a still pond. And slowly the heat filtered through the hops so that they started to steam. Then the vapour curled up almost invisibly through the throat of the roundel, but billowed from the mouth of the cowl as it mingled with the chill, evening air.

Now it was time for the worst part of hop drying, time for the pan of brimstone to be set on the hob of one fire and lit with a glowing coal. Soon the blue flames curled and the choking fumes rose, penetrating the hops to kill the insects but invading every corner of the oast house as well, to send us spluttering outside for deep breaths of clean autumn air.

Tea time had come and gone and now we left Checky to his night's vigil. Before I went to bed I would wander up the lane to visit the oast house again. Sometimes Checky would be tending his fires, pottering round the narrow passage that circled the roundel, bucket of lumps of anthracite in one hand, fire iron in the other. Sometimes the yellow glow of his hurricane lamp would be lighting up the top window and I'd find him standing on the five steps, the door to the drying floor open a crack as he peered inside to see how the hops were cooking.

'Everything okay?' I would ask.

He'd chuckle as he shut the door and came down the steps.

'Aye, they'm drawin' through a treat.'

Or perhaps he would look serious and say: 'Got some cold pockets in there by the looks on't. Someone must've stomped on the hops instead of shufflin' through them when we loaded up. The times I've said to be careful only to shuffle through 'em. Darn boys don't listen.' Stepping on the green hops tended to squash them tight on the hair so that hot air failed to draw through that particular spot leaving a cold pocket above. Checky always moaned about this. But, in point of fact, cold pockets all mixed in and soon dried out with the rest once he had turned the hops by shuffling them about when they were three parts dry. But hop drying was a jealously-guarded art that must be seen to be exacting. Attention had to be paid to the smallest detail that might mar the perfection of the dried sample.

And sometimes I would find Checky snoozing on the bags of straw which formed his makeshift bed beside the glowing entrance to the passage round the fires. The hurricane lamp would be hanging from a beam, the wick turned low but with just enough light to pick out the pockets of pressed hops already crowding the dark corner so that they looked like a group of conspiring giants. So if he was allowing himself forty winks everything must be fine. He caught up on his sleep whenever he could. But it depended on the wind, depended on the moisture, depended on all manner of things before he would allow himself to drop off. Later he would be up again, climbing the outside steps with the swinging light to test the hops, burying his arms into them elbow deep, extracting a double handful and rubbing them thoughtfully, throwing them back and perhaps easing through still sweating spots with the handle of the hay rake. Then down again to bank the fires, or damp them down, depending on a freshening breeze, depending on a lack of air, depending on how long he reckoned the oasting would take to finish without scorching. 'It all depends,' was the only answer I ever got if I asked a question.

About five in the morning, or six, or seven, it all depends, the oasting would be finished. Just dry enough but not too dry so that the pockets weighed light when the hops were pressed into them. And Checky would plough around into the hops, turning them out with a wide, wooden shovel, sending them fluttering down to the cooling floor to rise there in a great, glowing heap. Then he would sweep the hair clean with a broom of whispy faggots so that the yellow seeds that clung there went flying through the door and pelted on to the hops below like hail.

'You wants all the seeds, mind,' he would say, as he paused in his vigorous sweeping. 'Make sure they all goes into the pocket 'cos they weighs heavy.'

Later, before the hops got too cold, before they started to soak up the early morning mist outside into themselves, Checky began to press them into the pockets. And the heavy plunger scrunched down into the whispering hops, squeezing them into the swelling sides of the sacking until the weave squeaked and threatened to burst. And when the pocket was full, with a great bite of the oasting pressed into it, then the mouth was carefully rolled up and sewn, leaving an ear protruding at each end. And all that remained was to weigh the pocket, stencil on the weight and hump it over to the corner to join the growing gang of giants awaiting delivery to the hop factor.

18

ON THE LAST night of hop-picking we had our party. The
pickers had been paid off and departed early in the afternoon,
when the last bines were picked and the last shrieking picker
pitched into a bin. They departed laughing, waving, sun tanned,
well pleased with the proceeds from their holiday with pay.
Mrs Mabbs was the last to leave, her children crowding close to
her for once, under stern orders from Ethel that the last home
would miss his share out of the wages. And Mrs Mabbs walked
slowly, full bellied and puffing as she pushed her pram. It
looked as though she had only just made it to the end of hop-
picking before Number Eight arrived.

Soon Olive was busy with the preparations and when I found
her in the kitchen the table was loaded with a rolling heap of
large, scrubbed potatoes, a pudding basin full of home-made
butter, several loaves of bread and a huge wedge of cheese. And,
sternly to attention in two ranks across the end of the table,
stood twenty-six bottles of elderberry wine.

I looked at it all and whistled. 'Hell, woman, we're not expecting an army. There'll only be a few people who'll bother to come
out here after dark.'

'Better to have too much than too little. You never know.'

Mother arrived, swishing into the yard with her bell ringing.
She propped her bike against the fence and hurried into the
kitchen, face flushed and with her hair flying. She had volun-
teered to baby sit, to stay the night and take over the children so
that Olive could concentrate on the party.

So after tea we left her to it, kissed the kids goodnight and humped the food and wine to the oast house. I had warned Checky about the party and he had grunted and continued with his work. Now he greeted us with a stern stare. He still had the last oasting of hops to deal with and obviously it was sacrilege to use the oast house for a party at the same time.

But Olive said, brightly: 'You must try some of my elderberry wine, Mr Checksfield. Tell me if you think it's as good as your wife used to make.' She sloshed some into a glass and handed it to him.

Checky was really a beer man, with perhaps a whisky now and then as a special treat. But he took the wine, tossed it back rather like nasty medicine and rolled himself a fag as though to take the taste away. However, he accepted another glassful and now he sipped it and appeared to be enjoying it as he watched us take over his downstairs domain. We brought in apple boxes for seats, half cider barrels for tables and we lit candles and stuck them in their own grease, one for each table.

The flames flickered light up into the dark crevices of the beams. 'Oh, just look at all the cobwebs,' Olive sighed.

'Don't be so fussy,' I called, heaving a hop pocket to one side to give more room.

Checky chuckled: 'Cor, bless yer, nobody won't bother about cobwebs once they gets some o' this wine into 'em.' He walked over and picked up the basket of scrubbed potatoes. 'Here, I'll see to the spuds for ye. They'll want an hour or more in the hot ashes under the fires to cook 'em proper, I know.' Halfway back to the roundel, he called over his shoulder: 'I was jest going to see to me fires anyway.'

Just after it was dark Pete and Rose arrived. Pete pushed Rose in in front of him. He nodded and smiled self-consciously, red cheeks shining and hair smarmed down. And Rose kept repeating, 'I don't mind if I do', when we offered her a seat, a drink and a scalding spud. Almost immediately afterwards Bert sauntered in and behind him his parents, Jack and Mildred. They all sat around awkwardly, saying nothing but eating ernestly to cover their embarrassment, while Jack kept sampling the wine loudly, sucking at it as though it was steaming soup.

I tried a few topics of conversation. Olive provided some

rejoinders and each time Mildred contributed with a maniacal cackle. And I thought: God, we're in for a joyful evening, as I racked my brains for something else to say to liven up the proceedings until the wine took over.

Fortunately Tom and Ivy came to the rescue. As usual Ivy had picked more hops than anyone else and for several afternoons Tom had joined her, once he had dealt with his night's catch of rabbits. Now they had dressed for the occasion and it was the first time I had seen Ivy out of her dungarees. She wore a smart tweed two-piece that was obviously new and Tom's tattooed arms were covered with a check sports jacket over grey flannel trousers. His years in the navy had helped him with small talk, while Ivy's constant work among field gangs had made her used to the sound of her own voice in public.

Soon the ice was broken and hesitant conversation got going about hops and oasts and farming in general. And every now and then old Jack would slurp loudly at the wine, clear his throat and begin: 'I mind the time when...' only to find the rest of his dissertation overcome by other talk.

Bert's eyes were sparkling. He had polished off a couple of spuds, well washed down with wine, and now his cheeks were bulging with bread and cheese. He leant forward and a few crumbs flew as he spoke: 'I'll lay you've got your ol' mouth organ with yer, Tom. C'mon, give us a tune.'

Just then Checky came in again, down from one of his visits to check on the progress of the hops above. His cap was on the back of his head and his fag sparkled. As soon as he saw Tom produce his silver mouth organ from his top pocket, he started to hum in a wavering tenor. 'Aye, that's it,' he chuckled, 'let's be having a tune. I votes the Vicar of Bray.' And he launched into the song, gradually changing key until he was more or less in tune with Tom's accompaniment.

Once Tom had started he needed no prompting. Like a pub pianist, he switched from tune to tune with scarcely a break, old tunes, new tunes, tapping out the beat with his polished shoe on the hard, earth floor while we all joined in, now and then finding words, more often just shouting la, la, la.

It was when he paused for more refreshment that we heard the rich baritone come calling through the night. By now Checky was reclining comfortably on his bed of straw-filled sacks and from there he exclaimed: 'Cor, bugger me! That's old Boney Jackson, I'll bet a bob.'

And even as he spoke we heard the blacksmith's deep laugh and his push bike crash against the outside wall. He loomed into the candlelight like a great black skeleton. 'Here I be,' he declared, 'jest remembered you said you was havin' a party. Heard you singing comin' down the lane, I did. I likes a good sing-song, that I do.'

It was obvious that he had come from a session in the Six Bells. He belched loudly before starting on a baked potato, changed his mind and drained a glass of elderberry wine first. I hoped it would mix all right with beer. Certainly it did wonders for his voice because soon he was leading the singing in spite of his cadaverous cheeks being stuffed out with cheese and spuds.

The revving engine and the blaring hooter outside silenced a song in mid stanza.

'Who the hell's that?' Pete asked, suddenly serious.

'Who the hell d'you think?' Bert replied, laughing.

Mildred cackled. 'There's only one bleedin' hooter round 'ere like that. Ol' Stivvy Wild, that's who that be. Stivvy, and Reuben too, most like.'

Olive looked at me. She had been enjoying the sing-song, her face was flushed and already she was on her third glass of wine. 'The more the merrier!' She rose to meet the brothers amid the shouted greetings.

They settled beside a barrel and a guttering candle, apologising for their late arrival. Soon Stivvy laid his pipe to one side, Reuben removed his false teeth (but discreetly into a handkerchief because there were ladies present) and they set about bread and cheese, and potatoes brought hot from the ashes, as though they hadn't eaten all day. Probably they hadn't, although they'd had plenty of liquid refreshment before arriving.

Not that that stopped them enjoying the wine. They kept commenting on its warming qualities as we refilled their glasses. And as they joined in the sing-song, so Stivvy vied with Boney to hold on to the deep notes, conducting with his glass, urging Tom to linger over the spine-tingling passages so that they could savour the richness of the notes.

Stivvy's moustache quivered as he sang and his eyes watered as he gazed into Reuben's. Pete had dared to curl his arm

236

around Rose's neck while she leant her head gratefully on his shoulder. The intervals between Checky's inspections of the fires and the hops had grown longer and longer and now he was stretched out comfortably on his bed, occasionally throwing in a high tenor note if he thought one was called for. Old Jack gurgled steadily into his clay pipe, his head on his chest so that I thought he was asleep, but jerking up and looking round with spaniel eyes whenever a song ended. Mildred occasionally offered a high note, like a hen off the nest, continued to drink copiously and encouraged Bert to keep singing when his expression started to glaze. Ivy sang gazing into Tom's sucking face. And each time there was a lull for Tom to get his breath back, to wipe his lips and shake out saliva from his mouth organ, and have another drink, she would say: 'Knows all the tunes, my Tom do. Only got to hear a tune once an' 'ee can play it straight orf. Can't you, Tom?'

Now Boney seemed suddenly overwhelmed with religious fervour. It seemed as though the weight of his sins lay heavy on his shoulders. 'Rock of Ages,' he groaned, looking sorrowfully up into the dark beams, 'let's 'ave Rock of Ages. My old woman 'ud like that if 'er were 'ere.' And I thought; thank God she's not and wondered if she would dare to lock him out tonight, if he ever got home.

Tom poured more wine into his glass and drank it. 'Aye, in a minute, Boney. Rock of Ages it'll be if that's what you wants. But first I wants another spud and a nice big knob o' home-made butter.'

There was silence as he cut into the steaming potato.

Then Stivvy mused, slumped forward over the barrel and gazing at the candle. 'Darn me, Reuben, 'tis a long time since thee and I have sat aside a candle like this.'

'Aye,' Reuben agreed, solefully, ' 'tis that. Not since we was boys.'

'Aye, not since we was boys,' Stivvy repeated.

'Us used to go to bed by candlelight, didn't us? Used to stand the ol' candle right there aside the bed.' Reuben was gazing at it nostalgically.

Stivvy smirked. Then he chuckled. 'And d'ust remember the game we used to play? D'ust remember, Reuben? See who could be first to fart the candle out?'

237

There was a loud guffaw from Bert, a snort from Pete while Tom was covered with confusion because there were ladies present. He hurriedly finished his mouthful, washed it out with wine and said: 'Right, Boney. Here goes. Rock of Ages.'

And we all sang solemnly while Boney gazed heavenwards, sending rich notes reverberating into the rafters and curling through the cobwebs.

Stivvy and Reuben were the last to leave. And Boney Jackson was with them because they had promised him that he could put his bike in the emporium and they would drop him off in the village on their way home. The harvest moon was riding high, lighting the lane like day and making Boney's features more sepulchral than ever.

There was much banging of doors and an argument between Boney and Reuben as to who should sit in the middle.

'Ssh! Ssh!' Olive hissed, 'you'll wake the children.'

'Ssh!' Stivvy repeated, sternly, 'you'll wake the children.' And he started up the engine with a roar and promptly backed into the ditch.

I groaned. 'Oh God, we shall be here all night now.'

Presently we were all standing round the vehicle, gazing at it sorrowfully.

Reuben asked me: 'Soon pull us out with the tractor, couldn't you?'

'If you start that up you *will* wake the children,' Olive warned.

Boney kicked at one of the rear wheels, a little unsteadily. 'Ol' Colonel 'ud pull that out, no trouble at all. Pull 'er out easy, I'll lay.'

'Aye,' Stivvy grasped at this straw eagerly. 'Wouldn't make no noise neither.' He turned to Olive and hissed reassuringly: 'Wouldn't wake the children.'

Colonel was standing just inside his field behind us, a black statue in the moonlight as he slept the night away on all fours. He would not be too pleased to be called to duty at such an hour, and I said so.

Boney was instantly at my side, throwing a brawny arm over my shoulder. 'Now, you leave it all to I. Ol' Colonel knows I. You and your missus has given we a good party and you'm not to trouble yourselves 'bout this lil' difficulty. Ol' Colonel knows

238

I. 'E knows ol' Boney and between us we'll have this out the dick in no time.'

I did not feel like objecting. Let him get on with it. And soon he was leading the old horse out by his forelock. Evidently expecting that Boney would have rolled oats laid on, even at this late hour, Colonel followed him with all speed. Too much speed really, for Boney was none too steady on his pins, and as they reached the lane Colonel sort of overran him. The blacksmith stumbled, let go of the forelock and for a moment Colonel took fright and clattered round on the lane.

'Ssh!' hissed Stivvy, 'you'll wake the children.'

'Ssh!' Boney repeated, as he regained his balance. 'Ssh!' he said again to Colonel, as he re-caught his forelock. 'Ssh! You'll wake the children.' And now he walked on tiptoe as Colonel clumped after him into the stable.

By now Checky had appeared with the hurricane lamp. He patted his old horse on the rump, muttering endearments as he steadied himself against him and followed him into the stable. And Stivvy and Reuben rolled in after them, sshing to each other as they disappeared inside.

I was feeling none too steady on my pins either, so I leant back against the emporium.

Olive said: 'Aren't you going to help them?'

'Hell no. Let 'em get on with it. There's more than enough of them in there to harness him up.'

They were gone a long time. There were muttered orders and counter orders as the harness clinked. Every now and then someone said 'Ssh!' and later there were long silences, broken only by commands from Boney. He was humming. Then, quite clearly, 'Come on now, lift up, you ol' fool.' More humming, more orders, several choruses of 'Ssh!' as Boney threatened to break into song.

Then Checky came out of the stable, leading the way with the light. Behind him Boney led Colonel, with Stivvy and Reuben saying 'Ssh!' with each step.

As they came into the lane, into the full moonlight, Olive giggled and exclaimed: 'Whatever *have* they done?'

And along came Colonel, walking like a clown, but silently with each heavy hoof encased in a bag of hay.

I could scarcely push for laughing when Colonel took the

239

strain, Stivvy jerked the clutch and the rest of us heaved. But the wheels turned, the emporium lifted and slowly rolled back on to the lane.

When they had driven off we said goodnight to Checky as he returned to see to the last oasting of hops. Wrapped in arms we walked towards the house and paused over the gate leading into Colonel's field. Footloose again now he was moving slowly along the hedge to find an acceptable spot to continue his disturbed sleep.

And from across the silver field the heifers stood up, stretched and walked sedately over to see why everybody was up so late. The twins were only three months pregnant but they blew and fussed towards us like a couple of old matrons.

I leant on the gate and held out my free hand towards them.

Olive's arm tightened round my waist. 'Come on, it's too late now to start dreaming over a gate. The farm will still be there tomorrow.'

I smiled at her. Then I hugged her as we walked on to the house and crept inside to join our sleeping children.